STRUCTURED
Macroeconomics

FIRST EDITION

by Stephen Gillespie

GEORGE MASON UNIVERSITY

cognella®
academic publishing

Bassim Hamadeh, CEO and Publisher
Michael Simpson, Vice President of Acquisitions and Sales
Jamie Giganti, Senior Managing Editor
Miguel Macias, Graphic Designer
Marissa Applegate, Senior Field Acquisitions Editor
Luiz Ferreira, Senior Licensing Specialist
Sean Adams, Project Editor
Kat Ragudos, Interior Designer

First published in the United States of America in 2016 by Cognella, Inc.

Printed in the United States of America

ISBN: 978-1-63487-966-8 (pbk) / 978-1-63487-968-2 (br) / 978-1-63487-967-5 (sb)

www.cognella.com   800-200-3908

CONTENTS

INTRODUCTION

HOW TO USE THIS BOOK

Information is presented in "bitesize" blocks—either one or two-page units. The summary at the start of each unit describes the topic of the unit and gives the most important points to remember. The textbook is designed for use as a reference—its structure makes it easy to look up and read about particular topics.

This textbook follows a consistent structure throughout.

The topic for each unit is chosen at the level of detail that can reasonably be covered in one or two pages, so that it is easily "digestible." Each block is a self-contained unit—everything you need to know about that topic is there in that unit.

The first page of each chapter describes the overall topic of the chapter, summarizes the most important points about the overall topic, and lists the one and two-page units that expand upon various aspects of the overall chapter topic. The last page of each chapter is a more detailed summary of the most important information.

The title at the top of each one- or two-page unit describes the topic covered by the unit. Immediately following is a summary of the most important points to remember about the topic. The numbering of the units indicates whether a unit stands alone or there are other closely related units. For example, in chapter 9:

- Unit 2, Historical Examples of Fiscal Policy, and unit 3. Designing a Stimulus Policy, are both stand-alone units.
- Unit 4, Timing of Fiscal Policy, is an overview of the topic, closely related to units 4.1, 4.2, and 4.3, all of which cover sub-topics introduced in unit 4.

A topic typically is covered on 2 facing pages. There is no flipping of pages to look for information— everything you need to know about the topic is visible at once.

Unit # Topic Title	Detailed information
Topic Description/ summary	
Detailed Information	Charts, graphs, etc.
Page #	Ch. Title / Page #

The textbook is designed to be used as a reference—its structure makes it easy to look up and read about particular topics. With a standard textbook, if you want to look up some particular bit of information, you are probably in for a lengthy search—flipping through pages in what you hope is the correct chapter until you stumble across what you are looking for. With this structured textbook, the search process is much faster and easier.

For example, say you want to look up something about the natural rate of unemployment.
- First you turn to the chapter list at the front of the textbook and see that unemployment in general is covered in chapter 5.
- Then you turn to the first page of chapter 5 and see from the list of topics that the natural rate of unemployment is covered in unit 7.
- When you turn to unit 7, everything you need to know about the natural rate of unemployment is in front of you on the two facing pages.

Or say you want to know what Keynes thought about monetary policy.
- From the chapter list, you see that monetary policy is covered in chapter 12.
- From the list of topics on the first page of chapter 12, you see that Keynes' view of monetary policy is covered in unit 3.
- When you turn to unit 3, everything you need to know about Keynes' thoughts on monetary policy is in front of you on the two facing pages.

Suggested approach for using the textbook

1. Before going to class, do a cursory reading of the chapter that will be covered that day.
- This should be a quick reading. Don't try to master the material. Don't memorize anything. Don't pore over the charts and graphs. The purpose of a first reading is simply to get a feel for the overall topic.
- If possible, read the whole chapter at one sitting. But don't spend more than half an hour on it.
- An initial cursory reading will give you a general familiarity with the topic. Your instructor's lecture will then make a lot more sense to you.

2. After class, reread the chapter more slowly.
- This will reinforce the instructor's lecture and help you to nail down the important concepts.
- Pay particular attention to the graphs in the textbook—be sure you understand and can manipulate the graphs. Economists do a lot of their thinking with graphs.
- Two hours is a reasonable amount of time to invest.

3. To study for a test, start with the summaries at the end of the chapter. Any statement there that you are not certain you understand indicates a unit in the chapter that you need to refer back to.

CH ONE
INTRODUCTION TO MACROECONOMICS

Economics is "the study of mankind in the ordinary business of life." Macroeconomics is the study of aggregate behavior; that is, the economy as a whole. Macroeconomics is more controversial than microeconomics.

Economic models are a deliberate simplification of reality. They let us focus on a handful of key factors and influences. The simplest macroeconomic model is the production possibilities curve, which shows the various combinations of two different goods that can be produced with a society's resources.

The production possibilities curve illustrates the basic economic concepts of scarcity, opportunity cost, and efficiency. It can also be used as a simple model for economic growth.

1. WHAT IS MACROECONOMICS

Economics is "the study of mankind in the ordinary business of life." Macroeconomics is the study of aggregate economic behavior; that is, of the economy as a whole.

Alfred Marshall (1842–1924) was one of the most influential economists of all time. His book, *Principles of Economics* (1890), was the dominant economics textbook in English-speaking countries for generations. Marshall invented many of the graphs and models that appear in economics textbooks today—including this book.

Alfred Marshall defined economics as "the study of mankind in the ordinary business of life."

This is a wonderful definition, because it makes clear that economics is not some arcane field of study interesting and valuable only to a handful of dedicated practitioners. Rather, economics tells the story of ordinary people going about their everyday lives. Economics provides a set of tools and a unique point of view that enables anyone to better understand their society and how the larger economy affects them as individuals.

This study of mankind in the ordinary business of life is easy to see when we look at the field of microeconomics. Microeconomics examines how:

- A single consumer decides what to buy, what job to take, how much money to save
- A single producer decides what price to charge, how much to produce, how many workers to hire

The focus of microeconomics is narrow—the choices facing a single consumer or a single firm. The unit of analysis of micro (that is, the level at which economic inquiry is focused) is small.

In contrast, macroeconomics has a very broad focus—rather than modeling the behavior of individuals, it models the behavior of the economy as a whole, or of major sectors of the economy. The unit of analysis of macro is large.

An example should make this distinction clear.

> For microeconomics, *expenditures* means spending by an individual consumer. To investigate expenditures, a microeconomist looks at the consumer's income and preferences, and at the relative prices of goods and services.

For macroeconomics, *expenditures* means aggregate expenditures by the economy as a whole.

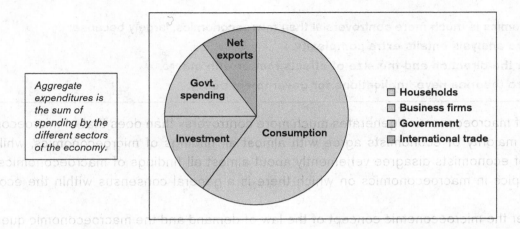

Aggregate expenditures is the sum of spending by the different sectors of the economy.

To investigate expenditures, a macroeconomist looks at disposable income, imports and exports, taxes, interest rates, and business expectations.

Macroeconomics deals extensively with the interactions between groups. Macro seldom examines any group in isolation; rather, macro most often examines a group in relation to other sectors of the economy.

For example, consider what the household sector does with its personal income. Among other things, households:

- Pay taxes to the government sector
- Purchase imported goods from the international trade sector
- Spend on goods and services produced by the business sector
- Put aside savings, which supports investment by the business sector

Interactions between groups are everywhere in the macro economy:

- Households are the customers for the goods and services produced by business firms
- Households also provide the labor and other resources business firms need to produce goods and services
- Wages and salaries paid by business firms provide the income households use to purchase goods and services
- Government tax policy influences how much income households have to spend, and also how much labor they sell to business firms

2. DIFFERENCES BETWEEN MACRO AND MICRO

Macroeconomics is much more controversial than microeconomics, largely because:
1. **Macro analysis entails extra complexity.**
2. **Both the direction and the size of effects matter with macro.**
3. **Macro theories have implications for government policy.**

The field of macroeconomics generates much more controversy than does that of microeconomics. The great majority of economists agree with almost all findings of microeconomics, while large numbers of economists disagree vehemently about almost all findings of macroeconomics. There are few topics in macroeconomics on which there is a general consensus within the economics profession.

Consider the microeconomic concept of the law of demand and the macroeconomic question of the impact of a minimum wage law. Ask any economist the micro question "Do demand curves slope downward?" and you will receive an unequivocal answer: "Yes, demand curves slope downward." However, if you ask economists the macro question "If the minimum wage is raised, will some low-skilled workers lose their jobs?" some will answer YES and some will answer NO. You will find this disagreement despite the fact that this appears to be a simple application of the universally accepted law of demand.

> *Raising the price (the wage rate) reduces the quantity demanded. That is, some workers lose their jobs.*

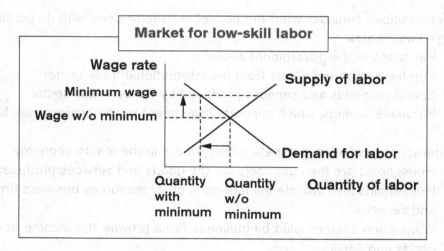

What accounts for macroeconomic topics being so much more controversial than microeconomic topics? The answer is three-fold:
1. Macroeconomic analysis is more complex than microeconomic analysis.
2. Both the direction and the size of effects matter with macroeconomics.
3. Macroeconomic theories have implications for government policy.

1. **Macroeconomic analysis is inherently more complex than microeconomic analysis.**

Partly this is because the scope of macro is larger. Microeconomics deals with the motives and behavior of a single consumer of a single firm, while macroeconomics deals with the behavior of large aggregates, entire sectors of the economy, or the economy as a whole. The focus of micro is narrow—the focus of macro is broad.

More significantly, micro, because of its narrow focus, can largely ignore how the individual or firm being studied interacts with others. For example, in the micro theory of perfect competition, the individual firm pays no attention to the behavior of other competing firms. But for macro, with its broader focus, interaction effects are much more important, and add greatly to the complexity of macro analysis. For example, the macro theory of the multiplier relies on a self-perpetuating series of interactions between the household and business sectors of the economy.

2. **For many macroeconomic topics, both the direction and the size of an effect matter.**

By contrast, microeconomics often concerns itself only with the direction of an effect. For example, the micro question "If the price of a good rises, what will happen to the quantity demanded?" is adequately answered by "If the price rises, the quantity demanded will fall." The direction of the effect is all that matters. The related macro question "What will happen if the government raises marginal tax rates on investment income?" is not adequately answered by "Raise tax rates and the volume of investment will decline." Knowing by how much investment will decline is crucial to deciding if higher investment tax rates would be a good source of revenue.

3. **Macroeconomic theories have implications for government policy, and actions in the political sphere have winners and losers.**

The transactions that microeconomics studies are typically win-win: voluntary exchange is mutually beneficial. When a consumer buys something from a retailer, both the consumer and the retailer are made better off. In contrast, government policy actions (which macroeconomics studies and informs) are typically redistributive—some folks are made better off and some folks are made worse off. For example, an agricultural price support program makes farmers better off (farm incomes rise) at the expense of making consumers worse off (food prices are higher).

Each side of any macro policy issue has its own economists who argue for policies that favor their own side. Economists, after all, are motivated by self-interest just as much as anybody else.

3. ECONOMIC MODELS

Economic models are a deliberate simplification of reality. They let us focus on a handful of key factors and influences. Economic models rely on the assumption of "all else being equal."

Models are everywhere in economics. Economists never look at the real world directly; they always view the world through the lens of the appropriate economic model. Economists use models to frame the questions they want to ask, to guide their investigations, and to assist in explaining their results.

At its most basic level, an economic model is a deliberate simplification of reality. Most of the complexity of the real world is simply assumed away by the model. The advantage of this is that it allows the researcher to focus on those key factors that are most relevant to the question being asked. An economic model is a tool that enables you to see the forest rather than a million trees.

> A demand curve is a simple economic model. It shows how the quantity of a good that consumers want to buy changes as the price of the good changes. We know that price is not the only thing that affects how much of a good consumers will buy—consumer purchases are also affected by income, preferences, prices of other goods, emotional mood, weather, whim, and who knows what else. But price is a key factor; and when we limit our focus only to price, we can see more clearly the effect it has.

The danger in using an economic model is that you might inadvertently exclude a factor that is critical to the question you are asking. A silly example should make this clear. Say you want to predict the position of the Earth relative to the sun, and that you know the Earth's current position and velocity. To predict the Earth's position in the future, you first model the Earth's motion. A very simple model of motion is Newton's first law: "A body in motion remains in constant motion in a straight line unless acted upon by an outside force." This model, however, will yield very poor results, because it excludes a factor critical to the question being asked—namely, a continually acting outside force: the sun's gravity.

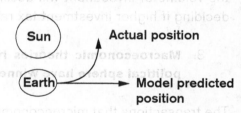

All economic models operate on the assumption of "all else being equal." This means that all factors not explicitly covered by the model are assumed to stay the same when the explicitly covered factors change.

To illustrate what this means, consider the demand curve for Coca-Cola. It predicts that, if the price of Coke falls, consumers will want to buy more Coke. But this assumes that nothing else relevant has changed along with the price of Coke. If "all else being equal" does not hold (for example, if the price of Pepsi-Cola also falls), then the prediction that more Coke will be purchased also might not hold.

Therefore, it is always important to check to see if there are any significant interaction effects in play.

A common criticism of economic models is that they are not realistic. However, as we have seen, economic models are not meant to be "realistic"—they are meant to be useful.

To illustrate the difference between realistic and useful, consider a model of when to pass on the highway.

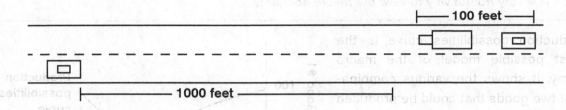

Velocities: Truck = 50 mph; Your car = 70 mph; Approaching car = 60 mph

The question we want to answer is: Is there enough time to pass the truck? We can model the situation as follows:

- Time to pass = Distance to truck ÷ (Velocity of your car - Velocity of truck)
- Time to arrive = Distance to truck ÷ (Velocity of approaching car + Velocity of truck)
- Pass if: Time to pass < Time to arrive

This is not a "realistic" model, in the sense that no driver actually makes the calculations in the model. Actually making the calculations would probably require a calculator, and by the time you determined that there was enough time to pass, the approaching car would likely be a mile or two past you in the opposite direction!

Nevertheless, this is a very "useful" model, because it lets us predict driver reaction to changes in a variety of factors. The driver will be less likely to try to pass the truck if:

- The truck is going faster
- The approaching car is closer
- Your car is going slower
- Your car is further behind the truck
- The approaching car is going faster

And it is also easy to incorporate other "all else being equal" factors into the model; things such as road conditions, weather conditions, acceleration speeds, and uncertain estimates of speeds and distances.

This model tells us a lot about how drivers in the real world behave, even though no driver ever actually does what the model says to do. *Useful* is better than *realistic*.

4. PRODUCTION POSSIBILITIES

A production possibilities curve is the simplest possible model of the macro economy. It shows what different combinations of two goods can be produced with an economy's existing resources. Though simple, it is a very fruitful way to view the macro economy.

A production possibilities curve is the simplest possible model of the macro economy. It shows the various combinations of two goods that could be produced with an economy's existing resources.

The production possibilities model is a massive simplification of the real world, where there are literally millions of different goods and services being produced. Because there are so many different goods, and because there are so many possible alternative uses for resources, and because the interrelationships between goods and resources are so complex, it is next to impossible to identify how changes in the production of one good affect the production of other goods. By simplifying down to only two products, the production possibilities model makes the task much simpler—we can focus on how changes in the production of one good affect the production of the single other good.

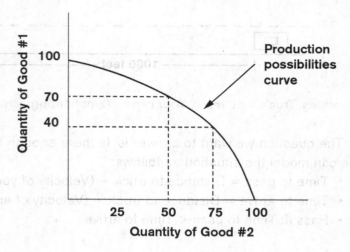

The production possibilities model asks the question: "What different combinations of the two goods can be produced by the society?"

- If all resources are applied to good #1, how much of good #1 can be produced?
- If all resources are applied to good #2, how much of good #2 can be produced?
- If resources are split between the two goods, how much of each can be produced?

The "all else being equal" assumption applies to the production possibilities model. The things that are held constant by the model are:
- The quantity of resources available to the society
- The quality of those resources
- The level of technology available to the society (that is, the methods by which the resources can be employed to produce the two goods)

The production possibilities model is certainly not realistic, but it is very useful.

The model nicely illustrates a number of key economic concepts.

Scarcity:

Resources are limited. Not all combinations of the two goods can be produced given the society's available resources. For example, the society shown on the previous page can't produce both 100 units of good #1 and 100 units of good #2 at the same time.

Opportunity cost:

There is always a trade-off between the two goods. In order to produce more of good #1, you must give up some production of good #2. If our sample society is currently producing seventy units of good #1 and fifty units of good #2, the cost of producing twenty-five more units of good #2 is thirty units of good #1 (the production of good #1 is reduced from seventy units to forty units).

Efficiency:

The combinations on the production possibilities curve itself are achieved only when all resources are used to their maximum. If our sample society is producing, for example, fifty units of good #1 and fifty units of good #2, then some resources are either unused or only partly used.

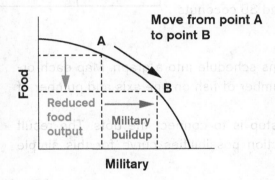

Move from point A to point B

The production possibilities model can be used to make societal trade-offs explicit.
For example: Famine in North Korea is partly due to its maintaining a large army. Resources used for the military aren't available for producing food.

The model can be used to show how changes in resources will affect the options available to a society.

A wide variety of situations can be modeled with a production possibilities curve simply by changing the goods listed on the horizontal and vertical axes.
- List "Investment Goods" and "Consumption Goods" to model economic growth.
- List "Guns" and "Butter" to model the impact of military spending.
- List "All other goods" on one axis to model the costs of any specific good.

4.1. CONSTRUCTING A PRODUCTION POSSIBILITIES CURVE

To construct a production possibilities curve, you first develop a schedule showing the possible combinations of two goods that an economy could produce, and then convert the schedule to a graph. The graph illustrates the key economic concepts of scarcity, efficiency, and opportunity cost.

The first step in constructing a production possibilities curve is to develop a schedule showing the possible combinations of two goods that an economy could produce.

To illustrate constructing a possible combinations schedule, imagine a simple society where the only activities are catching fish and gathering coconuts. There are four persons in the society, with varying skills in fishing and gathering coconuts, like so:

Person	Productivity		
	Fish		Coconuts
#1	4	or	5
#2	3	or	10
#3	2	or	15
#4	1	or	20

Possible combinations for this economy are:
- If all four persons only fish : 10 fish and 0 coconuts
- If three persons fish and one gathers coconuts : 9 fish and 20 coconuts
  - » Note: It's person #4, who is least efficient at fishing, who will gather coconuts instead: this is the most efficient use of resources.
- If two persons fish and two gather coconuts : 7 fish and 35 coconuts
- And so on …

Fish	Coconuts
10	0
9	20
7	35
4	45
0	50

The second step is to convert the possible combinations schedule into a graph. Map each ordered pair of fish and coconuts into a graph that shows number of fish on one axis and number of coconuts on the other axis.

The final step is to connect the dots. The result is the production possibilities curve for this simple society.

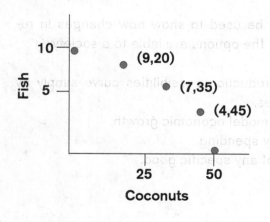

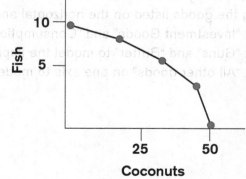

Connecting the dots creates much more information than was in the possible combinations table. The production possibilities curve divides the universe of all combinations of fish and coconuts into three distinct sets.
- Combinations inside the curve (area B)
- Combinations on the curve
- Combinations outside the curve (area A)

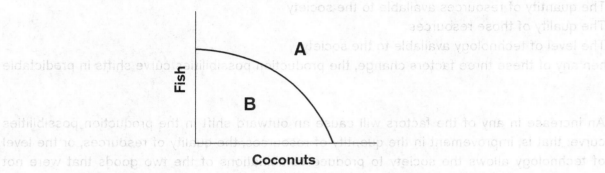

The production possibilities graph illustrates the key economic concepts of scarcity, efficiency, and opportunity cost.

Any combination of fish and coconuts in area A (outside the production possibilities curve) is unachievable given the society's existing resources and technology.
- This illustrates SCARCITY: There are limited resources available : We have to choose how to use those limited resources.

Any combination of fish and coconuts in area B (inside the production possibilities curve) or on the curve can be achieved. However, only points on the curve are using all resources to the best effect. At any point inside the curve, one or more of the fishers or coconut gatherers are not working as hard as they could.
- This illustrates EFFICIENCY: All resources are fully used.

Along the production possibilities curve, the only way to get more of one good is to give up some of the other good.
- This illustrates OPPORTUNITY COST: The true cost of catching more fish is that you will be able to gather fewer coconuts.

4.2. SHOWING CHANGES IN RESOURCES

When the resources available to a society change, the production possibilities curve shifts in predictable ways. The general shape of the production possibilities curve is due to the law of increasing costs.

A production possibilities curve holds constant:
- The quantity of resources available to the society
- The quality of those resources
- The level of technology available to the society

When any of these three factors change, the production possibilities curve shifts in predictable ways.

- An increase in any of the factors will cause an outward shift in the production possibilities curve: that is, improvement in the quantity of resources, the quality of resources, or the level of technology allows the society to produce combinations of the two goods that were not previously achievable.
- A decrease in any of the factors will cause an inward shift in the production possibilities curve: that is, some combinations previously available to the society can no longer be achieved.

Whether the shift in the production possibilities curve is more along the horizontal axis or more along the vertical axis depends on how the changes in resources and technology affect the production of each good. The examples that follow assume that the two goods being produced are books and food.

Example #1: An increase in all resources

Say, for example, that immigration brings in new workers with skills useful for the production of both food and books—not only farmers, millers, vintners, and the like, but also bookbinders, publishers, printers, and the like.
- There is an outward shift in the production possibilities curve along both the Books axis and the Food axis.

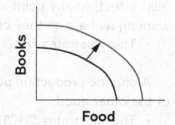

Example #2: A decrease in resources useful only for the production of 1 good

Say, for example, that a fire destroys a big fertilizer plant. This reduces the quantity of resources useful for food production, but causes no change in resources useful for book production.
- The production possibilities curve swings inward along the Food axis.

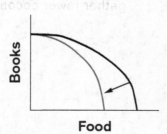

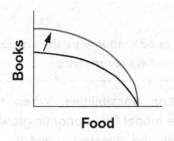

Example #3: Improvement in the technology used to produce one of the goods

Consider, for example, the invention of the printing press. This greatly reduced the cost of producing books, but was of no use in food production.

- The production possibilities curve swings outward along the Books axis.

In all of these examples, every production possibilities curve is concave from the origin. That is, production possibilities curves are not straight lines, but rather bulge outward from the origin.

- This shape of production possibilities curves is due to the law of increasing costs.

The law of increasing costs says:

> As you increase the production of one good in equal increments, there is an ever-increasing loss in the quantity of the second good that can be produced.

Consider these production possibilities:

Books	Food
0	20
1	18
2	14
3	8
4	0

The cost of the first unit of books is the loss of 2 units of food
- Food production declines from 20 to 18

The cost of the second unit of books is the loss of 4 units of food
- Food production declines from 18 to 14

The cost of the third unit of books is the loss of 6 units of food
- Food production declines from 14 to 8

The cost of the fourth unit of books is the loss of 8 units of food
- Food production declines from 8 to 0

The law of increasing costs works because not all resources are equally useful for the production of either good—some resources are more useful for food production, while other resources are more useful for book production.

- When we transfer resources from the production of books to the production of food, we always move the resources which are least useful for books (causing the smallest drop in book production) and most useful for food (causing the largest rise in food production).
- As we continue to transfer resources from books to food, those resources are increasingly ones more useful for books and less useful for food (if they were less useful for books and more useful for food, we would have moved them earlier).
- So the cost of additional food production continually increases.

4.3. SHOWING ECONOMIC GROWTH

A society's current choices between consumption goods and investment goods influences the shape of the production possibilities curve in the future. This is a simple model for economic growth.

A society's current production choices affect its future production possibilities. When the production possibilities curve is used to show this, it becomes a simple model for economic growth.

Broadly speaking, there are two types of goods: consumption goods and investment goods.

A consumption good is acquired by a household and used to satisfy the needs or wants of members of that household. It is not used to produce other goods, but rather is consumed: food that we eat, clothing that we wear, haircuts and manicures that we enjoy, books that we read, DVDs that we watch, and so on.

An investment good is acquired by a business firm and used to produce consumption goods or other investment goods. Investment goods are things like factories, machinery, power plants, business equipment, infrastructure, and so on. In effect, investment goods are new resources available to the society, and as such they expand an economy's production possibilities.

Society can choose to operate anywhere along this production possibilities curve. Where it chooses to operate today, affects the position of the curve in the future.

The particular combination of investment goods and consumption goods that a society chooses today, determines to what extent the society's production possibilities grow in the future.

A society that invests only a little will grow only slowly.

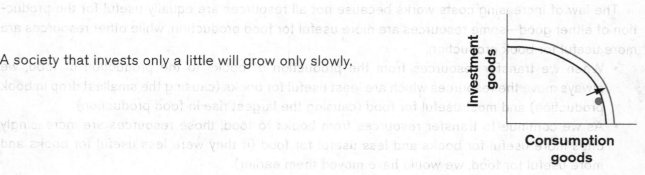

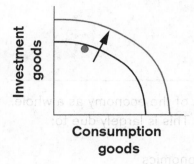

Foregoing consumption today can lead to greatly increased production possibilities in the future.

Though the production possibilities curve is a very simple and highly unrealistic model of growth, it nonetheless helps us to understand much real world behavior. Three examples:

1. The virtue of thrift

Put simply, thrift is spending less than you earn—saving rather than going into debt. The amount that you save (that you don't consume) is available to loan to businesses for them to invest. Thrift, then, is a "virtue" because, by moving society toward the investment end of the production possibilities curve, it encourages economic growth and rising prosperity.

2. Public education

A public education system is a choice by society to invest in human capital. By foregoing the current production that students could provide if they were instead in the labor force, society improves the quality of its labor resources, shifting out the production possibilities curve in the future.

3. Soviet Union during the Cold War

The Soviet Union was a command economy—overall production decisions were made by central planners. The Soviet leadership explicitly chose to move strongly toward the investment end of the production possibilities curve—they undertook massive infrastructure projects while severely limiting the production of consumer goods. As a result of this emphasis on investment, the growth rate of the Soviet economy in the 1950s and 1960s was much higher than that in the United States. However, the choice to severely curtail the production of consumption goods meant that the Soviet populace did not share in the benefits of growth, and growing popular dissent with the low living standards was a large factor in the eventual failure of the Soviet planned economy.

SUMMARY OF CHAPTER 1

Economics is the study of mankind in the ordinary business of life.

Macroeconomics is the study of aggregate economic behavior; that is, of the economy as a whole.
Macroeconomics is much more controversial than microeconomics. This is largely due to:

1. The extra complexity of macroeconomic analysis
2. Both the direction and the size of effects matter with macroeconomics
3. The fact that macroeconomic theories have implications for government policy

Economic models are a deliberate simplification of reality. They let us focus on a handful of key factors and influences.

Economic models rely on the assumption of "all else being equal."
A production possibilities curve is the simplest possible model of the macro economy.

- It shows what different combinations of two goods can be produced with an economy's existing resources.

Though simple, the production possibilities curve is a very fruitful way to view the macro economy.

To construct a production possibilities curve, first develop a schedule showing the possible combinations of two goods that an economy could produce, then convert the schedule to a graph.
A production possibilities curve illustrates a number of key economic concepts:

- SCARCITY: There are limited resources available. We have to choose how to use those limited resources.
- EFFICIENCY: All resources are fully used.
- OPPORTUNITY COST: The true cost of producing more of one good is that now you must produce less of the other good.

The law of increasing costs says: As you increase the production of one good in equal increments, there is an ever-increasing loss in the quantity of the second good that can be produced.

- This explains the concave shape of the production possibilities curve.

A society's current choices between consumption goods and investment goods influences the shape of the production possibilities curve in the future. This is a simple model for economic growth.

Credits

CH TWO

OVERVIEW OF THE U.S. ECONOMY

The U.S. economy is immensely complex, involving the production and consumption of literally millions of different products and services. U.S. producers and consumers operate through a complex set of interrelated product and resource markets. The U.S. economy is continually in motion, as consumers and producers react to ever-changing market conditions.

The U.S. labor force is both highly educated and highly mobile. Wages and salaries account for the bulk of the income of most Americans. Businesses have available an extensive infrastructure of capital goods that facilitate the production and distribution of goods and resources. Government, at various levels, plays a role in almost all aspects of economic life.

The U.S. economy is by far the largest in the world. International comparisons are legitimate, but can be misleading.

1. COMPLEXITY

The U.S. economy is immensely complex, involving the production and consumption of literally millions of different products and services. The focus of the economy has changed dramatically over time, with huge shifts from agriculture to manufacturing, and more recently from manufacturing to services.

The U.S. economy is immensely complex, producing and consuming literally millions of different products and services. The small portion of the Standard Industrial Classification system shown below gives a feel for the incredible variety of goods and services available in a modern economy.

Standard Industrial Classification Structure

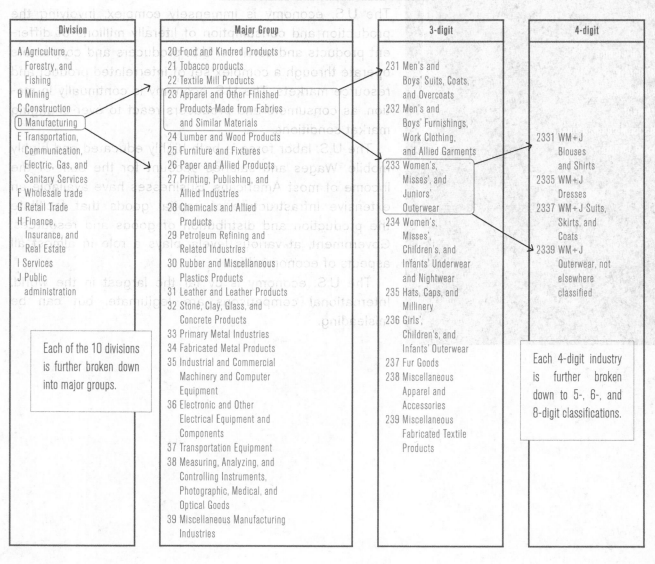

Division	Major Group	3-digit	4-digit
A Agriculture, Forestry, and Fishing	20 Food and Kindred Products	231 Men's and Boys' Suits, Coats, and Overcoats	
B Mining	21 Tobacco products		
C Construction	22 Textile Mill Products	232 Men's and Boys' Furnishings, Work Clothing, and Allied Garments	
D Manufacturing	23 Apparel and Other Finished Products Made from Fabrics and Similar Materials		2331 WM+J Blouses and Shirts
E Transportation, Communication, Electric, Gas, and Sanitary Services	24 Lumber and Wood Products	233 Women's, Misses', and Juniors' Outerwear	2335 WM+J Dresses
	25 Furniture and Fixtures		2337 WM+J Suits, Skirts, and Coats
	26 Paper and Allied Products		2339 WM+J Outerwear, not elsewhere classified
F Wholesale trade	27 Printing, Publishing, and Allied Industries	234 Women's, Misses', Children's, and Infants' Underwear and Nightwear	
G Retail Trade	28 Chemicals and Allied Products		
H Finance, Insurance, and Real Estate	29 Petroleum Refining and Related Industries	235 Hats, Caps, and Millinery	
I Services	30 Rubber and Miscellaneous Plastics Products	236 Girls', Children's, and Infants' Outerwear	
J Public administration	31 Leather and Leather Products		
	32 Stone, Clay, Glass, and Concrete Products	237 Fur Goods	
	33 Primary Metal Industries	238 Miscellaneous Apparel and Accessories	
	34 Fabricated Metal Products	239 Miscellaneous Fabricated Textile Products	
	35 Industrial and Commercial Machinery and Computer Equipment		
	36 Electronic and Other Electrical Equipment and Components		
	37 Transportation Equipment		
	38 Measuring, Analyzing, and Controlling Instruments, Photographic, Medical, and Optical Goods		
	39 Miscellaneous Manufacturing Industries		

Each of the 10 divisions is further broken down into major groups.

Each 4-digit industry is further broken down to 5-, 6-, and 8-digit classifications.

The focus of the U.S. economy has changed dramatically over the past 200 years. In 1800, the output of the economy was almost entirely from agriculture. The nineteenth century saw huge shifts away from agriculture into manufacturing. The twentieth century continued the shift away from agriculture with the dramatic rise of the services sector, which today dominates the U.S. economy.

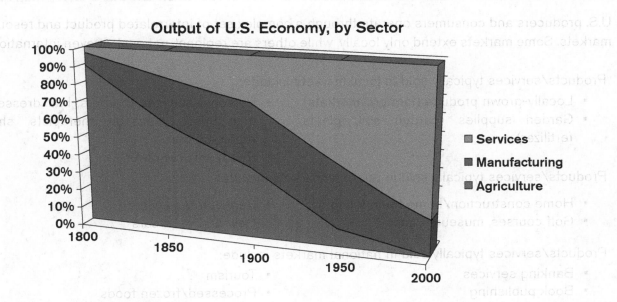

Output of U.S. Economy, by Sector

The particular companies operating in the economy also change greatly over time. *Fortune* magazine's ranking of U.S. companies by size began in 1955. Of the ten largest companies in 1955, only three are still in the top-ten list today—the others have fallen behind, merged with other companies, or disappeared entirely.

Fortune 500 ranking of largest U.S. companies

Rank	1955	1985	2014
1	General Motors	Exxon Mobil	Wal-Mart
2	Exxon Mobil	General Motors	Exxon Mobil
3	U.S. Steel	Mobil	Chevron
4	General Electric	Ford Motors	BerkshireHathaway
5	Esmark	Texaco	Apple
6	Chrysler	IBM	Phillips 66
7	Armour	DuPont	General Motors
8	Gulf Oil	AT&T	Ford Motors
9	Mobil	General Electric	General Electric
10	DuPont	Amoco	Valero Energy

Between 1955 and 1985, half of the largest companies changed.

Between 1985 and 2014, 6 of the largest companies changed.

2. EXTENT OF MARKETS

U.S. producers and consumers operate through a complex set of interrelated product and resource markets: local, regional, national, and international. The extent of a market is affected by transportation costs and trade barriers.

U.S. producers and consumers operate through a complex set of interrelated product and resource markets. Some markets extend only locally, while others are regional, national, or even international.

Products/services typically sold in local markets include:

- Locally-grown produce (farmers' markets)
- Garden supplies (garden soil, plants, fertilizer)
- Personal services (barbers, hair dressers, manicurists, massage therapists, shoe repair, tailors)
- Ready-mix concrete

Products/services typically sold in regional markets include:

- Home construction/home remodeling
- Golf courses, museums, zoos
- Real estate services
- New and used cars

Products/services typically sold in national markets include:

- Banking services
- Book publishing
- Tourism
- Processed/frozen foods

Products/services typically sold in international markets include:

- Fine wines
- Artwork
- Gem stones
- Rare minerals

Local labor markets typically handle jobs for:

- Unskilled labor
- Temporary labor
- Low-paying jobs in general

Regional labor markets typically handle jobs for:

- Computer programmers
- Nurses
- Teachers

National labor markets typically handle jobs for:

- Professional sports
- High-level management
- High-level government

International labor markets typically handle jobs for:

- Commodity traders
- Highly specialized skill

The extent of a market is affected by transportation costs. All else being equal, products that are heavy, bulky, or expensive to ship are more likely to be manufactured close to where they will be consumed.

- This is why steel mills historically have been located near deposits of iron ore, and petroleum refineries have been located near oil fields. The finished products are less expensive to ship than the raw materials, so the raw materials are consumed near to where they are produced.
- This is why gem cutters are not located near the mines. The cost of shipping raw gem stones is very low, so gem cutters can operate in more convenient locales.

If you purchase ready-mix concrete, it is almost certainly produced locally, because the cost of shipping heavy bulky concrete is very high.

If you purchase a smart phone, it might have been manufactured anywhere in the world, because the cost of shipping a small, light cell phone is very low.

The extent of a labor market is affected by commuting and relocation costs. All else being equal, jobs offering a lower wage are more likely to be filled by persons who live close to the job site. Higher salaries are needed to induce people to accept longer commutes or incur the expense of relocating closer to the job site.

- This is why there is usually a nation-wide search for top positions in major corporations. The pay for such jobs is so high that whoever is selected will certainly relocate.
- This is why fast food workers usually live nearby. The pay for such jobs is so low that it makes little sense to commute far to work one.

If you hire someone to clear snow from your driveway, they probably live close by, because driving a snow plow very far is expensive in both time and gasoline.

If you hire a new coach for your NBA basketball team, that person might currently live on the other side of the country. For what you will be paying, the coach will move.

The extent of a market can also be affected by trade barriers. Legal restrictions or ruinously high import tariffs can limit the extent of both product and labor markets.

- The U.S. government banned trade with Cuba after the communist takeover in 1959. Cuba's main exports were sugar and tobacco, and the trade embargo effectively converted international markets for both goods into national markets for U.S. consumers.
- If it were illegal for the owners of Japanese baseball teams to hire American players (as it once was), then the labor market for ballplayers in Japan would be national instead of international.

3. VARIABILITY

The U.S. economy is continually in motion. There are long-run ups and downs in the business cycle, and daily fluctuations in stock markets. Commodity prices in particular tend to be volatile.

The U.S. economy is always in motion, as millions of consumers and producers continually react to constantly changing market conditions.

Some changes occur over a period of years—long-term expansions and contractions called the business cycle. The U.S. economy has gone through ten business cycles since 1950—with each cycle averaging about six years in length.

Business cycle reference dates		Duration in Months			
		Contraction	Expansion	Cycle	
Peak	Trough	Peak to Trough	Previous trough to this peak	Trough from Previous Trough	Peak from Previous Peak
July 1953	May 1954	10	45	55	56
August 1957	April 1958	8	39	47	49
April 1960	February 1961	10	24	34	32
December 1969	November 1970	11	106	117	116
November 1973	March 1975	16	36	52	47
January 1980	July 1980	6	58	64	74
July 1981	November 1982	16	12	28	18
July 1990	March 1991	8	92	100	108
March 2001	November 2001	8	120	128	128
December 2007	June 2009	18	73	91	81

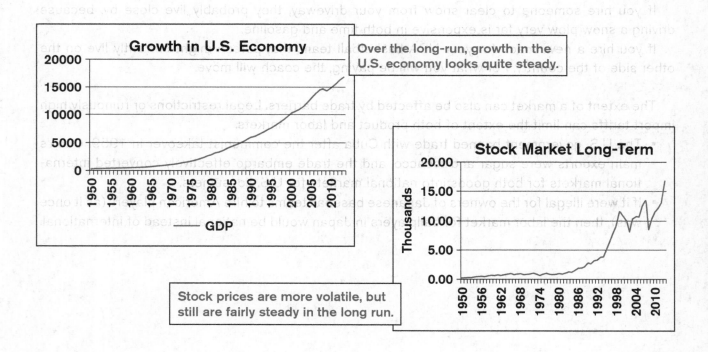

Growth in U.S. Economy

Over the long-run, growth in the U.S. economy looks quite steady.

Stock prices are more volatile, but still are fairly steady in the long run.

Stock Market Long-Term

But when viewed in the short run, changes are occurring on a daily basis.

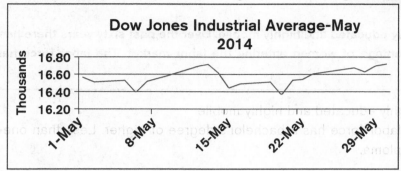

Dow Jones Industrial Average-May 2014

Stock indexes rise and fall minute by minute.

Prices of just about everything are subject to change at any time. Commodity prices in particular tend to be volatile, as the charts below indicate.

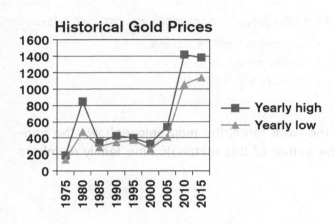

Historical Gold Prices

- Yearly high
- Yearly low

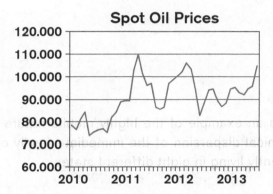

Spot Oil Prices

U.S. Export Corn Price Index, January 1989–October 2012

Corn

Wholesale Wheat Prices
World War I through The Great Depression

Wheat

High $2.45/bu 1920

Black Tuesday October 1929

Pearl Harbor Attack Dec. 1941

Armistice Nov. 1918

Low $0.49/bu 1932

4. LABOR FORCE

The U.S. labor force is both highly educated and highly mobile. Over the past sixty years there has been a dramatic increase in the percentage of women entering the labor market. The labor force has also become increasingly urban.

The U.S. labor force is both highly educated and highly mobile.

More than one-third of the labor force has a bachelor's degree or higher. Less than one-tenth does not have a high school diploma.

Level of education	Percent of labor force	Participation rate	Unemployment rate	Average weekly earnings
Less than high school	8.1%	44.2%	9.1%	$472
High school	26.9%	57.9%	6.5%	$651
Some college	27.7%	67.2%	5.5%	$727
With degree	37.4%	75.4%	3.2%	$1,199

The work force advantage of more education is clear. Persons with more education:

- Are more likely to enter the labor force
- Are more likely to find a job
- On average earn a larger income

As an example of the highly mobile nature of the work force, the map below shows the geographical dispersion of the immediate family of the author of this textbook: nine family members currently living in eight different states.

Geographic spread of the author's immediate family

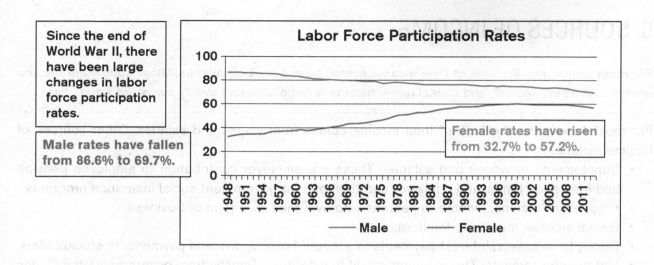

Labor Force Participation Rates

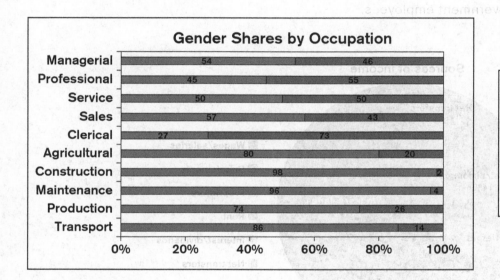

Gender Shares by Occupation

Occupation	Male	Female
Managerial	54	46
Professional	45	55
Service	50	50
Sales	57	43
Clerical	27	73
Agricultural	80	20
Construction	98	2
Maintenance	96	4
Production	74	26
Transport	86	14

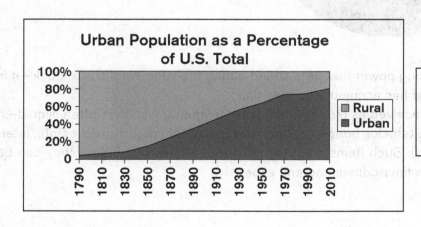

Urban Population as a Percentage of U.S. Total

Rural
Urban

5. SOURCES OF INCOME

For most Americans, the bulk of their income comes from wages or salaries. Other sources of income are rent, royalties, interest, and capital gains. Income is not distributed evenly across all Americans.

For most Americans, the bulk of their income comes from wages and salaries. Other sources of income include:

- Supplements to wages and salaries: These are employer contribution to employee pension and insurance funds, and employer contributions for government social insurance programs.
- Proprietors' income: Income to persons who own their own farm or business.
- Rental income: Income to landlords.
- Receipts on assets: Interest payments to account holders, dividend payments to stockholders.
- Net transfer receipts: This is benefits paid to individuals (mostly from government). It includes Social Security, Medicare, Medicaid, unemployment insurance, veterans' benefits, and pensions to retired government employees.

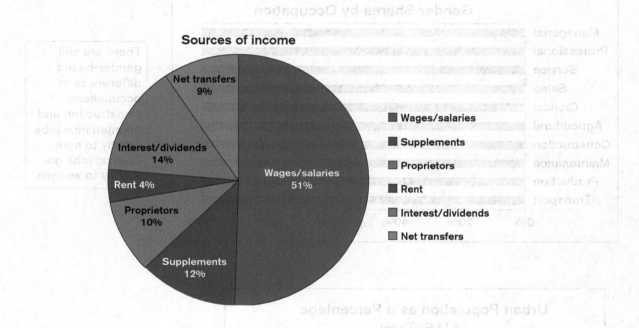

Income is a flow—it is purchasing power that gets added during the year. Wealth is a stock—it is the total of purchasing power that has accumulated over time.

Income is liquid—it is usually received as money and is easy to spend. Wealth is often illiquid—it resides in anything that has value (stocks, bonds, commodities, personal property, real estate, intellectual property rights, and so on). Such items must be converted into money before they can be spent, a process that can be both time-consuming and expensive.

Income is not equally distributed across all Americans. Income inequality has been increasing for the past thirty years. The table below shows the distribution of household income. In 2012, the richest 20% of U.S. households earned 51.0% of total income, while the poorest 20% of households earned 3.2% of total income. The richest 20% of households earned, on average, sixteen times as much income as the poorest 20% of households. Since 1982, the share of the highest fifth of households has increased by 13%, while the share of the lowest fifth has decreased by 20%.

Quintiles of Income

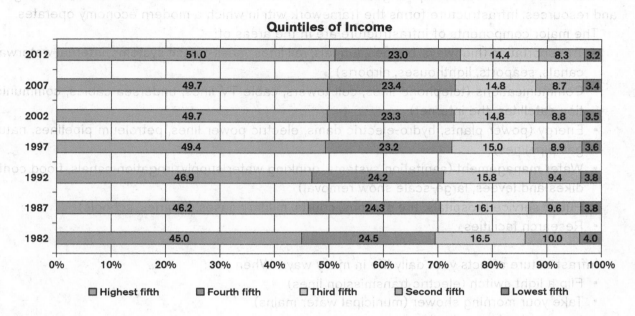

	Highest fifth	Fourth fifth	Third fifth	Second fifth	Lowest fifth
2012	51.0	23.0	14.4	8.3	3.2
2007	49.7	23.4	14.8	8.7	3.4
2002	49.7	23.3	14.8	8.8	3.5
1997	49.4	23.2	15.0	8.9	3.6
1992	46.9	24.2	15.8	9.4	3.8
1987	46.2	24.3	16.1	9.6	3.8
1982	45.0	24.5	16.5	10.0	4.0

The data on income inequality is real, but is also misleading in a number of ways.

- The income totals do not include the value of non-money transfer payments (things like food stamps, housing subsidies, school lunch programs). These benefits typically go to poorer households.
- The income totals are gross, not net of taxes. Taxes are disproportionately paid by richer households.
- Households with higher income tend to have more members than households with lower income (the lowest fifth contains many one-person households). This means that income inequality per-capita is lower than per household.
- Households in the higher fifths are more likely to be headed by persons in their prime working age, with full-time jobs. Many more households in the lower fifths are headed by retired persons or younger persons just starting their work career.

Most importantly, the data give the appearance of stability, but in reality there is tremendous mobility in the U.S. economy. People don't stay in the same income quintile their whole lives; many persons in lower fifths move up over time, while many persons in higher fifths move down over time.

6. INFRASTRUCTURE

Infrastructure is the set of capital goods that facilitates the production and distribution of goods and resources. This includes transportation, communications, and research facilities.

Infrastructure is the set of capital goods that facilitates the production and distribution of goods and resources. Infrastructure forms the framework within which a modern economy operates.

The major components of infrastructure are in the areas of:

- Transportation (highways, bridges, tunnels, rail lines, mass-transit systems, internal waterways, canals, seaports, lighthouses, airports)
- Communications (telephone lines, cell towers, cable TV lines, undersea cables, communication satellites, the internet)
- Energy (power plants, hydro-electric dams, electric power lines, petroleum pipelines, natural gas pipelines)
- Water management (sanitation systems, drinking water supply, irrigation canals, flood control dikes and levees, large-scale snow removal)
- Public service (hospitals, fire stations, courts, military bases, libraries, schools)
- Research facilities

Infrastructure affects your daily life in many ways. When you:

- Flip a light switch (electric transmission lines)
- Take your morning shower (municipal water mains)
- Use a toilet (sewer lines)
- Drive to work (highways, bridges)
- Tune in to the radio (transmission towers)
- Talk on your cell phone (cell towers)
- Use your smartphone's navigation feature (GPS satellites)
- Surf the internet (servers, routers)
- Stop at Starbucks (that coffee didn't walk here from Colombia)
- Relax in front of the TV (fiber optic cable lines)
- Cook dinner / heat your house (natural gas pipelines)
- Visit your parents three states over (airports)

The importance of infrastructure is most clearly seen when we lose its use. When Hurricane Katrina hit the East Coast, millions of people lost power, lost telephone service, lost access to clean water and sanitation, could not use flooded roads, could not reach hospitals or emergency care. Employees could not reach their places of work, stores could not get new supplies. Modern economic life is simply not possible without extensive infrastructure.

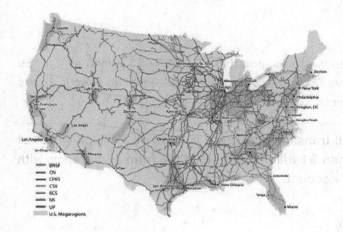

There are 140,000 miles of rail line in the U.S. rail network.

There are currently 7 large rail operators in the U.S.

There are 305,000 miles of natural gas transmission pipelines in the U.S. network.

The U.S. has 400 underground natural gas storage facilities.

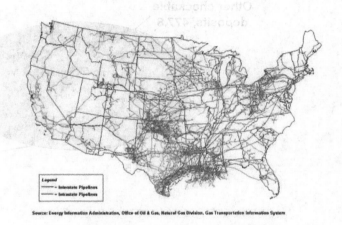

Source: Energy Information Administration, Office of Oil & Gas, Natural Gas Division, Gas Transportation Information System

Infrastructure is sometimes built and maintained by the government.
- Most highways are publically built and maintained.
- The Federal government runs nuclear research facilities in Hanford, Alamagordo, and Oak Ridge.

Sometimes infrastructure is privately owned, but assisted by the government.
- Railroad construction in the nineteenth century was privately funded, but greatly assisted by right-of-way land grants from the government.
- The government provides grants to support public and private academic research facilities.

Some infrastructure is privately owned and maintained.
- Cell towers are built and owned by the private service providers.
- Fiber optic cable networks are built and owned by cable TV companies.

7. MONEY ECONOMY

Money is the medium of exchange for almost all transactions, and there is nearly $3 trillion of it in the U.S. economy. In addition, people hold trillions more in a multitude of different financial assets. Funds flow through banks and various other types of financial intermediaries.

Money is the medium of exchange for almost all transactions. There is nearly $3 trillion worth of money in circulation in the U.S. economy. More than $1 trillion of this is in the form of currency, with most of the rest being in some type of checking account.

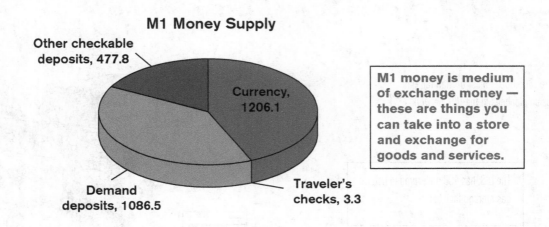

M1 Money Supply

Other checkable deposits, 477.8

Currency, 1206.1

Demand deposits, 1086.5

Traveler's checks, 3.3

M1 money is medium of exchange money — these are things you can take into a store and exchange for goods and services.

In addition, people hold trillions of dollars more in a multitude of near-monies. The most common of these is various types of savings accounts.

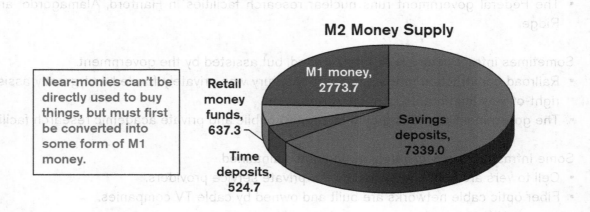

M2 Money Supply

Near-monies can't be directly used to buy things, but must first be converted into some form of M1 money.

M1 money, 2773.7

Retail money funds, 637.3

Savings deposits, 7339.0

Time deposits, 524.7

These trillions of dollars of funds flow through commercial banks, savings institutions, and other types of financial intermediaries.

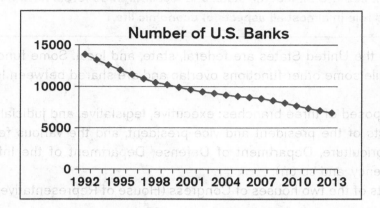

The number of banks in the U.S. has been declining steadily over the past 20 years. Although there have been a few bank failures, most of the decline is due to bank mergers.

Although only 10% of U.S. banks have deposits of over $1 billion, these banks have over 90% of total assets in the banking system.

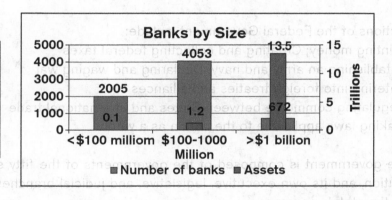

The banking sector is the most heavily regulated industry in the nation. Major government regulatory agencies include:
- Federal Reserve System: sets bank reserve requirements; examines the books of member banks
- Federal Deposit Insurance Corporation: insures depositor account to protect against loss in the event of bank failure; restricts the types of assets banks can hold
- Securities and Exchange Commission: requires disclosure of information; restricts insider trading

8. GOVERNMENT

There are three levels of government in the U.S.: federal, state, and local. All three levels have become larger over time. Government plays a role in almost all aspects of economic life.

The three levels of government in the United States are federal, state, and local. Some functions are unique to a particular level, while some other functions overlap and are shared between levels.

The federal government is composed of three branches: executive, legislative, and judicial.
- The executive branch consists of the president and vice-president, and the various federal agencies (Department of Agriculture, Department of Defense, Department of the Interior, Environmental Protection Agency, and so on).
- The legislative branch consists of the two houses of Congress (House of Representatives and Senate).
- The judicial branch consists of the Supreme Court and various federal courts.

Functions of the Federal Government include:
- Printing money; Creating and collecting federal taxes
- Establishing an army and navy; Declaring and waging war
- Entering into foreign treaties and alliances
- Regulating commerce between States and international trade
- Making laws applicable to the nation as a whole

State government is composed of the governments of the fifty states. Each state has its own constitution, and its own executive, legislative, and judicial branches. The chief executive of each state is the state's governor.

Typical functions of state governments include:
- Establishing local governments, state courts; creating and collecting state taxes
- Building and maintaining highways
- Issuing driver's licenses, marriage licenses, and the like; setting legal age for drinking, smoking, and the like; regulating intrastate commerce

Local government is composed of 30,000 municipal governments, 3,000 county governments, and 50,000 school and special districts. The structure and functions of these local governments vary widely.

Typical functions of local governments include:
- Public education
- Police and fire protection
- Public works (drinking water, sewers, wastewater and storm water management)
- Urban planning/zoning
- Parks and recreation

All three levels of government have grown over time. Government now plays a role in almost all aspects of economic life.

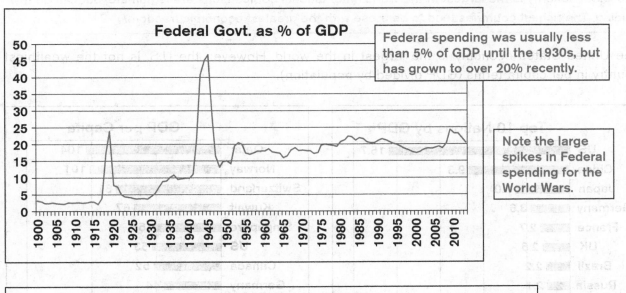

Federal Govt. as % of GDP

Federal spending was usually less than 5% of GDP until the 1930s, but has grown to over 20% recently.

Note the large spikes in Federal spending for the World Wars.

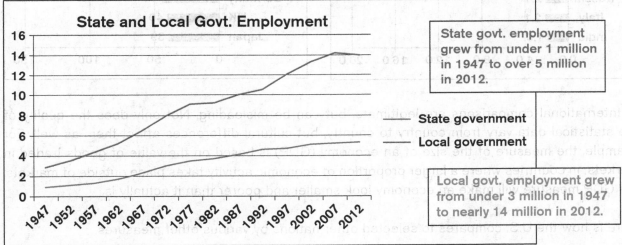

State and Local Govt. Employment

State govt. employment grew from under 1 million in 1947 to over 5 million in 2012.

Local govt. employment grew from under 3 million in 1947 to nearly 14 million in 2012.

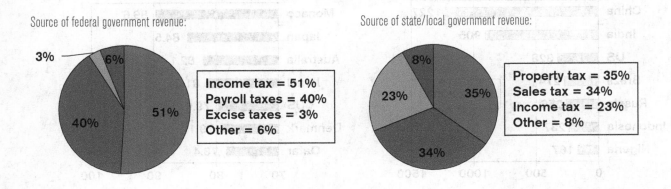

Source of federal government revenue:

Income tax = 51%
Payroll taxes = 40%
Excise taxes = 3%
Other = 6%

Source of state/local government revenue:

Property tax = 35%
Sales tax = 34%
Income tax = 23%
Other = 8%

9. INTERNATIONAL COMPARISONS

The U.S. economy is the largest in the world. International comparisons are legitimate, but can be misleading. The richest countries tend to be those with the greatest economic freedom.

The United States economy is the largest in the world. However, the U.S. is not the wealthiest country in per capita terms (GDP divided by population).

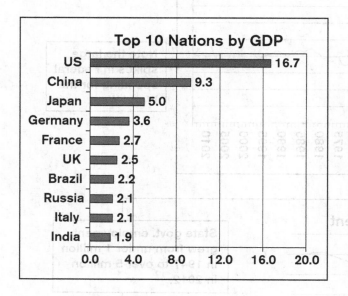

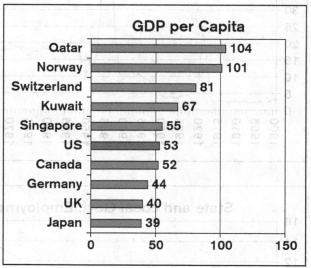

International comparisons are legitimate, but can be misleading. Not only does the quality of the statistical data vary from country to country, but cultural differences affect them as well. For example, the measure of the size of an economy (GDP) is based on the value of goods traded in markets; in countries where a larger proportion of economic activity takes place outside of markets, the GDP measure will make an economy look smaller and poorer than it actually is.

Here is how the U.S. compares to selected other nations by various other measures.

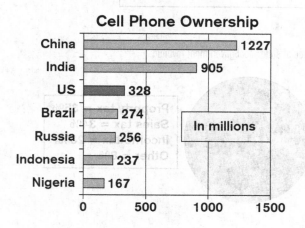

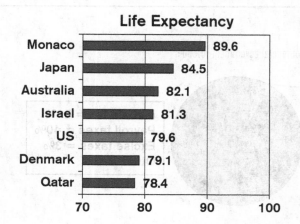

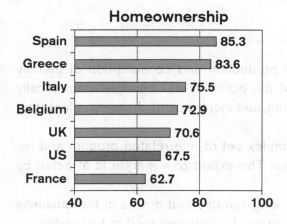

Homeownership

Spain	85.3
Greece	83.6
Italy	75.5
Belgium	72.9
UK	70.6
US	67.5
France	62.7

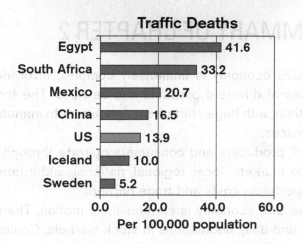

Traffic Deaths

Egypt	41.6
South Africa	33.2
Mexico	20.7
China	16.5
US	13.9
Iceland	10.0
Sweden	5.2

Per 100,000 population

The richest countries tend to be those with the greatest economic freedom. As the chart below indicates, countries that rank high in terms of economic freedom generally also rank high in terms of per capita GDP. Countries that rank low in terms of economic freedom generally also rank low in terms of per capita GDP.

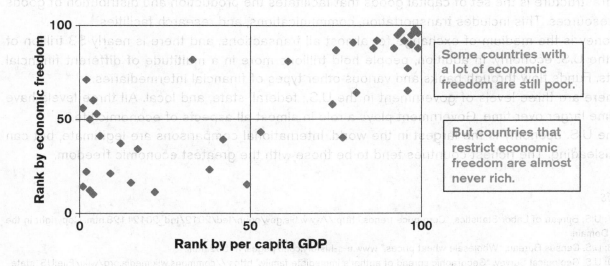

Some countries with a lot of economic freedom are still poor.

But countries that restrict economic freedom are almost never rich.

When markets are allowed to operate freely, they encourage efficiency, innovation, and productive activity. When productive behavior is rewarded, more of it occurs. Restrictions on markets (by corruption, by intrusive regulations, by limitations on labor or capital movement, by trade barriers) repress productive activity and make a nation poorer.

SUMMARY OF CHAPTER 2

The U.S. economy is immensely complex, involving the production and consumption of literally millions of different products and services. The focus of the economy has changed dramatically over time, with huge shifts from agriculture to manufacturing, and more recently from manufacturing to services.

U.S. producers and consumers operate through a complex set of interrelated product and resource markets: local, regional, national, and international. The extent of a market is affected by transportation costs and trade barriers.

The U.S. economy is continually in motion. There are long-run ups and downs in the business cycle and daily fluctuations in stock markets. Commodity prices in particular tend to be volatile.

The U.S. labor force is both highly educated and highly mobile. Over the past sixty years there has been a dramatic increase in the percentage of women entering the labor market. The labor force has also become increasingly urban.

For most Americans, the bulk of their income comes from wages or salaries. Other sources of income are rent, royalties, interest, and capital gains. Income is not distributed evenly across all Americans.

Infrastructure is the set of capital goods that facilitates the production and distribution of goods and resources. This includes transportation, communications, and research facilities.

Money is the medium of exchange for almost all transactions, and there is nearly $3 trillion of it in the U.S. economy. In addition, people hold trillions more in a multitude of different financial assets. Funds flow through banks and various other types of financial intermediaries.

There are three levels of government in the U.S.: federal, state, and local. All three levels have become larger over time. Government plays a role in almost all aspects of economic life.

The U.S. economy is the largest in the world. International comparisons are legitimate, but can be misleading. The richest countries tend to be those with the greatest economic freedom.

Credits

Fig 2.7: U.S. Bureau of Labor Statistics, "Corn price trends," http://www.bls.gov/opub/ted/2012/ted_20121128.htm. Copyright in the Public Domain.

Fig 2.8: U.S. Census Bureau, "Wholesale wheat prices," www.u-s-history.com/pages/h1532.html.

Fig 2.9: U.S. Geological Survey, "Geographic spread of author's immediate family," https://commons.wikimedia.org/wiki/File:US_state_outline_map.png. Copyright in the Public Domain.

Fig 2.9: U.S. Geological Survey, "Geographic spread of author's immediate family," https://commons.wikimedia.org/wiki/File:US_state_outline_map.png. Copyright in the Public Domain.

Fig 2.16: U.S. Energy Information Administration, "Natural gas pipelines," http://www.eia.gov/pub/oil_gas/natural_gas/analysis_publications/ngpipeline/ngpipelines_map.html. Copyright in the Public Domain.

CH THREE

REVIEW OF MICROECONOMICS

The foundation of economics is the idea that people respond to changing incentives, and that there are always opportunity costs for any action.

The laws of demand and supply form the basis for the simple market model. The intersection of the demand curve and the supply curve determines equilibrium price and equilibrium quantity.

The basic market model lets us predict what will happen to price and quantity if there is a change in any of the factors affecting either demand or supply.

1. FOUNDATION PRINCIPLES OF ECONOMICS

The six foundation principles of economics are:

1. **People respond to incentives.**
2. **There is no such thing as a free lunch.**
3. **No thing is just one thing; there are always at least two sides to every interaction.**
4. **The law of unanticipated influences.**
5. **The law of unintended consequences.**
6. **No one is, and no one ever can be, completely in control.**

There are six general principles that define the economist's "mind set." Economists view the world through the lens of these six principles.

1. People respond to incentives

Most simply: People want to get more of what makes them happy, and want to avoid what makes them unhappy. Therefore, when the benefits or costs associated with some action change, people change their behavior accordingly.

> For example:
> - When a lottery jackpot increases, more lottery tickets are sold.
> - When bus fare increases, fewer people ride the bus.
> - When an ice storm increases the danger of driving, fewer people go out on the road.
> - When dental technology makes routine dental care less painful, people visit the dentist more frequently.

People respond to incentives in consistent and predictable ways.

2. There is no such thing as a free lunch

Any use of a resource (be it money, possessions, talent, or even time) means that resource is no longer available to be used for anything else. The true cost (opportunity cost) of any activity is the value of what you give up when you choose to perform one activity rather than another.

> For example:
> - The money spent on a movie ticket can't also be spent on popcorn and a soda.
> - When you drive your car to work, that car is no longer available for your spouse to drive to the supermarket.
> - The time you spend reading this economics textbook can't be used on some other (more enjoyable?) activity.

There is no such thing as a free lunch, because there are always alternative uses for any resource—so there is always an opportunity cost.

3. **No thing is just one thing: there are always at least two sides to every interaction**

- For every buyer, there is a seller.
- For every borrower, there is a lender.
- Income to the employee is a cost to the employer.
- Expenditure to the consumer is revenue to the retailer.

There is little that we do that does not affect other persons as well.

4. **The law of unanticipated influences**

The world is highly inter-connected. Actions have consequences, and these consequences can sometimes be far off and completely unexpected.

For example: The collapse of the California house price bubble in 2007 led to towns in England laying off police and firefighters.
- How could this happen? What is the connection?
- Banks in Iceland had invested heavily in securitized debt obligations (packages of high-risk mortgages on California real estate). When California house prices fell dramatically, these securities lost most of their value, and the Icelandic banks became insolvent. Several English towns had made large deposits in the Icelandic banks (because of the high interest rates they were offering). When the banks went under, the English towns lost most of their deposits. This created a budget crisis for the English towns, which cut costs by laying off police and fire fighters.

So many things are connected in so many different ways, it is not possible to anticipate all the influences from any action.

5. **The law of unintended consequences**

People respond to changing incentives, but not always in the way intended by those who changed the incentives.

For example: The intent of red light cameras is to reduce the number of accidents caused by drivers running red lights. They do this by increasing the likelihood that a driver running a red light will receive a ticket. The cameras work—there are fewer accidents in intersections with the cameras. There is also an unintended consequence—more rear-end collisions as drivers slam on the brakes to avoid the risk of entering the intersection late and getting caught by the camera.

Because there are millions of people making their own decisions on how best to respond to changing incentives and opportunity costs, interacting in a myriad of ways, leading to unforeseen influences and unintended consequences:

6. **No one is, and no one ever can be, completely in control.**

2. THE LAW OF DEMAND

The law of demand states that the quantity demanded of a good is inversely related to its price. That is, if the price of a good rises, consumers will purchase less. Important factors influencing the level of demand include: the number of consumers, consumer income, consumer preferences, and the prices of related goods.

One of the most basic ideas in economics is the law of demand. This states that the quantity demanded of a good is inversely related to its price.

- If the price of a good rises, consumers will purchase less of the good.
- If the price of good falls, consumers will purchase more of the good.

The law of demand follows logically from the foundation economic principles that people respond to incentives and that there are opportunity costs associated with all actions. When the price of a good falls, this lowers the opportunity cost of buying the good, and people respond to the changed incentive by buying more of the good.

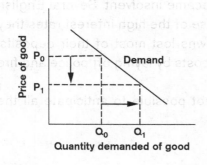

The demand curve does not have to be a straight line: it's just convenient to draw it that way.

What is important is that it slopes downward.

The demand curve models aggregate behavior, not individual behavior. It is certainly possible an individual consumer will continue buying the same amount of a good even after the price of the good rises. However, some consumers will buy less of the good, so that the aggregate quantity demanded will fall when the price rises.

The only things that change as you move along a demand curve are the price and quantity of the good. All other factors are held constant. The most important of these other factors are:

- The number of consumers
- Consumer income
- Consumer preferences
- Consumer expectations about future prices and income
- The prices of related goods

A change in any of these factors causes the entire demand curve to shift either inward or outward.

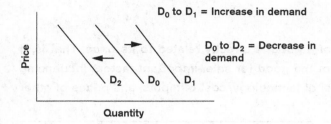

D₀ to D₁ = Increase in demand

D₀ to D₂ = Decrease in demand

An increase in demand means that, at any given price, the aggregate quantity demanded is now higher than it was before. A decrease in demand means that, at any given price, the aggregate quantity demanded is now lower than it was before.

Number of consumers:

- When the number of consumers rises, all else being equal, demand increases.
- When the number of consumers falls, demand decreases.

Consumer income:

- When consumers' income rises, demand for any normal good increases.
- If demand for a good falls when consumers' income rises, the good is called an inferior good.
- Inferior goods are typically low-cost, low-quality goods that consumers stop purchasing once they can afford something better.

Consumer preferences:

- Anything that causes consumers to like a good better will lead to an increase in demand.
  - » For example, publicity on health effects of apples leads to increased demand for apples.
- Anything that causes consumers to dislike a good more will lead to a decrease in demand.
  - » For example, a new report linking margarine to heart disease leads to decreased demand for margarine.

Expectations:

- If consumers expect the price of a good to increase in the future, current demand will increase (buy the good before the price rise).
- If consumers expect their income to rise in the future, current demand for all normal goods will increase (extra spending now will be paid out of extra income in the future).

Prices of related goods: Goods can be related to each other in two ways:

Goods can be substitutes for each other; that is, you can use one good in place of the other: Pepsi-Cola for Coca-Cola; a mobile phone for a land line; satellite TV for cable TV.

- With substitutes, an increase in the price of one leads to increased demand for the other

Goods can be complements for each other; that is, the complementary goods are often used together: golf clubs and golf balls; steak and steak sauce; automobiles and gasoline.

- With complements, an increase in the price of one leads to decreased demand for the other.

3. THE LAW OF SUPPLY

The law of supply states that the quantity supplied of a good is directly related to its price. That is, if the price of a good rises, producers will offer more of the good for sale. Important factors influencing the level of supply include: the number of sellers, level of technology, cost of inputs, and prices of other goods.

Going hand-in-hand with the law of demand is the law of supply. This states that the quantity supplied of a good is directly related to its price.

- If the price of a good rises, producers will offer more of the good for sale.
- If the price of a good falls, producers will offer less of the good for sale.

The law of supply follows logically from the foundation economic principles that people respond to incentives and that there are opportunity costs associated with all actions. When the price of a good rises, this lowers the opportunity cost of using resources to produce that good, and people respond to the changed incentive by producing more of the good.

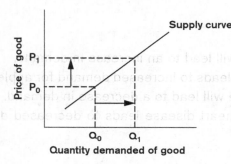

The supply curve does not have to be a straight line; it's just convenient to draw it that way.

What is important is that it slopes upward.

The supply curve models aggregate behavior; that is, it shows the production decisions of all producers combined. The supply curve is meaningful only when there is competition among producers. It is competition that forces producers to charge a price based on the costs of production. When there is only a single producer (a monopolist), the price can (and will) be set higher than cost.

The only things that change as you move along a supply curve are the price and quantity of the good. All other factors are held constant. The most important of these other factors are:
- The number of sellers
- Costs of inputs to the production process
- The level of technology
- Producer expectations about future prices and costs
- The prices of other goods that could be produced using the producer's resources

A change in any of these factors causes the entire supply curve to shift either inward or outward.

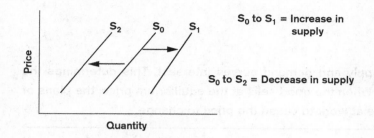

An increase in supply means that, at any given price, the aggregate quantity supplied is now higher than it was before. A decrease in supply means that, at any given price, the aggregate quantity supplied is now lower than it was before.

Number of sellers:

- When there are more sellers, all else being equal, supply increases.
- When there are fewer sellers, supply decreases.

Costs of inputs to the production process:

- When prices for the resources that are needed to produce a good go up, supply decreases—because the opportunity cost of producing the good has increased.
- When prices for inputs go down, supply increases.

Level of technology:

- The level of technology influences supply by affecting the costs of production.
- New inventions and innovations that lower the costs of producing a good lead to an increase in supply.

Expectations:

- If producers expect the price of a good to increase in the future, they cut back on current supply (hold back inventory to take advantage of the future price rise).
- If producers expect the cost of inputs to their production process to rise in the future, they expand current supply (produce more before the prices of their inputs increase).

Prices of other goods that could be produced using the producer's resources:

- Resources generally can be used to produce more than just one particular good; for example, resources used to produce upholstered sofas can quite easily be used to produce upholstered chairs instead.
- When the selling price of (for example) chairs rises, this decreases the opportunity cost of producing chairs, and increases the opportunity cost of producing sofas; the quantity supplied of chairs increases, and the supply of sofas decreases.

4. EQUILIBRIUM

Equilibrium in a market comes where the supply and demand curves intersect. This determines the equilibrium price and the equilibrium quantity. When the good sells at the equilibrium price, the plans of all buyers and sellers are met; there is no force at work to cause the price to change.

Just like on a treasure map, in economics X marks the spot. The intersection of the supply and demand curves marks the spot of market equilibrium, and determines both equilibrium price and equilibrium quantity.

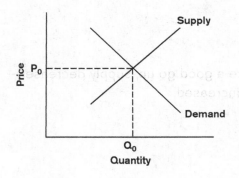

Equilibrium means "at rest."

At equilibrium there is no force at work to cause the price to change.

The demand curve represents the plans of buyers in the market—how much they intend to buy at each price. The supply curve represents the plans of sellers in the market—how much they intend to offer for sale at each price. At the equilibrium price, the plans of all buyers and sellers are met.

- Any buyer who wants to buy at that price finds a seller willing to sell at that price.
- Any seller who offers to sell at that price finds a buyer willing to buy at that price.
- Quantity demanded = Quantity supplied.

Each point along the demand curve represents the value that consumers place upon the good. The available quantity goes to those consumers who value it the highest.

Each point along the supply curve represents the cost of manufacturing the good. The goods are sold by those producers who can manufacture at the lowest cost.

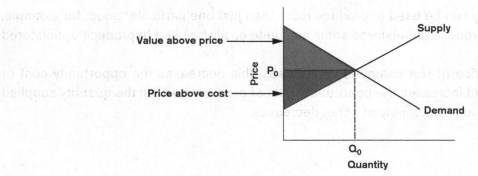

What happens if the going price is higher than the equilibrium price?

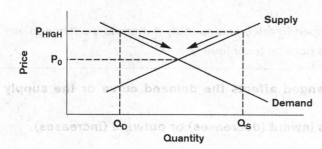

At P$_{HIGH}$, the quantity supplied is greater than the quantity demanded: there is excess supply.

Plans of buyers and sellers do not match: At P$_{HIGH}$, sellers offer more for sale than buyers are willing to buy.

- This mismatch puts pressure on the price to fall.
- If a store has more of some good than they want to have, what do they do? They hold a sale—they lower the price.

As the price falls below P$_{HIGH}$, quantity demanded increases along the demand curve, and quantity supplied decreases along the supply curve. So long as there is excess supply, there is pressure on the price to continue falling. This adjustment only stops when price falls to the equilibrium price and quantity demanded again equals quantity supplied.

What happens if the going price is lower than the equilibrium price?

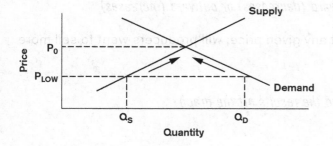

At P$_{LOW}$, the quantity demanded is greater than the quantity supplied: there is excess demand.

Plans of buyers and sellers do not match: At P$_{LOW}$, buyers want to purchase more than sellers are willing to provide.

- This mismatch puts pressure on the price to rise.
- If a store has a waiting line to buy some good, what do they do? They order more, and raise the price.

As the price rises above P$_{LOW}$, quantity demanded decreases along the demand curve, and quantity supplied increases along the supply curve. So long as there is excess demand, there is pressure on the price to continue rising. This adjustment only stops when price rises to the equilibrium price and quantity demanded again equals quantity supplied.

5. USING THE SUPPLY/DEMAND MODEL

The basic market model lets us predict what will happen to price and quantity if there is a change in any of the factors affecting either demand or supply. The general technique is:

1. **Identify whether the factor that has changed affects the demand curve or the supply curve.**
2. **Identify whether the affected curve shifts inward (decreases) or outward (increases).**
3. **Read the results off of the graph.**

The basic market model of supply and demand lets us predict what will happen to equilibrium price and equilibrium quantity if there is a change in any of the factors that affect either demand or supply.

- Remember that the only thing that changes along the demand and supply curves is the price of the good: all other factors are held constant.
- When one of these other factors changes, the entire demand curve or supply curve shifts

In order to predict how equilibrium values will change, follow a three-step general technique.

Step #1 : Identify whether the factor affects the demand curve or the supply curve

That is, does the factor influence the behavior of consumers (demand curve) or the behavior of producers (supply curve)?

Step #2 : Identify whether the affected curve shifts inward (decreases) or outward (increases)

That is, will consumers want to buy more or less at any given price; will producers want to sell more or less at any given price?

Step #3 : Draw the supply/demand graph, and then read the results off the graph

That is, let the model do the thinking for you.

   Here are the factors that influence consumers. A change in any of these will cause a shift in the demand curve.

- The number of consumers
- Consumer income
- Consumer preferences
- Consumer expectations
  » That the price of the good will change in the future
  » That consumer income will change in the future
- Prices of related goods
  » Substitute goods
  » Complement goods

Here are the factors that influence producers. A change in any of these will cause a shift in the supply curve.

- The number of sellers
- Costs of production
    » Level of technology
    » Prices of inputs to the production process
- Producer expectations
    » That the price of the good will change in the future
    » That the prices of inputs will change in the future
- Prices of alternate goods that could be produced with the available resources

Be careful when you draw the new demand or supply curve. If you think of an increase (decrease) as a shift up (down), it is easy to make a mistake.

- Ask if, at the given price, you will buy (sell) more or less after the change in the underlying factor
- Think of the curves as shifting in or out rather than as shifting up or down

If you do the first two steps correctly, the graph will show you what will happen to equilibrium price and equilibrium quantity.

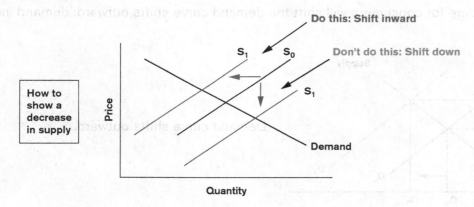

- If the demand curve shifts, the intersection of the new demand curve with the supply curve shows the new equilibrium values.
- If the supply curve shifts, the intersection of the new supply curve with the demand curve shows the new equilibrium values.

It is possible to reason out the answer without using the graph, but it is very easy to make a mistake if you don't use the graph.

5.1. SHIFTS IN A SINGLE FACTOR

When only a single underlying factor changes, only one of the curves shifts. We can be certain about the direction of the resulting change in both the equilibrium price and the equilibrium quantity.

When only a single underlying factor changes, then only one of the curves shifts.
- Either demand shifts or supply shifts, but not both.

Because only one curve shifts, we can be certain about the direction of the change in both equilibrium price and equilibrium quantity. We can't predict the size of the change in the equilibrium values, but we can predict the direction of the change.

Example #1 : Consumer income rises

Step #1 - Will this affect supply or demand?
- Consumer income influences the behavior of consumers, so the demand curve will shift.

Step #2 - Will demand increase or decrease?
- Rising income for consumers will shift the demand curve shifts outward: demand increases.

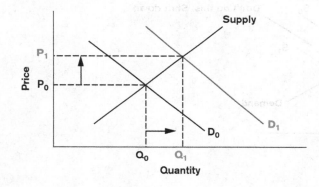

Demand curve shifts outward.

Step #3 - Read the answer from the graph.
- Equilibrium price increases.
- Equilibrium quantity increases.

Example #2 : Increase in input prices

Step #1 - Will this affect supply or demand?
- Input prices influence the behavior of producers, so the supply curve will shift

Step #2 - Will supply increase or decrease?
- Rising input prices increase the costs of production and shift the supply curve shifts inward: supply will decrease.

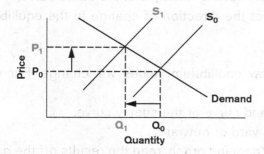

Supply curve shifts inward.

Step #3 - Read the answer from the graph.
- Equilibrium price increases.
- Equilibrium quantity decreases.

Example #3 - Decrease in the price of a substitute good

Step #1 - Will this affect supply or demand?
- The prices of related goods influences the behavior of consumers, so the demand curve will shift inward

Step #2 - Will demand increase or decrease?
- A decrease in the price of a substitute for the good will increase the quantity demanded for the substitute, but will decrease demand for the good itself.

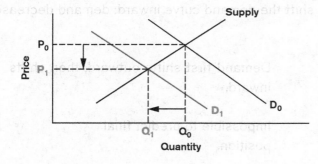

Demand curve shifts inward.

Step #3 - Read the answer from the graph.
- Equilibrium price decreases.
- Equilibrium quantity decreases.

5.2. SHIFTS IN TWO OR MORE FACTORS

When two or more underlying factors change at the same time, it may not be possible to predict the direction of the change in both equilibrium price and equilibrium quantity. However, the general approach to follow is still the same.

When more than one underlying factor changes at the same time, there can be shifts in both the demand curve and the supply curve, or there can be off-setting changes in the same curve.

- In either case, it might not be possible to predict the direction of change in the equilibrium values.

Follow the same general approach to determine how equilibrium values will change. For each change in an underlying factor:

Step #1: Identify whether the factor affects the demand curve or the supply curve.

Step #2: Identify whether the affected curve shifts inward or outward.

Step #3: After all changes are reflected in the supply/demand graph, read the results off the graph.

Off-setting changes in a single curve

- We can predict the change in direction of neither equilibrium price nor equilibrium quantity

Example: Consumer incomes increase at the same time that consumer preferences for a good decline.

Step #1 - Will this affect supply or demand?

- Consumer income and consumer preferences both influence the behavior of consumers, so the demand curve will shift.

Step #2 - Will demand increase or decrease?

- Rising income for consumers will shift the demand curve outward: demand increases.
- Declining preferences for the good will shift the demand curve inward: demand decreases.

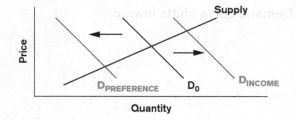

Demand first shifts outward, then shifts inward.

Impossible to predict final position.

Step #3 - Read the answer from the graph.
- Impact on equilibrium values depends on which influence is stronger.
- If influence of income rise is stronger, equilibrium price and equilibrium quantity both increase.
- If influence of preference decline is stronger, equilibrium price and quantity both decrease.

Changes in both demand and supply at the same time

- We can predict the change in direction of either price or quantity, but not both.

Example: Increase in demand along with an increase in supply
   The increase in demand (by itself) causes equilibrium price to increase and equilibrium quantity to increase. The increase in supply (by itself) causes equilibrium price to decrease and equilibrium quantity to increase.
- Both changes cause equilibrium quantity to increase, so we can predict that equilibrium quantity will increase.
- The two changes have off-setting effects on equilibrium price, so we can't predict what will happen to equilibrium price.
- The final effect on equilibrium price depends on which of the changes is stronger.

A large increase in demand, coupled with a small increase in supply, leads to a higher equilibrium price.

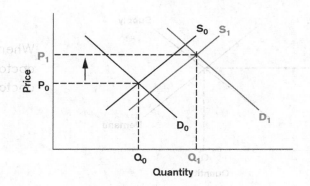

A small increase in demand, coupled with a large increase in supply, leads to a lower equilibrium price.

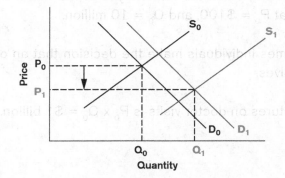

5.3. EXAMPLE: MARKET FOR MEDICAL SERVICES

The demand/supply model for the market for medical services shows how consumer decisions are based on marginal costs, and why this makes it so hard to control total costs.

From what we hear on the news, there are two major problems with health care in the U.S. today:
1. Too many people do not have health insurance.
2. Healthcare costs too much.

Our simple supply/demand market model reveals that fixing one of these problems will make the other problem worse.
- The demand/supply model for the market for medical services shows how consumer decisions are based on marginal costs rather than full costs, and why this makes it so hard to control the total costs for medical care.

Example: The medical service for visits to a doctor's office
A person without health insurance faces the following situation:

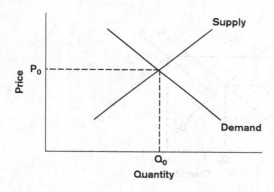

When persons without health insurance visit a doctor, they pay the full price charged by the doctor.

You visit a doctor only when the value to you of the visit is at least as great as its cost to you. Let's assume that $P_0 = \$100$, and $Q_0 = 10$ million.

Ten-million times individuals make the decision that an office visit to a doctor is worth at least $100 to themselves.

Total expenditures on doctor visits is $P_0 \times Q_0 = \$1$ billion.

A person with health insurance faces a different situation:

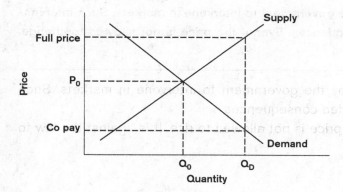

When a person with health insurance visits a doctor, they pay only their insurance co pay amount (typically much less than the full price).

You visit a doctor only when the value to you of the visit is at least as great as its cost to you. When someone has health insurance, the cost of another visit to them is lower, so (following the law of demand) they purchase more office visits.

- People visit the doctor far more often when it costs them (for example) $20 rather than when it costs them $100

The insurance co pay is the MARGINAL cost of the doctor visit. It is how much additional you must pay to obtain one additional visit.

The insurance co pay is not the FULL cost of the doctor visit. The difference between the co pay and the full cost is paid by the insurance company. The insurance company gets the revenue it pays from the insurance premiums paid by persons who buy insurance policies. So, in actuality, consumers do pay the full price for the doctor visits.

But the full price is not the same equilibrium price paid by persons without health insurance. Because the marginal cost of visits is lower for those with health insurance, a larger quantity of visits is demanded. In order to induce doctors to provide the higher quantity of visits, the price of a visit rises (following the law of supply).

Let's assume that P_{FULL} = $200, and Q_D = 20 million.

- Total expenditures on doctor visits now is $P_{FULL} \times Q_D$ = $4 billion.

In other words, when more people get health insurance, the cost of health care rises.

5.4. EXAMPLE: PRICE CEILINGS AND PRICE FLOORS

Price ceilings and price floors are tools used by the government to intervene in markets. Such intervention usually causes unfortunate unintended consequences. Even if the price is not allowed to change, markets still find a way to reach equilibrium.

Price ceilings and price floors are tools used by the government to intervene in markets. Such intervention usually causes unfortunate unintended consequences.

A price **CEILING** sets a limit above which the price is not allowed to rise. It is against the law to charge a price higher than the price ceiling.

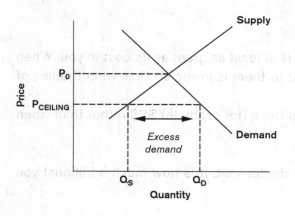

A price ceiling creates a disequilibrium situation. The quantity demanded is greater than the quantity supplied.

A price **FLOOR** sets a limit below which the price is not allowed to fall. The government guarantees that the producers will receive a price at least as high as the price floor.

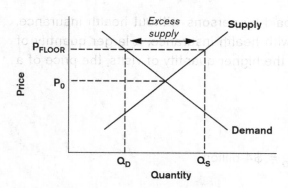

A price floor creates a disequilibrium situation. The quantity supplied is greater than the quantity demanded.

With both price ceilings and price floors, the plans of the buyers do not match the plans of the sellers. This creates disequilibrium in the market. Normally markets return to equilibrium by means of changes in the price. Price ceilings and price floors prevent this, so markets are forced to reach equilibrium in other ways.

Example of a price ceiling: Rent Control

The intent of rent control is to make rental housing more affordable for low-income persons. The result of rent control is excess demand—some people who want to rent an apartment at the ceiling price are unable to do so.

Normally, excess demand is resolved when the price rises. Rent control blocks the price rising, so instead:

- Landlords impose quasi-price increases: they impose or increase security deposits, pet fees, utility charges, and the like.
- The quality of apartments is allowed to deteriorate, as landlords reduce maintenance efforts to save costs.
- Queuing develops in order to ration the available apartments among the larger number of potential renters—this increases the real opportunity cost of trying to rent.
- Discrimination becomes easier and less costly—with a waiting list of potential renters, landlords can avoid those with "undesirable" traits.

Are low-income renters made better off by rent control?

- Some are better off; most are worse off.

Example of a price floor: Minimum Wage

The intent of the minimum wage is to increase income to low-skilled workers. The result of the minimum wage is an excess supply of labor and unemployment—some low-skill workers who want a minimum wage job can't get one.

Normally, excess supply is resolved when the price falls. The minimum wage blocks the wage rate falling, so instead:

- Producers substitute higher-skill labor and more-advanced technology for the now relatively more expensive low-skill labor.
- Low-skill workers are more likely to be unemployed, and with longer periods of unemployment.
- Low-skill workers have fewer opportunities to increase their human capital with on-the-job experience, which reduces their chances of ever advancing to better higher-paying jobs.

Are low-skill workers made better off by the minimum wage?

- Some are better off; most are worse off.

SUMMARY OF CHAPTER 3

The six foundation principles of economics are:
1. People respond to incentives.
2. There is no such thing as a free lunch.
3. No thing is just one thing; there are always at least two sides to every interaction.
4. The law of unanticipated influences.
5. The law of unintended consequences.
6. No one is, and no one ever can be, completely in control.

The law of demand states that the quantity demanded of a good is inversely related to its price. That is, if the price of a good rises, consumers will purchase less.
- Important factors influencing the level of demand include the number of consumers, consumer income, consumer preferences, and the prices of related goods.

The law of supply states that the quantity supplied of a good is directly related to its price. That is, if the price of a good rises, producers will offer more for sale.
- Important factors influencing the level of supply include the number of sellers, level of technology, cost of inputs, and the prices of other goods that could be produced with the same resources.

Equilibrium in a market comes where the supply and demand curves intersect. This determines the equilibrium price and the equilibrium quantity.
- At equilibrium, the plans of all buyers and all sellers are met.
- Markets reach equilibrium by means of price changes.

The basic market model lets us predict what will happen to equilibrium price and quantity if there is a change in any of the factors affecting either supply or demand. The general technique for using the market model is:
1. Identify whether the factor affects the demand curve or the supply curve.
2. Identify whether the affected curve shifts inward (decreases) or outward (increases).
3. Draw the supply/demand graph, and then read the results off the graph.

When only a single factor changes, we can predict the direction of change of both equilibrium price and equilibrium quantity. When two or more factors change at the same time, it may not be possible to predict the direction of the change in both equilibrium price and equilibrium quantity.

CH **FOUR**

GROSS DOMESTIC PRODUCT

The size of the U.S. Economy is measured as the Gross Domestic Product (GDP). GDP is produced by the Bureau of Economic Analysis as part of the National Income and Product Accounts (NIPA).

GDP is the market value of all final goods and services produced within the U.S. during the calendar year. The measure itself is quite accurate, but there are problems with using GDP as a measure of economic well-being.

GDP is the sum of expenditures by the four major sectors of the economy (GDP=C+I+G+NE). When comparing GDP from one year to the next, use real GDP rather than nominal GDP.

1. MEASURING THE MACRO ECONOMY

How large is the U.S. economy? We measure the U.S. economy as a whole as Gross Domestic Product (GDP). We measure various sectors of the U.S. economy using the National Income and Product Accounts (NIPA).

How large is the U.S. economy? There are many ways to answer this; we could look at:

- The size of the U.S. labor force
- The total amount of available capital
- The stock of natural resources
- Total retail or wholesale revenue

All of these get at some aspects of the economy. However, in its broadest sense, the question means, "What is the total amount of economic activity?"

However we define it, there are many reasons why it is valuable to know the size of the economy.

- To track economic growth over time
- To help assess the effectiveness of government macroeconomic policy
- To alert decision makers when policy changes are needed
- To enable comparisons with the economies of other nations

There is no perfect way to measure the total amount of economic activity. The best method that has yet been developed is to approximate total economic activity by measuring the value of the goods and services produced in the economy. This is called a nation's Gross Domestic Product (GDP).

The U.S. GDP is broken down by major sectors in the National Income and Product Accounts (NIPA). The table below shows the size of the total U.S. economy in 2013, by quarter, along with the size of the household, business, international trade, and government sectors of the U.S. Economy.

Table 1.1.5. Gross Domestic Product (S millions)	2013			
	I	II	III	IV
Gross Domestic Product	16,535.3	16,661.0	16,912.9	17,080.7
Personal consumption expenditures	11,379.2	11,427.1	11,537.7	11,640.7
Gross private domestic investment	2,555.1	2,621.0	2,738.0	2,780.5
Net exports of goods and services	−523.1	−509.0	−500.2	−456.8
Government consumption expenditures	3,124.1	3,121.9	3,137.5	3,116.2

GDP data is found on the Bureau of Economic Analysis website: www.bea.gov.

2. CIRCULAR FLOW DIAGRAMS

Circular flow diagrams provide a useful visual tool to illustrate the interactions between the various sectors of the economy. They show both real flows (goods and services) and financial flows (dollars).

A circular flow diagram is a useful visual tool to illustrate the interactions between the various sectors of the economy.

There are four components to a circular flow diagram:

- Two or more sectors of the economy: these are major parts of the economy, such as households, business firms, government, agriculture, manufacturing, services
- One or more markets : through which the sectors interact
- Real flow arrows : transfers of goods/services/resources between sectors
- Financial flow arrows : transfers of dollars between sectors

The real and financial flows move in opposite directions, with the financial flow representing the value of the real flow.

Every interaction has at least two sides:

- What is a purchase for households is sales for business firms.
- What is revenue for business firms is expenditures for households.

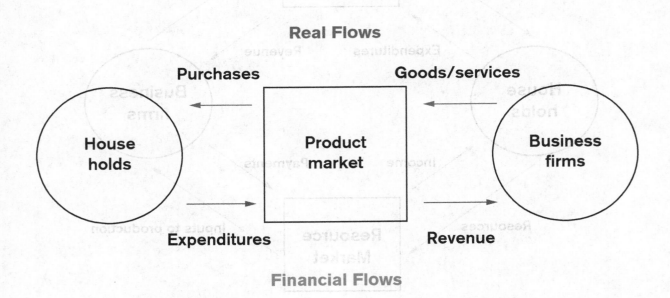

2.1. TWO-SECTOR CIRCULAR FLOW

A two-sector circular flow diagram shows how households and business firms interact by means of product markets and resource markets.

A two-sector circular flow consists of:
- The household sector and the business firms sector
- A product market and a resource market
- Four sets of matching real and financial flows

The blue arrows show real flows. The red arrows show financial flows.
- All the flows are the same size.

Business firms sell goods and services to households through the product market.

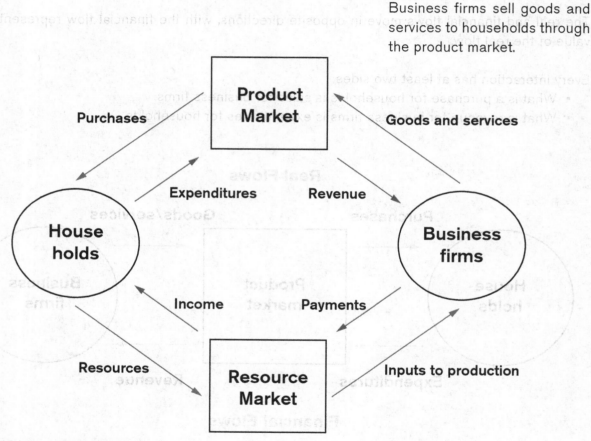

Households provide labor and other inputs to business firms through the resource market.

2.2. THREE-SECTOR CIRCULAR FLOW

A three-sector circular flow diagram adds government to the household and business sectors. Government interacts with the other sectors both directly and also through product and resource markets.

A three-sector circular flow diagram adds government to the household and business sectors. Government activity consists of:

- Obtaining (and selling) labor and other inputs through the resource market
- Purchasing (and selling) goods and services through the product market
- Interacting directly with the other sectors: providing services and transfer payments, and collecting taxes

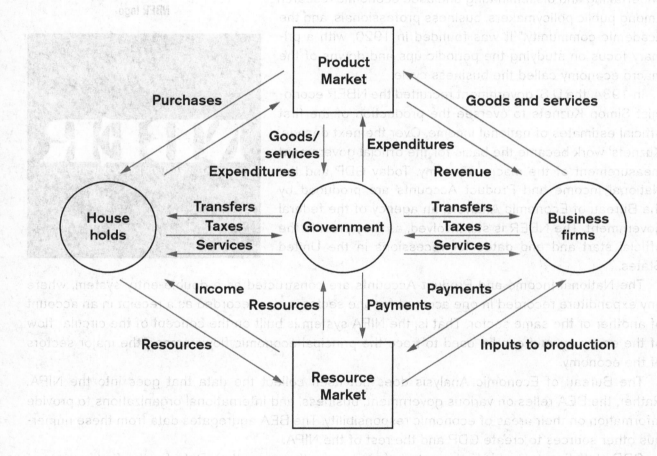

Note that the direct government flows to households and business firms do not have to balance. That is, taxes from households are not necessarily equal to the sum of transfers and services from government to households.

3. GROSS DOMESTIC PRODUCT

Gross Domestic Product (GDP) is the most important measure of the size of the U.S. economy. It is produced by the Bureau of Economic Analysis. GDP is only one part of the National Income and Product Accounts (NIPA).

The standard measure for the size of the U.S. economy is the Gross Domestic Product (GDP). GDP is part of a comprehensive macroeconomic measurement project called the National Income and Product Accounts (NIPA).

The modern concept of GDP was developed by the National Bureau of Economic Research (NBER). The NBER is an American private non-profit research association "committed to undertaking and disseminating unbiased economic research among public policymakers, business professionals, and the academic community." It was founded in 1920, with a primary focus on studying the periodic ups and downs of the macro economy called the business cycle.

NBER logo

In 1934, the U.S. government recruited the NBER economist Simon Kuznets to oversee the production of the first official estimates of national income. Over the next decade, Kuznets' work became the basis for the official government measurement of the macro economy. Today GDP and the National Income and Product Accounts are produced by the Bureau of Economic Analysis, an agency of the federal government. The NBER is still involved, as they provide the official start and end dates for recessions in the United States.

The National Income and Product Accounts are constructed as a double-entry system, where any expenditure recorded in one account for one sector is also recorded as a receipt in an account of another or the same sector. That is, the NIPA system is built on the concept of the circular flow of the economy, and can be used to trace the principal economic flows among the major sectors of the economy.

The Bureau of Economic Analysis does not itself collect the data that goes into the NIPA. Rather, the BEA relies on various government, business, and international organizations to provide information on their areas of economic responsibility. The BEA aggregates data from these numerous other sources to create GDP and the rest of the NIPA.

GDP statistics are published quarterly (once every three months). Data for the first quarter of the year (January–March) is first published the following month (April). At the time of the writing of this textbook (March 2014), the most recent GDP statistics available were for the fourth quarter of 2013.

Bureau of Economic Analysis

News

- U.S. Economy at a Glance
- Current Releases
- News Release Archive

U.S. Economic Accounts

National   Gross Domestic Product (GDP)   Personal Income and Outlays
Consumer Spending   Corporate Profits   Fixed Assets   Research and
Development Satellite Account

This is what you see when you go to www.bea.gov. Click here to get to the GDP data.

⌄ SECTION 1 - DOMESTIC PRODUCT AND INCOME

Table 1.1.1. Percent Change From Preceding Period in Real Gross Domestic Product (A) (Q)

Table 1.1.2. Contributions to Percent Change in Real Gross Domestic Product (A) (Q)

Table 1.1.3. Real Gross Domestic Product, Quantity Indexes (A) (Q)

Table 1.1.4. Price Indexes for Gross Domestic Product (A) (Q)

Table 1.1.5. Gross Domestic Product (A) (Q)

Table 1.1.6. Real Gross Domestic Product, Chained Dollars (A) (Q)

Table 1.1.6A. Real Gross Domestic Product, Chained (1937) Dollars (A)

Table 1.1.6B. Real Gross Domestic Product, Chained (1952) Dollars (A) (Q)

Table 1.1.6C. Real Gross Domestic Product, Chained (1972) Dollars (A) (Q)

Table 1.1.6D. Real Gross Domestic Product, Chained (1992) Dollars (A) (Q)

Here is the menu of the various tables that are available.

Table 1.1.5. Gross Domestic Product

[Billions of dollars] Seasonally adjusted at annual rates
Last Revised on: February 28, 2014 - Next Release Date March 27, 2014

Table 1.1.5. is nominal GDP. The default is to show quarterly data.

The first line is GDP as a whole. The following lines are for the various components of GDP.

Line		2013			
		I	II	III	IV
1	**Gross domestic product**	16,535.3	16,661.0	16,912.9	17,080.7
2	**Personal consumption expenditures**	11,379.2	11,427.1	11,537.7	11,640.7
3	Goods	3,851.8	3,848.5	3,912.8	3,933.2
4	Durable goods	1,244.8	1,257.5	1,274.0	1,275.0
5	Nondurable goods	2,607.0	2,591.0	2,638.8	2,658.2
6	Services	7,527.4	7,578.6	7,624.8	7,707.6
7	**Gross private domestic investment**	2,555.1	2,621.0	2,738.0	2,780.5
8	Fixed investment	2,491.7	2,543.8	2,593.2	2,634.2
9	Nonresidential	2,001.4	2,030.6	2,060.5	2,103.3
10	Structures	429.1	452.6	470.7	475.9
11	Equipment	928.0	934.5	935.8	959.1
12	Intellectual property products	644.3	643.5	654.1	668.2
13	Residential	490.3	513.2	532.6	531.0
14	Change in private inventories	63.4	77.2	144.8	146.3

3.1. DEFINITION OF GDP

GDP is the market value of all final goods and services produced within the U.S. during the calendar year. GDP excludes used goods, intermediate goods, and goods not sold in markets.

Gross Domestic Product (GDP) is the market value of all final goods and services produced within the United States during the calendar year. Let's examine this definition of GDP in more detail to see what is included, and what is excluded, from this definition of U.S. economic activity.

Market Value

GDP only includes goods and services that are sold through markets. Non-market goods and services are excluded from GDP. Non-market goods and services are typically activities performed within and for one's own household; things such as:
- Meals prepared at home
- Childcare provided by parents for their own children
- Do-it-yourself repairs around your own property

Non-market goods/services are excluded from GDP because there is no objective way to measure their value. Values of market goods/services are objectively measured by the prices they sell at; non-market goods/services have no prices.

Final Goods

Final goods are items purchased and consumed by consumers. GDP excludes intermediate goods. An intermediate good is something that is used up in producing a final good. For example:
- Cotton used to produce yarn is an intermediate good.
- Yarn used to produce fabric is an intermediate good.
- Fabric used to produce clothing is an intermediate good.
- Clothing is a final good, as it is bought and consumed rather than being used to produce something else.

Intermediate goods are excluded from GDP in order to avoid double counting them. The value that is added by intermediate goods (cotton, yarn, fabric) is captured by the price of the final good (clothing).

Within the United States

GDP includes the production of foreign-owned companies operating inside the U.S. GDP excludes the production of U.S.-owned companies operating outside the U.S. The reason for this is that GDP is measuring economic activity inside the country; the ownership of the economic activity is irrelevant to the size of that activity.

During the Calendar Year

GDP excludes the value of used goods. So, for example, the price you pay for a three-year-old auto from a used car lot is excluded from GDP. It is excluded because the value of the used item was already counted in GDP during the year when the used item was produced.

Underground Economy

The underground economy is economic activity that takes place off-the-books. That is, economic activity that does not get reported, and so can't be counted. This includes:
- Small cash transactions like a child's lemonade stand, payment to a teenager who mows lawns in the neighborhood, a babysitter's payment, a tip jar in a restaurant.
- Barter—that is, direct exchange of goods/services for other goods/services
- Illegal activities—things like drugs, prostitution, smuggling, where both parties have strong incentives to keep the transaction secret

We would like to include the value of underground economic activity in GDP, but are unable to do so.

In or Out of GDP?

Situation	In or Out?	Reason
American steel purchased by Japanese auto manufacturers, and used to produce cars in Japan	IN	The steel is a "final" good as soon as it leaves the U.S.
Oil changes you perform yourself on your new car	OUT	Work you do for yourself is not a market transaction.
Household services provided by illegal immigrants whose employers do not report their earnings or pay taxes on them	OUT	These services are not reported; they are part of the underground economy.
Haircuts performed by an Iranian immigrant at a local barbershop	IN	This is a service provided inside the U.S.; the nationality of the service provider is irrelevant.
American rice purchased by American cereal manufacturers as input for making puffed rice cereal	OUT	This rice is an intermediate good used in the production of cereal.
DVRs manufactured by Sony (a Japanese-owned company) at their plant in Kentucky	IN	Because it is made inside the U.S.
A set of World Book encyclopedias bought from a used book store	OUT	Because this is not current production.

Gross Domestic Product 67

3.2. QUALITY OF GDP MEASUREMENT

Accuracy of the GDP measurement is shown by comparing GDP as the sum of expenditures (C+I+G+NE) to GDP as the sum of incomes. GDP is often assumed to indicate a nation's economic well-being, but there are serious deficiencies to GDP as a measure of well-being.

The question of the quality of the GDP measurement has two aspects.
- How accurately do we measure what we say we are trying to measure?
- How close does what we are trying to measure match what we would actually like to measure?

GDP is intended to measure the size of the economy. How accurately does it do this? Before answering this question, let us first acknowledge the very real operational difficulties inherent to the measuring process. The BEA, although it constructs the GDP measure, does not itself collect most of the needed data. Data used by the BEA is collected by various government agencies, trade associations, and international organizations. These organizations collect the data for their own purposes, using their own definitions and time periods. The BEA frequently must adjust the data to fit the GDP framework. The BEA also frequently must fill gaps in the data by estimation, interpolation, and other methods.

The data used by BEA are usually available only after some lag. In general, the longer the lag time, the better the data become. This means that the most recent GDP estimates get revised as better and more complete data are received. For example, here is how estimates of GDP growth changed over a three-month period in 2014.
- In February 2015, the "advance" estimate for the fourth quarter of 2014 was reported as +2.6%.
- In March 2015, the "preliminary" estimate revised this to +2.2%.
- In April 2015, the "final" estimate kept it at +2.2%.

The best estimate of the accuracy of the GDP measurement may come from comparing two different ways to measure GDP.
- The expenditures approach adds together spending on final goods and services by the various major sectors of the economy.
- The income approach adds together the incomes earned through the production of the final goods and services.

The two different approaches should result in the same total measure of GDP, but they don't. In 2011:

Expenditures	Income
Consumption = 10,711.8 Investment = 2,232.1 Government = 3,158.7 Net exports = -568.7	Wages/salaries = 8,286.6 Taxes = 1,037.1 Profits = 3,811.2 Fixed capital = 2,457.6 Statistical discrepancy = -53.7
GDP = 15,533.8	GDP = 15,587.5

The statistical discrepancy is an entry made so that the 2 methods sum to the same total. It is an indication of the margin of error in the measurement:

In 2011 = 0.35%

GDP is often interpreted as a measure of a nation's economic well-being; a rising GDP means that the nation is better off, while a falling GDP means that the nation is worse off.

There are a number of serious problems with using GDP as a measure of economic well-being.

1. GDP does not count non-market goods.
    - Child care provided by parents is not counted in GDP, but child care provided at a daycare center is. GDP rises when stay-at-home parents enroll their children in daycare instead; but does less parental care improve our well-being?
    - Meals prepared at home are not counted in GDP, but restaurant meals are. GDP rises when people eat out more; but does a steady diet of restaurant food improve our health and well-being?

2. GDP does not account for environmental damage caused by production activities.
    - When a forest is clear cut, GDP captures the value of the harvested timber, but it does not count the cost of the subsequent soil erosion.

3. GDP does not count the underground economy.
    - The amount of economic activity that goes unreported varies widely from one country to the next—this type of activity is especially common in developing countries. GDP comparisons make poor countries look much worse than they actually are.

There have been several attempts to develop alternatives to GDP that would better measure a nation's well-being. For example:
- The Index of Social Health has been constructed by the Institute for Innovation in Social Policy at Vassar College since 1987. It is a composite measure based on sixteen social indicators, including: infant mortality, high school dropout rates, unemployment, poverty levels among the elderly, food insecurity, and income inequality.
- The United Nations Human Development Index was developed in 1990 by the economists Mahbub ul Haq and Amartya Sen. It is a composite statistic of life expectancy, education, and income indexes.

The main challenge for any alternative measure is to define what contributes to (or detracts from) well-being. This invariably involves subjective judgment—and so creates controversy. For example, the Human Development Index has been criticized for having an ideological bias towards egalitarianism and "Western" models of development—concepts that seem obviously good to some and are decisively rejected by others.

3.3. REAL VS. NOMINAL GDP

Nominal GDP is the value of goods and services calculated using their current prices. Nominal GDP increases when the economy grows, but also increases when there is inflation. Real GDP removes the effect of inflation, so that we can see if the economy has actually grown. This is done by using the GDP deflator.

Nominal GDP is the value of goods and services calculated using their current prices. Chart #1 shows the calculation of GDP in a simple society that produces only 3 goods.

Chart #1 - Nominal GDP

Good	Quantity	X	Price	=	Value
A	100	X	10	=	1000
B	50	X	5	=	250
C	250	X	3	=	750
			GDP	=	2000

$$GDP = \sum Q_i P_i$$

Nominal GDP increases when the economy grows—when a larger quantity of goods and services is produced. To show this, chart #2 repeats the calculations in chart #1, but with double the quantity of each good. Nominal GDP is now twice as large as it was before.

Chart #2 - Nominal GDP, with double the quantities

Good	Quantity	X	Price	=	Value
A	200	X	10	=	2000
B	100	X	5	=	500
C	500	X	3	=	1500
			GDP	=	4000

However, nominal GDP also increases when there is inflation—when the market prices of goods rise. To show this, chart #3 repeats the calculations in chart #1, but with double the prices of each good. Nominal GDP is again twice as large as it was before.

Chart #3 - Nominal GDP, with double the prices

Good	Quantity	X	Price	=	Value
A	100	X	20	=	2000
B	50	X	10	=	500
C	250	X	6	=	1500
			GDP	=	4000

In both chart #2 and chart #3, nominal GDP is twice as large as in chart #1.
- In chart #2 we have twice the real goods and services as in chart #1.
- In chart #3 we have the same real goods and services as in chart #1, we just pay twice as much for them.

"Real" GDP removes the effect of inflation, so we can see if the economy has actually grown.
  To convert nominal GDP to real GDP, divide nominal GDP by the GDP deflator (then multiply by 100).
  • The GDP deflator is an index which shows by how much the general price level has risen.

Year	Nominal GDP	GDP deflator	Real GDP	Percentage change from 2009	
				Nominal	Real
2009	14,417.9	100	14,417.9	-	-
2010	14,958.3	101.210	14,779.4	3.7	2.5
2011	15,533.8	103.198	15,052.4	7.7	4.4
2012	16,244.6	105.002	15,470.7	12.7	7.3
2013	16,979.5	106.590	15,759.0	17.8	9.3

Sample calculation: In 2010, 14,958.3 × 100/101.210 = 14,779.4

Note that:
  • The price level was rising over this entire period (GDP deflator is larger each year).
  • Because prices were rising, nominal GDP is larger than real GDP.
  • Nominal GDP rose by 17.8% from 2009 to 2013.
      » More than half of this increase came from an increase in real goods and services (9.3 / 17.8 = 52%).
      » The remainder of this increase comes from prices being higher in 2013 than in 2009

On the Bureau of Economic Analysis website (www.bea.gov):
  • GDP deflator values are shown in table 1.1.4.
  • Nominal GDP values are shown in table 1.1.5.
  • Real GDP values are shown in table 1.1.6.

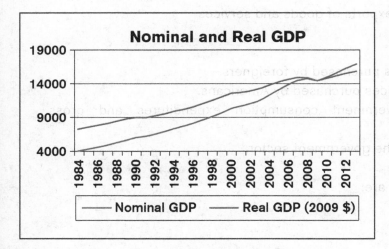

Nominal and Real GDP

Over this 30-year period, nominal GDP rises more steeply than does real GDP, because the price level was rising over this period.

Nominal and real GDP are the same in 2009 (the year whose $ are used to calculate real GDP).

Prior to 2009, real GDP is higher; after 2009, nominal GDP is higher.

4. COMPONENTS OF GDP

GDP is the sum of expenditures by the four major sectors of the economy. Consumption (spending by households) + Investment (spending by business firms) + Government purchases + Net Exports (spending by international trade sector). GDP = C + I + G + NE.

GDP is most commonly measured as the sum of expenditures by the four major sectors of the economy: households, business firms, government, and international trade.

   Spending by the household sector = Personal consumption expenditures
- This is mainly purchases of new goods and services by individuals from private businesses.

The components of consumption are:
- Durable goods: commodities with an average life of at least three years
- Non-durable goods: all other commodities
- Services: things consumed at the time and place of purchase

Spending by the business sector = Gross private domestic investment
- This consists of both fixed investment and changes in private inventories.

The components of investment are:
- Residential: single-family and multi-family homes
- Non-residential structures: business offices, factories, hotels, mines
- Non-residential equipment and software: business machinery, equipment, vehicles, and computer software
- Change in private inventories: change in the physical volume of inventories, valued in average prices of the period

Spending by international trade sector = Net exports of goods and services
- Defined as exports minus imports

Exports are U.S.-produced goods and services purchased by foreigners.
Imports are foreign-produced goods and services purchased by Americans.
Spending by government sector = Government consumption expenditures and gross investment
- This is the measure of final demand by the government sector.

The components of government expenditures are:
- National defense
- Other federal government
- State and local government

Table 1.1.5. Gross Domestic Product
[Billions of dollars] Seasonally adjusted at annual rates
Last Revised on: February 28, 2014 - Next Release Date March 27, 2014

Line		2013			
		I	II	III	IV
1	**Gross domestic product**	16,535.3	16,661.0	16,912.9	17,080.7
2	**Personal consumption expenditures**	11,379.2	11,427.1	11,537.7	11,640.7
3	Goods	3,851.8	3,848.5	3,912.8	3,933.2
4	Durable goods	1,244.8	1,257.5	1,274.0	1,275.0
5	Nondurable goods	2,607.0	2,591.0	2,638.8	2,658.2
6	Services	7,527.4	7,578.6	7,624.8	7,707.6
7	**Gross private domestic investment**	2,555.1	2,621.0	2,738.0	2,780.5
8	Fixed investment	2,491.7	2,543.8	2,593.2	2,634.2
9	Nonresidential	2,001.4	2,030.6	2,060.5	2,103.3
10	Structures	429.1	452.6	470.7	475.9
11	Equipment	928.0	934.6	935.8	959.1
12	Intellectual property products	644.3	643.5	654.1	668.2
13	Residential	490.3	513.2	532.6	531.0
14	Change in private inventories	63.4	77.2	144.8	146.3
15	**Net exports of goods and services**	-523.1	-509.0	-500.2	-456.8
16	Exports	2,214.2	2,238.9	2,265.8	2,320.1
17	Goods	1,531.6	1,548.8	1,572.1	1,614.9
18	Services	682.6	690.2	693.7	705.2
19	Imports	2,737.3	2,747.9	2,766.0	2,776.9
20	Goods	2,281.9	2,288.7	2,304.5	2,309.6
21	Services	455.3	459.3	461.5	467.3
22	**Government consumption expenditures and gross investment**	3,124.1	3,121.9	3,137.5	3,116.2
23	Federal	1,255.0	1,252.6	1,251.2	1,224.8
24	National defense	775.8	776.3	777.3	753.7
25	Nondefense	479.2	476.3	473.9	471.1
26	State and local	1,869.1	1,869.3	1,886.3	1,891.4

Data for the 4 sectors are on lines 2, 7, 15, and 22.

Services are the largest part of consumption.

Imports are larger than exports.

State and local government are larger than the federal government.

Since government goods and services are seldom sold, they are valued as the cost of the inputs used to produce them.

Our standard definition of the total macro economy is:

GDP = C + I + G + NE

  = Consumption + Investment + Government expenditures + Net exports

5. NATIONAL INCOME ACCOUNTING

GDP is the top of the National Income and Product Accounts (NIPA). Other important NIPA measures include Net Domestic Product, National Income, Personal Income, and Disposable Income.

GDP is the top measure in the National Income and Product Accounts (NIPA), but it is not the only measure. Other important NIPA measures include Net Domestic Product, National Income, Personal Income, and Disposable Income.

Net Domestic Product (NDP)

Net domestic product is the market value of final goods and services, less depreciation of capital. That is, NDP is GDP minus the fixed capital that is used up in producing it.

NDP is important because it indicates the level of production that can be sustained over time. It is a measure of the level of consumption that can be maintained while leaving capital assets intact.

National Income (NI)

National income is the total income earned by all factors of production. It is calculated as Net Domestic Product plus net foreign factor income.
- Net foreign factor income is the value of U.S. resources purchased by foreigners, minus the value of foreign resources purchased by Americans.

NI is important because it indicates the value of the resources available to the nation.

Personal Income (PI)

Personal income is that portion of National Income that comes to the household sector. The portions of NI that do not come to households are:
- Indirect business taxes (sales taxes, import tariffs, and the like)
- Corporate profits
- Interest and miscellaneous payments
- Social Security taxes

Additional income comes to households through:
- Transfer payments (Social Security payments, government pensions, and the like)
- Capital income (interest and dividend payments)

PI is important because households are the largest sector of the economy.

Disposable Income (DI)

Disposable income is the amount of income actually available to households for their use. Disposable income is Personal Income minus the income taxes that the household pays.

DI is important because it shows the amount that consumers can dispose of themselves; it shows how much consumers can spend or save.

How the NIPA goes from GDP to Disposable Income:

	2010	2011	2012	% change 2010-2012
GDP	14,958.3	15,533.8	16,244.6	8.60
Less: depreciation	2,381.6	2,452.6	2,542.9	6.77
NDP	12,576.7	13,081.3	13,701.7	8.95
Plus: foreign income	720.2	802.8	818.6	13.66
Less: income to foreigners	514.1	542.1	565.7	10.04
Less: statistical discrepancy	43.1	-53.7	-17.0	-
National Income	12,739.5	13,295.7	13,954.6	9.54
Less: corporate profits	1,740.6	1,877.7	2,009.5	15.45
Less: indirect business taxes	1,001.2	1,037.2	1,065.6	6.43
Less: interest/misc. payments	595.0	562.7	518.8	-12.81
Less: Social Security taxes	984.1	918.2	950.7	-3.39
Plus: transfer payments	2,276.9	2,306.9	2,358.3	3.58
Plus: interest and dividends	1,739.6	1,884.6	1,958.5	12.60
Personal Income	12,435.2	13,191.3	13,743.8	10.52
Less: personal taxes	1,191.5	1,404.0	1,498.0	25.72
Disposable income	11,243.7	11,787.4	12,245.8	8.91

Note annotations on the table:
- Note that NI is larger than NDP—we export more resources than we import.
- Here is that statistical discrepancy again.
- Social Security taxes actually fell from 2011 to 2012

Note that the various components of the NIPA do not all grow at the same rate. For example, note that:
- Corporate profits grew much faster than the economy as a whole.
- Indirect business taxes grew at a slower pace than GDP.
- Disposable income grew at a slower rate than Personal income, because personal taxes grew at a rate about 3 times that of the economy as a whole.

SUMMARY OF CHAPTER 4

The size of the U.S. economy is measured as the Gross Domestic Product (GDP). GDP is produced by the Bureau of Economic Analysis as part of the National Income and Product Accounts (NIPA).

Circular flow diagrams are visual tools that illustrate the interactions between various major sectors of the economy.

Find GDP data at: www.bea.gov.

The definition of GDP is: The market value of all final goods and services produced within the U.S. during the calendar year

The accuracy of the GDP measurement is shown by comparing GDP as the sum of expenditures (C+I+G+NE) to GDP as the sum of incomes. The size of the "statistical discrepancy" indicates that the GDP measure is quite accurate.

Problems with using GDP as a measure of economic well-being include:
- Does not include non-market goods/services
- Does not account for changes in environmental quality
- Does not count activity in the underground economy

Nominal GDP is the value of goods and services calculated using their current prices. Nominal GDP increases when the economy grows, but also increases when there is inflation. Real GDP removes the effect of inflation, so that we can see if the economy has actually grown.

GDP is the sum of expenditures by the four major sectors of the economy: (C+I+G+NE)
- Consumption + Investment + Government expenditures + Net exports

Other important aggregate measures include:
- Net Domestic Product : GDP minus depreciation
- National Income: Total income to all factors of production
- Personal Income: Total income to the household sector
- Disposable Income: Personal income minus personal taxes

Credits

Fig 4.5: "NBER Logo," http://www.nber.org/img_2009/NBER_logo_2014.jpg.
Fig 4.6: Bureau of Economic Analysis, www.bea.gov. Copyright in the Public Domain.
Fig 4.10: Bureau of Economic Analysis, "Gross Domestic Product," http://www.bea.gov/iTable/index_nipa.cfm. Copyright in the Public Domain.

CH FIVE

UNEMPLOYMENT

Everyone age sixteen or older is either employed, unemployed, or not in the labor force. Information on unemployment and the labor force can be found on the Bureau of Labor Statistics website.

Month-to-month changes in labor force totals are relatively small. This hides massive churning in labor markets, as millions of people change their labor force status each month.

There are four general types of unemployment: seasonal, frictional, structural, and cyclical. The natural rate of unemployment is when there is zero cyclical unemployment.

1. LABOR FORCE CONCEPTS

Everyone age sixteen or older is either employed, unemployed, or not in the labor force. The unemployment rate is the number of persons unemployed divided by the number of persons in the labor force.

Everyone age sixteen or older is either employed, unemployed, or not in the labor force. Intuitively:
- Employed = You have a job
- Unemployed = You don't have a job, but you want one
- Not in the labor force = You don't have a job, and don't want one

The unemployment rate is the percentage of persons in the labor force who are unemployed.
- Unemployment rate = Number unemployed / Number in labor force
- Number in labor force = Number employed + Number unemployed

The labor force participation rate is the percentage of persons who are in the labor force.
- Labor force participation rate = Number in labor force / Number in population
- Number in population = Number in labor force + Number not in labor force

Labor force statistics in the United States are created by the combined efforts of the Census Bureau and the Bureau of Labor Statistics. The Census Bureau collects the basic data with its monthly Current Population Survey. The Bureau of Labor Statistics takes the data collected by Census, then calculates and publishes the labor force statistics.

The Current Population Survey consists of monthly personal visits or telephone interviews to 60,000 U.S. households. The Census field representative determines the status of each eligible member of the household by asking a series of questions, including:
- Last week, did you do any work for pay or profit?
- Last week, did you have a job from which you were temporarily absent?
- What was the main reason you were absent from work last week?
- Have you been doing anything to find work during the last four weeks?
- Last week, could you have started a job if one had been offered?

A person is classified as employed if they did any work in the last week for pay or profit, if they did any unpaid work in their family business or farm, or if they had been temporarily absent from their job (for vacation, illness, family obligation, on strike, bad weather, and the like).

A person is classified as unemployed if they did not have a job last week, had actively looked for work in the prior four weeks, and would have been available for work if offered a job. Actively looking for work includes things like going to job interviews, sending out resumes, answering job ads, and the like.

A person is classified as not in the labor force if they did not have a job, and either had not looked for one in the past four weeks or would not have been available to work if offered a job.

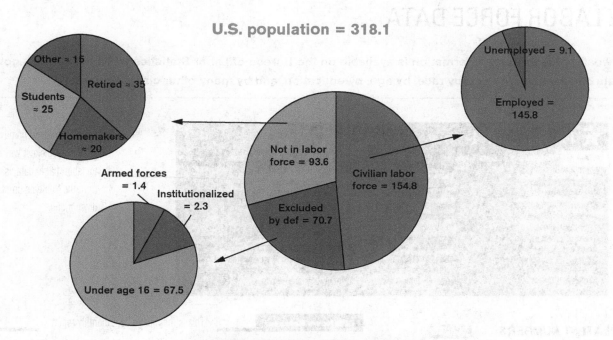

U.S. population = 318.1

Other ≈ 15
Retired ≈ 35
Students ≈ 25
Homemakers ≈ 20

Not in labor force = 93.6

Civilian labor force = 154.8

Unemployed = 9.1
Employed = 145.8

Armed forces = 1.4
Institutionalized = 2.3
Excluded by def = 70.7

Under age 16 = 67.5

Examples of determining labor force status:

Linda Coleman is a homemaker. Last week, she was occupied with her normal household chores. She neither held a job nor looked for a job. Her eighty-year-old father who lives with her has not worked or looked for work because of a disability. *Linda and her father are not in the labor force.*

George Lewis is sixteen years old, and he has no job from which he receives any pay or profit. However, George does help with the regular chores around his father's farm and spends about twenty hours each week doing so. *George is employed; he is an unpaid family worker.*

Yvonne Bennett reported that two weeks ago she applied for a job as a receptionist at the Capitol Travel Agency and the Equity Mortgage Lending Company. *Yvonne is unemployed because she made a specific effort to find a job within the prior four weeks and is presently available for work.*

Marcus Green was laid off from the Hotshot Motor Company when the firm began retooling to produce a new model car. Marcus knows he will be called back to work as soon as the model changeover is completed. *Marcus is unemployed because he is waiting to be recalled from layoff.*

Mrs. Jenkins tells the interviewer that her daughter, Katherine Marie, was thinking about looking for work in the prior four weeks but knows of no specific efforts she has made. *Katherine Marie does not meet the activity test for unemployment and is, therefore, counted as not in the labor force.*

James Kelly and Elyse Martin attend Jefferson High School. James works after school at the North Star Cafe, and Elyse is seeking a part-time job at the same establishment (also after school). *James' job takes precedence over his non-labor force activity of going to school, as does Elyse's search for work; therefore, James is counted as employed and Elyse is counted as unemployed.*

2. LABOR FORCE DATA

A wealth of labor force information is available on the Bureau of Labor Statistics website (www.bls.gov). Data can be found by sex, by race, by age, by education, and by many other classifications.

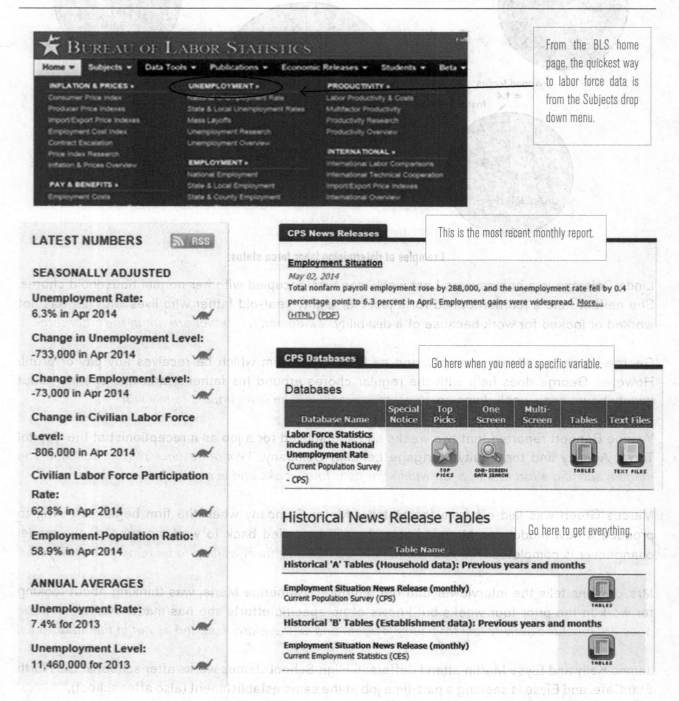

Here are some of the major ways in which labor force data are available:

Table A-1. Employment status of the civilian population by sex and age
Table A-2. Employment status of the civilian population by race, sex, and age
Table A-4. Employment status of the civilian population 25 years and over by educational attainment
Table A-8. Employed persons by class of worker and part-time status
Table A-9. Selected employment indicators
Table A-10. Selected unemployment indicators, seasonally adjusted
Table A-11. Unemployed persons by reason for unemployment
Table A-12. Unemployed persons by duration of unemployment
Table A-13. Employed and unemployed persons by occupation, not seasonally adjusted

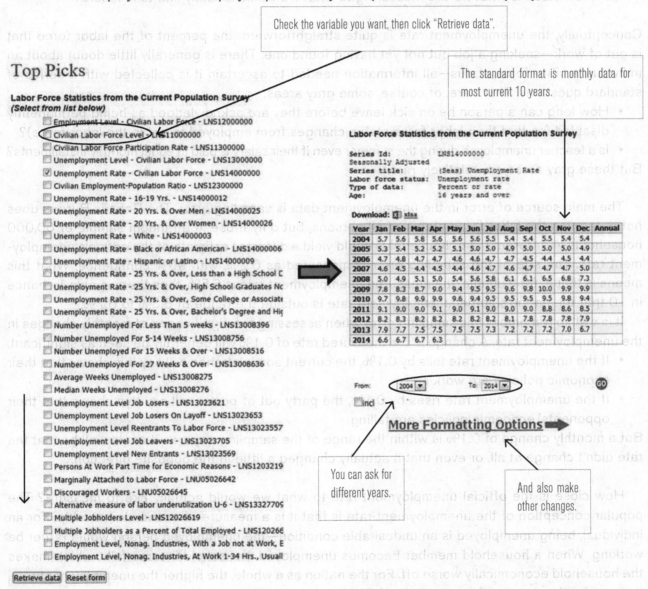

Check the variable you want, then click "Retrieve data".

The standard format is monthly data for most current 10 years.

Top Picks

Labor Force Statistics from the Current Population Survey
(Select from list below)

- Employment Level - Civilian Labor Force - LNS12000000
- Civilian Labor Force Level - LNS11000000
- Civilian Labor Force Participation Rate - LNS11300000
- Unemployment Level - Civilian Labor Force - LNS13000000
- ☑ Unemployment Rate - Civilian Labor Force - LNS14000000
- Civilian Employment-Population Ratio - LNS12300000
- Unemployment Rate - 16-19 Yrs. - LNS14000012
- Unemployment Rate - 20 Yrs. & Over Men - LNS14000025
- Unemployment Rate - 20 Yrs. & Over Women - LNS14000026
- Unemployment Rate - White - LNS14000003
- Unemployment Rate - Black or African American - LNS14000006
- Unemployment Rate - Hispanic or Latino - LNS14000009
- Unemployment Rate - 25 Yrs. & Over, Less than a High School D
- Unemployment Rate - 25 Yrs. & Over, High School Graduates No
- Unemployment Rate - 25 Yrs. & Over, Some College or Associate
- Unemployment Rate - 25 Yrs. & Over, Bachelor's Degree and Hig
- Number Unemployed For Less Than 5 weeks - LNS13008396
- Number Unemployed For 5-14 Weeks - LNS13008756
- Number Unemployed For 15 Weeks & Over - LNS13008516
- Number Unemployed For 27 Weeks & Over - LNS13008636
- Average Weeks Unemployed - LNS13008275
- Median Weeks Unemployed - LNS13008276
- Unemployment Level Job Losers - LNS13023621
- Unemployment Level Job Losers On Layoff - LNS13023653
- Unemployment Level Reentrants To Labor Force - LNS13023557
- Unemployment Level Job Leavers - LNS13023705
- Unemployment Level New Entrants - LNS13023569
- Persons At Work Part Time for Economic Reasons - LNS1203219
- Marginally Attached to Labor Force - LNU05026642
- Discouraged Workers - LNU05026645
- Alternative measure of labor underutilization U-6 - LNS1332770S
- Multiple Jobholders Level - LNS12026619
- Multiple Jobholders as a Percent of Total Employed - LNS12026E
- Employment Level, Nonag. Industries, With a Job not at Work, E
- Employment Level, Nonag. Industries, At Work 1-34 Hrs., Usuall

Retrieve data   Reset form

Labor Force Statistics from the Current Population Survey

Series Id:	LNS14000000
Seasonally Adjusted	
Series title:	(Seas) Unemployment Rate
Labor force status:	Unemployment rate
Type of data:	Percent or rate
Age:	16 years and over

Download: ☒ xlsx

Year	Jan	Feb	Mar	Apr	May	Jun	Jul	Aug	Sep	Oct	Nov	Dec	Annual
2004	5.7	5.6	5.8	5.6	5.6	5.6	5.5	5.4	5.4	5.5	5.4	5.4	
2005	5.3	5.4	5.2	5.2	5.1	5.0	5.0	4.9	5.0	5.0	5.0	4.9	
2006	4.7	4.8	4.7	4.7	4.6	4.6	4.7	4.7	4.5	4.4	4.5	4.4	
2007	4.6	4.5	4.4	4.5	4.4	4.6	4.7	4.6	4.7	4.7	4.7	5.0	
2008	5.0	4.9	5.1	5.0	5.4	5.6	5.8	6.1	6.1	6.5	6.8	7.3	
2009	7.8	8.3	8.7	9.0	9.4	9.5	9.5	9.6	9.8	10.0	9.9	9.9	
2010	9.7	9.8	9.9	9.9	9.6	9.4	9.5	9.5	9.5	9.5	9.8	9.4	
2011	9.1	9.0	9.0	9.1	9.0	9.1	9.0	9.0	9.0	8.8	8.6	8.5	
2012	8.2	8.3	8.2	8.2	8.2	8.2	8.2	8.1	7.8	7.8	7.8	7.9	
2013	7.9	7.7	7.5	7.5	7.5	7.5	7.3	7.2	7.2	7.2	7.0	6.7	
2014	6.6	6.7	6.7	6.3									

From: 2004 ▼   To: 2014 ▼   GO

☐ include

More Formatting Options ➡

You can ask for different years.

And also make other changes.

3. QUALITY OF UNEMPLOYMENT DATA

Ask yourself two questions:

1. How accurately are we measuring what we say we want to measure?
2. How close is what we are measuring to what we would actually like to measure?

The question of the quality of the unemployment data has two aspects:

1. How accurately are we measuring what we say we want to measure?
2. How close is what we are measuring to what we would actually like to measure?

Conceptually, the unemployment rate is quite straightforward: the percent of the labor force that is out of work—seeking a job but not yet having found one. There is generally little doubt about an individual's labor force status—all information needed to ascertain it is collected with a series of standard questions. There are, of course, some gray areas:

- How long can a person be on sick leave before they are acknowledged as being permanently disabled (so that their labor force status changes from employed to not in the labor force)?
- Is a teacher unemployed during the summer even if their salary is paid in equal monthly installments?

But these gray areas are relatively rare.

The main source of error in the unemployment data is sampling error. The Census Bureau does not determine the labor force status of all persons, but only those in a random sample of 60,000 households. A different set of households could yield a different estimate of the nation's unemployment rate. The size of the sampling error is measured as 0.2%, with 90% confidence. What this means is that if, for example, the measured unemployment rate is 6.5%, then there is only 1 chance in 10 that the nation's actual unemployment rate is outside the range of 6.3% to 6.7%.

It is well to remember this sampling error when assessing the significance of monthly changes in the unemployment rate. A change in the measured rate of 0.1% will generally be seen as significant.

- If the unemployment rate falls by 0.1%, the current administration will say this shows that their economic policies are working.
- If the unemployment rate rises by 0.1%, the party out of power will say this shows that their opponents' economic policies are failing.

But a monthly change of 0.1% is within the range of the sampling error, so it could well be that the rate didn't change at all, or even that it actually changed a little in the opposite direction.

How close is the official unemployment rate to what we would actually like to measure? The popular conception of the unemployment rate is that it is a measure of economic hardship. For an individual, being unemployed is an undesirable condition—the unemployed person would rather be working. When a household member becomes unemployed, household income falls, which makes the household economically worse off. For the nation as a whole, the higher the unemployment rate, the greater the degree of economic hardship.

There are a number of ways in which the official unemployment rate understates economic hardship. That is, that economic conditions might be worse than the official unemployment rate suggests.

1. When someone has been unemployed for a long time, and has had no success in finding a job, they can become discouraged and give up. They stop actively seeking a job, because they think they won't find one. When this happens, the discouraged worker is classified as not in the labor force, and is no longer counted as unemployed.
2. A person with a part-time job is counted as employed, even if that person would much rather have a full-time job, but is unable to find one.
3. A highly skilled person working a low-skill job is underemployed. They qualify for a better job, but are unable to find one. In the official data, the underemployed worker is still counted as employed.
4. When the head of a household is working in a low-wage job, their low income certainly causes economic hardship. Nevertheless, low-wage workers are simply counted as employed.

There are also a number of ways in which the official unemployment rate overstates economic hardship. That is, economic conditions might be better than the official unemployment rate suggests.

5. Many households have more than one wage earner. One member of the household becoming unemployed does not mean that the household loses its only source of income.
6. Workers who are not the head of household tend to have a more casual attachment to the labor force. They may repeatedly shift in and out of the labor force as circumstances change. Consider a teenager who seeks a part-time job simply to earn a little spending money. Being unemployed is unfortunate for the teenager, but is hardly economic hardship for the household.
7. Unemployment insurance programs replace a significant portion of the income lost for many unemployed workers.
8. Most unemployed persons find another job relatively quickly. A short period of unemployment, while unpleasant, is probably not a large economic hardship.

The Bureau of Labor Statistics acknowledges these criticisms of the official unemployment rate. In response, BLS provides a number of alternate measures of unemployment.

Table A-15. Alternative measures of labor underutilization
[Percent]

Measure	Not seasonally adjusted			Seasonally adjusted					
	Apr. 2013	Mar. 2014	Apr. 2014	Apr. 2013	Dec. 2013	Jan. 2014	Feb. 2014	Mar. 2014	Apr. 2014
U-1 Persons unemployed 15 weeks or longer, as a percent of the civilian labor force	4.3	3.7	3.3	4.1	3.6	3.4	3.5	3.5	3.2
U-2 Job losers and persons who completed temporary jobs, as a percent of the civilian labor force	3.9	3.7	3.2	4.1	3.5	3.5	3.5	3.5	3.4
U-3 Total unemployed, as a percent of the civilian labor force (official unemployment rate)	7.1	6.8	5.9	7.5	6.7	6.6	6.7	6.7	6.3
U-4 Total unemployed plus discouraged workers, as a percent of the civilian labor force plus discouraged workers	7.6	7.2	6.3	8.0	7.2	7.1	7.2	7.1	6.7
U-5 Total unemployed, plus discouraged workers, plus all other persons marginally attached to the labor force, as a percent of the civilian labor force plus all persons marginally attached to the labor force	8.5	8.1	7.2	8.9	8.1	8.1	8.1	8.0	7.6
U-6 Total unemployed, plus all persons marginally attached to the labor force, plus total employed part time for economic reasons, as a percent of the civilian labor force plus all persons marginally attached to the labor force	13.4	12.8	11.8	13.9	13.1	12.7	12.6	12.7	12.3

Long-term unemployed

Discouraged workers

Part-time, but want full-time

4. LABOR MARKET FLOWS

Month-to-month changes in labor force totals are relatively small. This hides massive churning in labor markets, as millions of people change their labor force status each month.

Stock is a static concept. It is the measure of the size of something at a point in time. Flow is a dynamic concept. It is the size of the movement between two points in time.

Month-to-month changes in labor force totals (the stocks of employed, unemployed, and not in the labor force) are relatively small. This hides massive churning in labor markets, as millions of people change their labor force status each month. That is, stability in labor market stocks hides great volatility in labor market flows.

There are many reasons why unemployed persons might leave the labor force.

- Discouraged workers decide that the likelihood of their finding a job is so low that it isn't worth the effort to keep looking.
- Some persons might suspend their job search while going back to school to learn new skills or earn a degree, or while they relocate to an area with better job opportunities.
- Changing personal circumstances might lead some persons to stop looking for a job (perhaps declining health or the birth of a grandchild).

There are also reasons why employed persons might leave the labor force.

- Retirement.
- A student who had been working a summer job returns to school.
- A young couple has their first child, and one of them quits work to be a full-time parent.
- Changing personal circumstances might lead some persons to quit their job (perhaps the need to care for an invalid parent or winning the lottery).

And there are also many reasons why persons might enter the labor force.

- Students graduate and start looking for a job.
- Homemakers might decide to find a paying job once their children have grown.
- Teenagers might want to earn a little spending money from working a part-time job.
- Children become legally able to take a job when they turn sixteen.

The diagram at the top of the next page shows labor market stocks and flows for the United States between March 2014 and April 2014. The changes in the stocks are much smaller than the flows. For example, the stock of employed increased by 677 thousand, but over 10 million persons moved in or out of employment.

Change from March 2014 to April 2014:

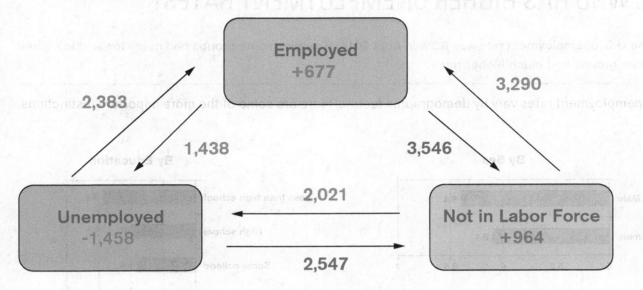

The population of the United States is highly mobile. Every year large numbers of persons change their jobs, their residences, their occupations, and their education.

Employment mobility:
The average American worker will hold more than eleven different jobs over their career. One-third of these jobs last no longer than one year, and only thirty-percent last longer than five years.

Geographic mobility:
Three percent of the population moves across state lines every year, with ten percent moving at least once in a five-year period. Over half of Americans currently live in a different state than at birth.

Occupational mobility:
Over a two-year period, about twenty percent of workers in low-wage occupations move upward to high-wage occupations (from 16.8% of service workers to 27.7% of clerical workers). A somewhat lower percentage of workers in high-wage occupations move downward to low-wage occupations (from 8.0% of professional/technical workers to 20.6% of craft workers).

Educational mobility:
At present over 4 million persons age thirty-five or over are enrolled in degree-granting educational institutions. Annual business expenditures on employee training exceed $100 billion.

5. WHO HAS HIGHER UNEMPLOYMENT RATES?

The U.S. unemployment rate was 6.3% in April 2014. However, some groups had much lower rates, while other groups had much higher rates.

Unemployment rates vary by demographic factors. Here are some of the more important distinctions.

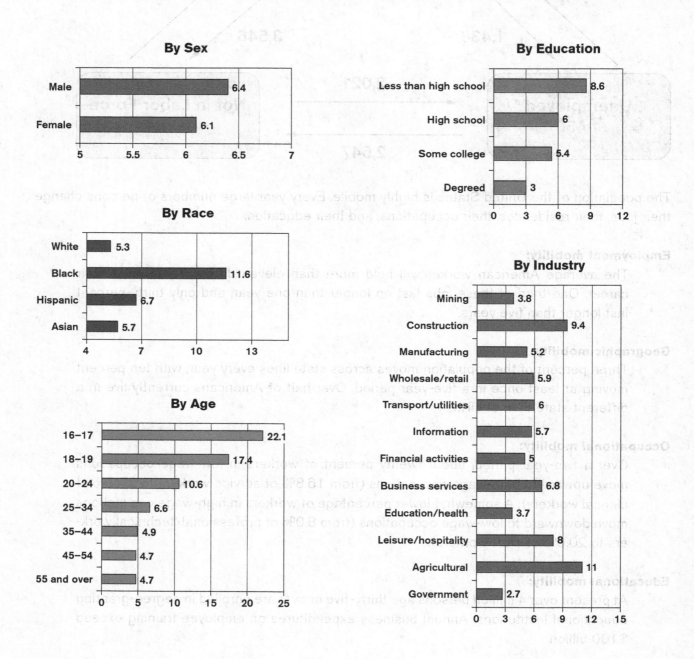

6. TYPES OF UNEMPLOYMENT

There are four general types of unemployment: seasonal, frictional, structural, and cyclical. The economic hardship caused by unemployment, and the appropriate policies in response, differ greatly between the four types of unemployment.

People become unemployed for various reasons. The economic hardship caused by unemployment, and the appropriate polices in response differ greatly depending upon the cause of the unemployment.

Seasonal unemployment is caused by predictable patterns of change in the supply of or demand for labor. Examples of seasonal unemployment include:
- K-12 teachers during the summer when school is out
- Snow ski instructors in the summer; water ski instructors in the winter
- Construction workers in areas where harsh weather conditions shut down construction sites
- Teenagers in the summer, when a flood of students looking for temporary jobs swamps the job market

Frictional unemployment is brief periods of unemployment caused by people moving between jobs. Examples of frictional unemployment include:
- A teacher hired in May for a position that will start in the fall
- Someone who quits their current job in order to devote full time to obtaining a better position
- A spouse who quits their current job to follow their partner who has gotten a promotion in another city

Structural unemployment is caused by sudden drops in demand in particular labor markets, in conditions where workers lack mobility. Examples of structural unemployment include:
- Coal miners in Appalachia; Auto workers in Detroit; Inner-city teenagers

Cyclical unemployment is caused by a fall in the demand for labor across many labor markets at the same time. Cyclical unemployment occurs during recessions.

The degree of economic hardship caused by each type of unemployment is affected by several factors:
- Is the unemployment expected, or unpredictable?
- Is the unemployment voluntary or involuntary?
- How long is the period of unemployment?
- How costly is it for workers to adjust to changes in labor conditions?

Unemployment causes little economic hardship when it is expected, voluntary, short-lived, and when workers are highly mobile. Unemployment causes more economic hardship when it is unpredictable, involuntary, long-term, and when workers lack mobility.

6.1. SEASONAL UNEMPLOYMENT

Seasonal unemployment is caused by predictable changes in labor demand and labor supply at certain times of the year.

Seasonal unemployment is caused by predictable changes in labor demand/supply at certain times of the year.

Demand predictably falls for:

- Retail sales workers in January (after the Christmas sales rush ends)
- Teachers in the summer (when school is out)
- Construction workers in Northern states in the winter (when weather conditions hinder outdoor construction work)

Supply predictably rises for:

- Low-skilled temporary labor in the summer (as students are released from school)

Workers in such occupations can anticipate being unemployed at certain times during the year.

Seasonal unemployment is most common in January and February (as temporary retail hires are released) and in June and July (when there is a glut of students seeking temporary employment). Seasonal unemployment seldom accounts for more than ten percent of the total unemployed.

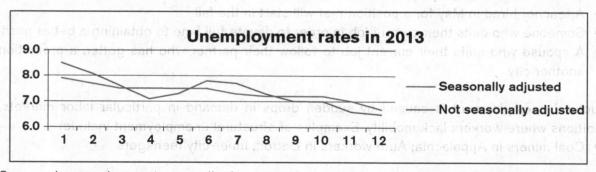

Seasonal unemployment generally does not cause great economic hardship, because:

- The periods of likely unemployment are predictable, and so can be planned for.
- The unemployment is generally short-term.
- Individuals voluntarily choose occupations where seasonal periods of unemployment are likely.
- Persons subject to seasonal unemployment tend to be less strongly attached to the labor force—they are more likely to think of themselves as being seasonally employed than as being seasonally unemployed.

Many communities have summer youth work programs designed to increase demand for temporary labor during the out-of-school months. Little is done to mitigate other sources of seasonal unemployment—probably because it is recognized that seasonal unemployment causes little economic hardship. In many states, the seasonally unemployed are not even eligible to collect unemployment insurance benefits.

6.2. FRICTIONAL UNEMPLOYMENT

Frictional unemployment is people who are in-between jobs. It is the cost we pay for mobility in labor markets.

Frictional unemployment is people who are temporarily between jobs.

- Demand for labor decreases in an industry, and some workers get laid off. These workers are frictionally unemployed while they look for similar work in other local firms, or relocate to where job opportunities are brighter, or learn new skills so they can find work in some other occupation.
- The supply of labor increases in an occupation (perhaps there is a bumper crop of new graduates in the field) and some workers are unable to find jobs. These workers are frictionally unemployed until they find a job in their chosen field, or take a temporary job in some other occupation, or relocate, or go back to school to earn a degree in another field.

Frictional unemployment can be thought of as the cost we pay for well-functioning labor markets. Employers don't necessarily hire the first applicant; nor do workers necessarily accept the first job offer. Companies may need to widen their search for good job applicants. Job seekers may need to consider relocating or career change. It takes time and effort to find good matches between jobs and workers. It is only because employers are willing to leave positions temporarily unfilled, and workers are willing to accept temporary unemployment, that labor markets are able to make good matches.

Frictional unemployment is relatively stable. This is because the level of frictional unemployment is largely determined by the institutional structure of labor markets—the mechanisms by which employers find job applicants and workers learn of job opportunities. Frictional unemployment tends to change slowly, because labor market mechanisms tend to change slowly. Frictional unemployment probably averages around five percent.

Frictional unemployment generally does not cause great economic hardship. Frictional unemployment is generally short-term. It is not that the frictionally unemployed can't find jobs, but rather that they are unwilling to take just any job—they voluntarily choose to spend more time unemployed in order to end up with a better job than if they accepted the first offer.

Public policies designed to improve the efficiency of labor markets (and lower frictional unemployment) include assistance in job search, retraining programs, and laws prohibiting discrimination in hiring. The public policy with the largest effect on frictional unemployment is probably state unemployment insurance (UI) programs. UI benefit payments offset part of the loss in income for a job loser, and so allow the job loser to spend more time looking for a better job—this increases the level of frictional unemployment. Policy makers must balance the benefits of better job matching against the cost of higher frictional unemployment.

6.3. STRUCTURAL UNEMPLOYMENT

Structural unemployment can occur when, for one reason or another, it is very costly to adjust to changes in labor markets.

Structural unemployment results from a lack of labor market mobility. Normally, when labor demand falls in an industry, the laid-off workers adjust to the changed labor market by switching to other occupations or relocating to other areas where job opportunities are better. When, for one reason or another, it is very costly for workers to adjust, structural unemployment occurs.

Structural unemployment can develop in a single geographically dispersed industry. The best example of this is probably the nuclear bomb making industry. With the end of the cold war, demand for nuclear bomb workers dropped dramatically, and many nuclear physicists lost their jobs. The skills possessed by these highly educated workers had little application outside nuclear bomb making. Unwilling to accept serious underemployment (at much lower salaries), many remained structurally unemployed.

However, structural unemployment usually is based on geography. When one industry dominates a geographic area, and demand for that industry's output falls, structural unemployment is likely to develop. The best examples of this are coal miners in Appalachia and auto workers in Detroit. It proved very costly for workers to adjust to their changed labor markets, because:

- There were too few other industries in the area to absorb the large number of workers laid off from the dominant industry.
- The workers' specialized skills were ill-suited for use in other industries.
- Relocation was very expensive: the laid off were generally older workers with stronger ties to the local community, who would suffer a large financial loss if they tried to sell their homes in the depressed local housing market.

When structural unemployment occurs, it causes great economic hardship. However, it doesn't occur very often. U.S. labor markets tend to be highly mobile. The unemployed tend to be younger, and younger workers are more geographically mobile.

Public policies to deal with structural unemployment vary from one case to the next. They can include things such as:

- Relocation assistance
- Retraining programs
- Establishment of enterprise zones or tax breaks to encourage economic development in the depressed region
- Direct subsidization of the depressed industry

6.4. CYCLICAL UNEMPLOYMENT

Cyclical unemployment results from a general decline in labor demand over broad portions of the economy.

Cyclical unemployment results from a general decline in labor demand over broad portions of the economy. Cyclical unemployment occurs during downturns in the business cycle (hence its name). The rise in unemployment during a recession comes from an increase in cyclical unemployment.

Cyclical unemployment has the potential to cause severe and widespread economic hardship. When labor demand falls for a particular industry, occupation, or region, workers adjust by moving to where job opportunities are better. But when labor demand falls in general during a recession, adjustment stalls because there is nowhere better to go. Laid-off workers can't move to other industries that are hiring if there are no other industries hiring.

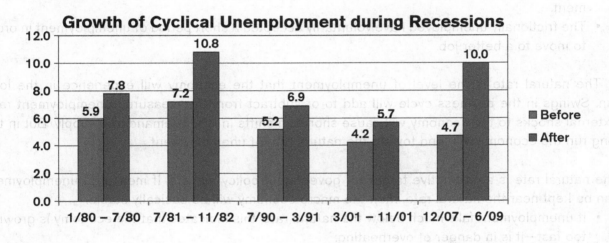

Cyclical unemployment is likely to be long-term. Many of the cyclically unemployed will not find jobs until the economy as a whole recovers; that time is measured in months or years, not in weeks. The longer a person is unemployed, the more severe is the economic hardship. Long-term unemployment tends to exhaust household savings, increase household debt, and put home ownership at risk. It causes households to skimp on medical care and postpone or cancel investments in education and other forms of human capital. The longer a worker is unemployed, the greater their loss of job skills, and the harder it is to find a new job.

The only effective remedy for cyclical unemployment is economic growth. Expansionary fiscal and monetary policies are designed to increase output and thereby increase the demand for labor.

7. NATURAL RATE OF UNEMPLOYMENT

The natural rate of unemployment is when there is no cyclical unemployment. It is also called "full" employment. At the natural rate of unemployment, the economy is operating at the level of potential GDP.

The natural rate of unemployment is what unemployment would be if there were no cyclical unemployment. It occurs when the economy is growing at its average long-term rate: neither growing at a faster rate (so that the economy is overheating) nor at a slower rate (so that the economy is falling into recession). The natural rate of unemployment is also called "full" employment.

The natural rate of unemployment consists of the sum of seasonal unemployment and frictional unemployment. This means that the natural rate can be thought of as the "voluntary" unemployment rate.
- The seasonally unemployed have voluntarily taken jobs with predictable periods of unemployment.
- The frictionally unemployed have voluntarily accepted a short period of unemployment in order to move to a better job.

The natural rate is the level of unemployment that the economy will experience in the long run. Swings in the business cycle will add to or subtract from the measured unemployment rate. External shocks to the economy will cause short-run shifts in labor demand and supply. But in the long run the economy will tend toward the natural rate of unemployment.

The natural rate is an attractive target for government policy makers. If measured unemployment can be kept near the natural rate, then the macro economy will be basically stable.
- If unemployment falls much below the natural rate, this indicates that the economy is growing too fast—it is in danger of overheating.
- If unemployment rises much above the natural rate, this indicates that the economy is growing too slowly—it is in danger of falling into recession.

The natural rate is also attractive as a target because this is the level that minimizes the economic hardship caused by unemployment. At the natural rate, unemployment is:
- Voluntary: individual persons accept their bout of unemployment as a reasonable price to pay for future economic gains.
- Short: measured in weeks, not in months or years.
- Dynamic: labor markets are continually changing, continually creating new opportunities for a mobile workforce.

Potential GDP is the output that the economy produces when unemployment is at the natural rate. To set an unemployment target of the natural rate is equivalent to setting an output target of potential GDP.

The main difficulty in using either the natural rate or the level of potential GDP as targets for macroeconomic policy, is that neither of them can be directly measured.

- When Census field representatives ask their standard questions to identify labor force status, there is nothing that distinguishes between those unemployed that contribute to the natural rate and those that do not. BLS cannot aggregate the data to calculate the natural rate.
- When the Bureau of Economic Analysis aggregates expenditures to measure GDP, there is no way to say that this expenditure is part of potential GDP and that expenditure is not.

Potential GDP and the natural rate of unemployment are theoretical concepts, not measurable objects. They are real, but they can't be measured. In addition, both are continually changing. Setting the natural rate as a goal is like shooting at an invisible target that never stands still!

> Estimates of the natural rate have changed over time:
> 1978 = 4%
> 1983 = 6-7%
> 1991 = 5.5%
> 1999 = 5.3%
> 2004 = 5.1%

What determines the level of the natural rate of unemployment?

It is affected by three general factors.

1. The efficiency of labor markets
   - How much time and effort is needed for workers to identify and assess their job opportunities?
   - How much time and effort is needed for employers to identify and assess their job applicants?
   - How do laws and government regulations affect the hiring process?

2. The variability of job opportunities and applicants
   - The greater the variability in the quality of job applicants, the more time and effort companies will invest in trying to find the top candidate.
   - The greater the variability in the quality of job opportunities, the more time and effort workers will invest in trying to find the best offer.

3. Characteristics of the work force
   - Some groups tend to have higher unemployment rates—the young, the poorly educated, those with weaker attachment to the labor force.
   - If these groups grow to comprise a larger proportion of the population, the natural rate of unemployment could be expected to rise.

SUMMARY OF CHAPTER 5

Everyone age sixteen or older is either employed, unemployed, or not in the labor force.
- Employed = You have a job
- Unemployed = You don't have a job, but you want one
- Not in the labor force = You don't have a job, and don't want one

The unemployment rate is the number of persons unemployed divided by the number of persons in the labor force.

The labor force participation rate is the number of persons in the labor force divided by the number of persons in the population.

Labor force information can be found on the Bureau of Labor Statistics website: www.bls.gov

Unemployment is measured quite accurately, but is not necessarily a good indicator of overall economic hardship.

Month-to-month changes in labor force totals are relatively small. This hides massive churning in labor markets, as millions of people change their labor force status each month.

Unemployment rates tend to be lower than the national average for white workers, older workers, and workers with more education.

The four general types of unemployment are seasonal, frictional, structural, and cyclical.
- Seasonal unemployment is caused by predictable changes in labor demand and labor supply at certain times of the year.
- Frictional unemployment is people who are in-between jobs.
- Structural unemployment can occur when it is very costly to adjust to changes in labor markets.
- Cyclical unemployment results from a general decline in labor demand over broad portions of the economy.

The natural rate of unemployment is when there is no cyclical unemployment. It is also called "full" employment.

At the natural rate of unemployment, the economy is operating at the level of potential GDP.

Credits

CH **SIX**

INFLATION

Inflation is a general increase in the price level. Inflation is measured using a price index.

The most common price indexes are:

- CPI = Consumer Price Index = Prices at the retail level
- PPI = Producer Price Indexes = Prices at the whole-sale level
- GDP deflator = Prices paid by major sectors of the economy

Price indexes are used to convert nominal values to real values.

Inflation redistributes income in unpredictable ways. It distorts investment and savings decisions.

1. WHAT IS INFLATION?

Inflation is a general increase in the price level. It is measured with a price index. The most common price indexes are the CPI, the PPI, and the GDP deflator.

Common sense says that inflation is when things cost more. While this is true, it is also deceptive; inflation is not caused by an increase in the price of any particular good, but by a general increase in the price level.

Product	Price 30 years ago	Price today	Percentage increase
Gasoline	$1.21	$3.36	178%
College tuition	$5,504	$35,116	538%
Baseball salary	$371,571	$3,650,257	882%

> There have been large increases in the price for each of these, but, by themselves, they are not inflation.

Prices on goods and services change all of the time—prices on some goods go up, prices on some goods go down, while prices of still other goods stay the same. For example, in 2013:
- The prices of potatoes rose; the price of apples fell; the price of soups did not change.
- The prices of propane gas rose; the price of floor covering fell; the price of gasoline did not change.
- The price of women's dresses rose; the price of women's footwear fell; the price of men's shirts did not change.
- The price of hospital services rose; the price of televisions fell; the price of telephone service did not change.

With this continual mix of rising, falling, and stable prices, how can we tell if prices in general have risen? The only way to tell is by the use of a price index.

A price index is a way to combine the prices of a mix of different goods and services into a single number. A price index, therefore, is a measure of the general price level. An increase in the general price level, indicated by a rise in the price index, means that there is inflation.

A price index does not show the actual prices of any individual good or service. Rather, it shows how the total amount needed to purchase a particular set (a market basket) of goods and services has changed over time.

Year	Imaginary Price Index
2001	90
2002	95
2003	98
2004	100
2005	108
2006	113
2007	125
2008	130
2009	135
2010	145

If X is the amount needed to buy the specified market basket, then:

$$X_{2010}/X_{2004} = 1.45$$

This means that, for each $1.00 spent on the market basket in 2004, it was necessary to spend $1.45 in 2010 to buy the same items.

The base year of this imaginary index is 2004. This means that 2004 is the year whose prices are being compared against.

By definition, any price index has a value of 100 in its base year.

The most commonly used price indexes in the United States are:
1. The Consumer Price Index (CPI)
   - This is produced by the Bureau of Labor Statistics (BLS).
   - It measures changes in the prices paid by consumers for final goods and services.

2. Producer Price Indexes (PPI)
   - These are also produced by the Bureau of Labor Statistics.
   - They measure changes in the prices paid by businesses at the wholesale level.

3. GDP deflators
   - These are produced by the Bureau of Economic Analysis (BEA).
   - They measure year-to-year changes in the prices paid by major sectors of the economy.

2. CONSTRUCTING A PRICE INDEX

To construct a price index, select a market basket of goods and services, assign appropriate weights to each item, and then measure the prices of each good in two different periods.

There are four basic steps involved in constructing a price index:
1. Select a market basket of goods and services.
2. Assign appropriate weights to each item in the market basket.
3. Measure the prices of each good in two different time periods.
4. Multiply the price of each good by its weight, and sum the products.

The price index is the ratio of the summed total in the second period to the summed total in the first period.

Step #1: Select a market basket

The particular goods and services that go into the market basket depend on what type of inflation you want to measure. The items selected for the market basket should be typical of the items purchased by the targeted audience.
- For example, say you want to measure inflation in grocery prices. You might load your market basket with a gallon of milk, a dozen eggs, a pound of hamburger, a box of cereal, and so on.

Step #2: Assign appropriate weights

Weights indicate the importance of each item in the market basket. We are not interested merely in what items are purchased, but also in how many units of each item are purchased.
- For our grocery price index, we might weight each item in our market basket by the average number of that item purchased by the typical consumer.

Step #3: Measure the prices of each good in two different time periods

It is important that the exact same items are priced in the two periods. We do not want to be literally comparing apples and oranges.
- For our grocery price index, if we price a gallon of whole milk in the first period, we need to make sure that we price a gallon of whole milk (not a quart, and not low-fat milk) in the second period too.

Step #4: Multiply price times quantity

The weights stay the same; only prices change from period to period. For the first period, multiply the price of each good in period 1 times the quantity of that good sold in period 1. For the second period, use the new prices (prices in the second period), but keep the same weights (the first period quantities).

Here is a simple example of the process:

Our market basket consists of the four listed goods.

Here are the prices of those four goods in the first period.

Here also are the average quantities of those goods sold in the first period. These first-period quantities are the weights for the goods in the market basket.

First Period

Item	Quantity	X	Price	=	Total
Milk	10	X	3	=	30
Eggs	5	X	2	=	10
Hamburger	3	X	5	=	15
Cereal	3	X	4	=	12
			Sum	=	67

In the second period, the prices of most of our market basket goods have changed.

- The price of milk has fallen.
- The prices for eggs and hamburger have risen.
- The price of cereal has not changed.

We don't need to know the average quantities of the goods that sold in period 2, because we use the same weights in each period.

Second Period

Item	Quantity	X	Price	=	Total
Milk	10	X	2	=	20
Eggs	5	X	4	=	20
Hamburger	3	X	6	=	18
Cereal	3	X	4	=	12
			Sum	=	70

The price index is the ratio of the summed totals in the 2 periods.

$$70/67 = 1.05 \times 100 = 105$$

← Multiply by 100 to convert the ratio into an index value.

Our grocery price index increased by five percent in the second period.

3. COMMON PRICE INDEXES

The 3 most common price indexes in use in the United States are the Consumer Price Index (CPI), Producer Price Indexes (PPI), and the GDP deflator.

The 3 most common price indexes used in the U.S. are:

1. The CPI (Consumer Price Index)
2. The PPI (Producer Price Indexes)
3. The GDP deflator

The choice as to which of these indexes is the best to use depends on what you are trying to do with it.

The Consumer Price Index (CPI) is a measure of the average change over time in the prices paid by urban consumers for a market basket of consumer goods and services. It reflects spending patterns for about eighty-seven percent of the U.S. population. The CPI is constructed once a month by the Bureau of Labor Statistics (BLS), using current prices for about 80,000 items in over 200 categories.

The CPI market basket is developed from detailed expenditure information provided by families on what they actually bought. The most recent Consumer Expenditure Survey (2009-2010) interviewed 7,000 families quarterly and collected detailed spending diaries from an additional 7,000 families. The specific stores at which prices are collected each month are selected based on a Point-of-Purchase Survey that identifies where consumers purchased various types of goods.

Major uses for the CPI are as:
- An overall macroeconomic indicator
- A deflator of other economic series
- A means of adjusting dollar values

The CPI is the best index to use for adjusting payments to consumers, and for identifying the real impact of price changes on consumers.

Consumer Price Index - All Urban Consumers

Series Id: CUUR0000SA0
Not Seasonally Adjusted
Area: U.S. city average
Item: All items
Base Period: 1982-84=100
Download: fjj.xls

> Here is data for the overall CPI for the past 10 years.

> The default format on the BLS webpage is to give monthly data for 10 years.

> In 2007 BLS began reporting to 3 decimal places – I wish they hadn't.

Year	Jan	Feb	Mar	Apr	May	Jul	Jul	Aug	Sep	Oct	Nov	Dec	Annual	HALF1	HALF2
2004	185.2	186.2	187.4	188.0	189.1	189.7	189.4	189.5	189.9	190.9	191.0	190.3	188.9	187.6	190.2
2005	190.7	191.8	193.3	194.6	194.4	194.5	195.4	196.4	198.8	199.2	197.6	196.8	195.3	193.2	197.4
2006	198.3	198.7	199.8	201.5	202.5	202.9	203.5	203.9	202.9	201.8	201.5	201.8	201.6	200.6	202.6
2007	202.416	203.499	205.352	206.686	207.949	208.352	208.299	207.917	208.490	208.936	210.177	210.036	207.342	205.709	208.976
2008	211.080	211.693	213.528	214.823	216.632	218.815	219.964	219.086	218.783	216.573	212.425	210.228	215.303	214.429	216.177
2009	211.143	212.193	212.709	213.240	213.856	215.693	215.351	215.834	215.969	216.177	216.330	215.949	214.537	213.139	215.935
2010	216.687	216.741	217.631	218.009	218.178	217.965	218.011	218.312	218.439	218.711	218.803	219.179	218.056	217.535	218.576
2011	220.223	221.309	223.467	224.906	225.964	225.722	225.922	226.545	226.889	226.421	226.230	225.672	224.939	223.598	226.280
2012	226.665	227.663	229.392	230.085	229.815	229.478	229.104	230.379	231.407	231.317	230.221	229.601	229.594	228.850	230.338
2013	230.280	232.166	232.773	232.531	232.945	233.504	233.596	233.877	234.149	233.546	233.069	233.049	232.957	232.366	233.548
2014	233.916	234.781													

The Producer Price Index (PPI) is a family of indexes that measures the average change over time in the selling prices received by domestic producers of goods and services. About 10,000 PPIs for individual products and groups of products are released by the BLS each month. PPIs cover nearly all goods-producing industries and about seventy-two percent of the output of the service sector.

Major uses for the PPI are as:
- An overall macroeconomic indicator
- A deflator of other economic series
- A basis for escalating purchase and sales contracts

A PPI is the best index to use for adjusting sales contracts to account for changes in input prices, and for identifying the real impact of price changes on producers.

Producer Price Index Industry Data

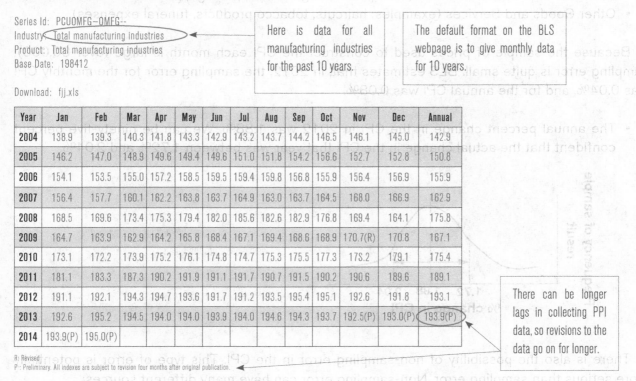

Series Id: PCUOMFG--OMFG--
Industry: Total manufacturing industries
Product: Total manufacturing industries
Base Date: 198412

Download: fjj.xls

Here is data for all manufacturing industries for the past 10 years.

The default format on the BLS webpage is to give monthly data for 10 years.

Year	Jan	Feb	Mar	Apr	May	Jun	Jul	Aug	Sep	Oct	Nov	Dec	Annual
2004	138.9	139.3	140.3	141.8	143.3	142.9	143.2	143.7	144.2	146.5	146.1	145.0	142.9
2005	146.2	147.0	148.9	149.6	149.4	149.6	151.0	151.8	154.2	156.6	152.7	152.8	150.8
2006	154.1	153.5	155.0	157.2	158.5	159.5	159.4	159.8	156.8	155.9	156.4	156.9	155.9
2007	156.4	157.7	160.1	162.2	163.8	163.7	164.9	163.0	163.7	164.5	168.0	166.9	162.9
2008	168.5	169.6	173.4	175.3	179.4	182.0	185.6	182.6	182.9	176.8	169.4	164.1	175.8
2009	164.7	163.9	162.9	164.2	165.8	168.4	167.1	169.4	168.6	168.9	170.7(R)	170.8	167.1
2010	173.1	172.2	173.9	175.2	176.1	174.8	174.7	175.3	175.5	177.3	178.2	179.1	175.4
2011	181.1	183.3	187.3	190.2	191.9	191.1	191.7	190.7	191.5	190.2	190.6	189.6	189.1
2012	191.1	192.1	194.3	194.7	193.6	191.7	191.2	193.5	195.4	195.1	192.6	191.8	193.1
2013	192.6	195.2	194.5	194.0	194.0	193.9	194.0	194.6	194.3	193.7	192.5(P)	193.0(P)	193.9(P)
2014	193.9(P)	195.0(P)											

R: Revised
P: Preliminary. All indexes are subject to revision four months after original publication.

There can be longer lags in collecting PPI data, so revisions to the data go on for longer.

The GDP Deflator is based on chain-type quantity and price indexes developed by the Bureau of Economic Analysis. A chain-type index does not use fixed weights, but rather directly compares prices and quantities from one year to the next. The BEA calculates deflators separately for each component of the GDP measure.

The principal use for the GDP deflator is to convert nominal values to real values in the National Income and Product Accounts. It is the best index to use for this purpose because it is a broader based index than either the CPI or the PPI.

4. QUALITY OF THE CPI

The CPI is a broad-based index that well represents the typical purchases of urban consumers. The CPI is not a true cost-of-living index, as it does have some known, relatively small, biases.

The CPI is a broad-based index that well represents the typical purchases of urban consumers. Expenditures are classified into 8 major groups:
- Food and Beverages (examples: breakfast cereal, milk, coffee, chicken, wine, snacks)
- Housing (examples: rent of primary residence, fuel oil, bedroom furniture)
- Apparel (examples: men's shirts and sweaters, women's dresses, jewelry)
- Transportation (examples: new vehicles, airline fares, gasoline, motor vehicle insurance)
- Medical care (examples: prescription drugs, physicians' services, eyeglasses)
- Recreation (examples: televisions, toys, pets, sports equipment, admissions)
- Education and Communication (examples: college tuition, postage, phone service, software)
- Other Goods and Services (examples: haircuts, tobacco products, funeral expenses)

Because the sample of prices used to construct the CPI each month is large (over 80,000), sampling error is quite small. BLS estimates that, in 2012, the sampling error for the monthly CPI was 0.04%, and for the annual CPI was 0.08%.

- The annual percent change in the CPI in 2012 was 1.88%. We can be ninety-five percent confident that the actual change in the CPI that year was between 1.72% and 2.04%.

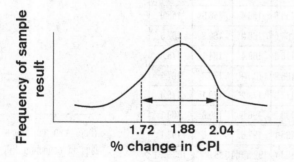

95% of samples fall within 2 standard deviations from the mean.

There is also the possibility of non-sampling error in the CPI. This type of error is potentially more serious than sampling error. Non-sampling error can have many different sources:
- Mistakes in data collection: the BLS data collector might record a price incorrectly, price the wrong item, or even make up a price to avoid doing their work.
- Time lags in conducting survey: data collection is spread over a three-week period each month, and prices will vary somewhat depending on when during that period they are collected.
- Operational difficulties: for example, how do you identify the price of a new or used car, where the price actually paid depends partly on the bargaining skill of the consumer?

- Quality changes: items in the market basket change over time, as producers make improvements. BLS attempts to adjust for the value of product improvements, but this is inherently a subjective process.

We would like the CPI to measure changes in consumers' cost of living, but the CPI is not a true cost-of-living index. In the broadest sense, consumer well-being is affected by many things that are not included in the CPI—for example, safety, health, water quality, crime. More narrowly, the CPI suffers from a problem called substitution bias.

The CPI measures price change for a fixed market basket. But consumers do not always purchase exactly the same set of goods and services. As prices change, consumers tend to substitute goods whose prices are rising faster with goods which have become relatively less expensive. This means that the price increase on the goods that consumers actually buy is smaller than what the CPI measures—there is an upward bias to the CPI. It is estimated that the bias is in the range of 0.3-0.4 percent annually. If, for example, annual inflation was measured at 2.5%, removing substitution bias from the CPI would probably result in the measured inflation rate dropping to 2.1-2.2%.

BLS publishes two alternative measures to the CPI for all urban consumers.

The CPI-W is for urban wage earners and clerical workers. This index has more limited coverage than the regular CPI; the CPI-W covers about thirty-two percent of the U.S. population, while the regular CPI covers eighty-even percent. The CPI-W once was the standard measure for inflation, until BLS expanded the definition to provide more comprehensive coverage. The CPI-W is still the preferred index for use in many union wage escalation contracts, since it more directly reflects expenditure patterns for union members.

The Chained CPI attempts to adjust for the substitution bias known to be present in the regular CPI. It does this by using estimates of current expenditures in place of the fixed expenditure weights used by the regular CPI. The chained CPI typically increases somewhat slower than does the regular CPI, but is also subject to larger revisions, since estimates of current expenditures are not as accurate as the lagged expenditure data used in the regular CPI. The chained CPI is considered by BLS to be an experimental index, and is not currently used as an adjustment mechanism in any federal government program.

Comparison of recent inflation estimates for the three versions of the CPI:

Year	CPI	CPI-W	Chained CPI
2008	3.9	4.1	3.7
2009	-0.4	-0.7	-0.4
2010	1.7	2.1	1.4
2011	3.1	3.3	3.1
2012	2.1	2.1	1.9

The close relationship among all 3 versions of the CPI is obvious.

Note that the chained CPI tends to show slightly lower inflation than does the regular CPI.

5. USING PRICE INDEXES

Price indexes are used to convert nominal to real values. With a price index we can calculate the purchasing power of the dollar, the real wage rate, and the real interest rate.

Price indexes are used to convert nominal values to real values. A nominal value is simply the price of an item in dollars. In contrast, a real value is the opportunity cost of an item— that is, the real goods and services that must be given up to purchase the item. Real and nominal values differ when there have been changes in the overall price level.

Convert nominal to real by multiplying the nominal price by a ratio of price indexes.
- The top of the ratio is the index in the year whose dollar is used for the real series.
- The bottom of the ratio is the index in the year of the nominal price.

Gasoline prices over time				
Year	Nominal price	Price index	Real price (1980 $)	Real price (2014 $)
1980	1.21	82.4	1.21	3.45
1990	1.04	130.7	0.66	1.87
2000	1.37	172.2	0.66	1.87
2010	2.66	218.1	1.01	2.86
2014	3.36	234.8	1.18	3.36

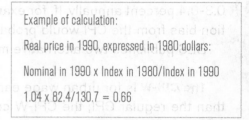

Example of calculation:

Real price in 1990, expressed in 1980 dollars:

Nominal in 1990 x Index in 1980/Index in 1990

1.04 x 82.4/130.7 = 0.66

When there is inflation, the change in the nominal series is larger than the change in the real series. Over the thirty-five years shown in the table above:
- Nominal gas prices increased by 178% (3.36 – 1.21) /1.21 = 1.78
- Real gas prices actually decreased by 2% (1.18 – 1.21) /1.21 = –0.02

No matter what year's dollars are used for the real series, the percentage change over time is the same.
- From 1980 to 2014: using 1980 $, decrease by 2%; using 2014 $, decrease by 2%

The BLS website has a tool called the inflation calculator, which can be used to convert nominal prices to real prices.

$3.45 is the real value of the 1980 price of $1.21, expressed in 2014 dollars.

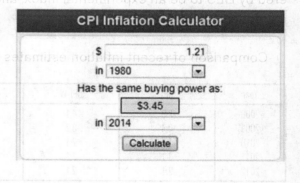

CPI Inflation Calculator

$ 1.21
in 1980

Has the same buying power as:

$3.45

in 2014

Calculate

With a price index we can calculate the purchasing power of the dollar.

- Purchasing power of the dollar = $100 / price index

Consumer Price Index	
Year	Price index
1970	38.8
1980	82.4
1983	99.6
1990	130.7
2000	172.2
2010	218.1
2013	233.0

A dollar was worth $2.58 in 1970

- $100 /38.8 = $2.58

A dollar was worth $1.00 in 1983

- $100 /99.6 = $1.00

A dollar was worth $0.43 in 2013

- $100 /233.0 = $0.43

With a price index, we can calculate the real wage rate. What matters most to workers is not how many dollars are in their paychecks, but rather how many real goods and services they can buy with those dollars. Consider how the real value of the minimum wage has changed over time.

Federal Minimum Wage – Hourly Rate			
Year	Nominal minimum wage rate	Price index (CPI)	Real minimum wage rate (2013 $)
1938	0.25	14.1	4.13
1950	0.75	24.1	7.25
1968	1.60	34.8	10.71
1980	3.10	82.4	8.77
1997	5.15	160.5	7.48
2009	7.25	214.5	7.88
2013	7.25	233.0	7.25

The nominal minimum wage is about 10 times higher today than in 1950, but in real terms, in 2013, it is the same!

Using a price index we can calculate the real interest rate. The inflation rate is the percentage change in the price index. The real interest rate is the nominal interest rate minus the rate of inflation. For example:

Year	Price index	Inflation rate	Nominal interest rate	Real interest rate
1	100.0	-	-	-
2	110.0	10%	11%	1%
3	115.5	5%	8%	3%

Even though the nominal interest rate fell in year 3, the real interest rate rose.

6. PROTECTING AGAINST INFLATION

Inflation reduces the value of fixed income and fixed assets. Protection against inflation is provided by COLA (cost of living adjustment) clauses and by TIPS (Treasury inflation protected security).

Inflation reduces the value of fixed income and fixed assets.

Inflation erodes value			
Year	Fixed income	Price index	Value of income
1	1000	100.0	1000
2	1000	105.0	952.38
3	1000	110.3	907.03
4	1000	115.8	863.56
5	1000	121.6	829.53
6	1000	127.6	783.51

> At 5% inflation, a fixed income of $1,000 loses more than 21% of its value in just five years.

Protection against inflation-caused loss of value in fixed income is provided by COLA (cost of living adjustment) clauses. COLAs are valuable when an income source is fixed in dollar terms. For example:

- Social Security might pay a retiree a fixed amount of $1,200 per month.
- A union wage contract might specify that a worker received $15 per hour.

Without protection, inflation steadily erodes the purchasing power of those on a fixed income.

A COLA protects against inflation by guaranteeing that the fixed income (the nominal amount) will increase when there is inflation. Typically, the fixed income increases when the price index increases. Here is how a COLA protects Social Security recipients.

Year	CPI	Inflation	COLA	Social Security payment	
				Nominal	Real (2000 $)
2000	172.2	-	-	1,200.00	1,200.00
2001	177.1	2.8%	2.6%	1,231.20	1,197.14
2002	179.9	1.6%	1.4%	1,248.44	1,195.00
2003	184.0	2.3%	2.1%	1,274.65	1,192.91

> The real value has hardly changed, because the nominal value has increased.

The Social Security example seems to show that a COLA provides very good protection against inflation. This is not necessarily true. The CPI represents the cost of the market basket typically purchased by all urban consumers. If an individual's typical expenditures differ from the CPI market basket, and the items the individual purchases more of have prices increasing faster than average, then inflation will erode that person's purchasing power even with a COLA clause.

- This is the situation with many Social Security recipients. Being on average older, they tend to use more medical care; and prices for medical care have been increasing faster than average.

Protection against inflation-caused loss of value in fixed assets is provided by TIPS (Treasury inflation protected security). U.S. savings bonds and Treasury bills guarantee a rate of return specified as a nominal interest rate. For example, a $1,000 Treasury bill paying 4% interest, will, in one year, be worth $1,040 —a 4% rate of return. However, if there is inflation, the real value will be less than $1,040—real interest rate = nominal interest rate minus inflation.

TIPS protects against inflation by guaranteeing a real rate of return. For example, say you buy a $1,000 1-year TIPS paying 4% interest, and then there is 2% inflation. At the end of the year, the TIPS will be worth $1,060—the promised 4% rate of return is adjusted up to 6% to offset the 2% inflation.

Because a TIPS carries a real interest rate, and a comparable non-TIPS security carries a nominal interest rate, the TIPS rate will generally be lower than the non-TIPS rate (that is, the TIPS costs more to buy).

Here is how interest rates on the two types of securities compare:

5-year Treasury Securities			
Year	Interest rates		Expected Inflation
	TIPS	Non-TIPS	
2003	1.27	2.97	1.70
2006	2.28	4.75	2.47
2009	1.06	2.20	1.14
2012	-1.19	0.76	1.95

The difference between non-TIPS and TIPS (between nominal and real interest rates) is the purchasers' expectation of inflation over the life of the security.

• In 2003 : 2.97 – 1.27 = 1.70

How good is the TIPS protection against inflation? That depends on the accuracy of the purchasers' inflation expectations. If investors accurately predict future inflation over the life of the security, then the TIPS provides very good protection. However, if inflation runs lower than investors expected, then TIPS is not such a good value; in effect, in this case investors will have paid too much for the TIPS; they will have bought too much inflation protection.

Year	Inflation over 5 years		Prediction error
	Expected	Actual	
2003	1.70	3.18	1.48
2004	2.39	2.56	0.17
2005	2.55	2.20	-0.35
2006	2.47	2.20	-0.27
2007	2.28	2.06	-0.22

Except for 2003 (the first year that TIPS were offered), investors' predictions of future inflation have been quite accurate.

But, if investors collectively under-predict future inflation (as they did in 2004), then TIPS is an even better bargain; in effect, investors will have gotten more inflation protection than they paid for.

7. PROBLEMS CAUSED BY INFLATION

Inflation redistributes income in unexpected ways. It distorts investment and saving decisions. Resources must be expended to predict and adjust for inflation.

There are three general types of problems caused by even a moderate level of inflation:
1. Unexpected redistribution of income, and the appearance of unfairness
2. Errors in investment and savings decisions
3. Expenditure of real resources to predict and adjust to inflation

There are economic winners and losers whenever inflation occurs. And the winning or losing seems to be unrelated to the ordinary virtues of effort and prudence. Inflation redistributes income in unexpected ways. When inflation is higher than was expected, it favors borrowers (who now can pay back their loans with dollars that are worth less) and hurts lenders. When inflation is lower than expected, it favors lenders and hurts borrowers.

Inflation distributes income away from those on fixed incomes by eroding the real value of that income. This can lead persons to feel that their hard work and thrift are being punished rather than rewarded.

Inflation redistributes income away from households and business firms, and toward government in two ways:
- Rising nominal incomes push taxpayers into higher tax brackets where they are taxed at a higher rate.
- Inflation reduces the real value of government debt (so that the government can pay off its obligations to investors with dollars that are worth less); this is called monetizing the debt.

Inflation distorts investment decisions. Inflation causes real values to be lower than nominal values, and can lead investors to misjudge the actual business conditions. For example:
- You project that revenue for your business will rise by ten percent over the next five years. Should you invest in a new factory to increase your inventory? If there is no inflation, then a revenue increase means that you will be selling more goods, and so need to produce more. But if inflation is two percent per year or higher, then the projected revenue increase will all be from higher prices—you won't be selling more real goods, and so don't need to produce more.

Another example: You determine that a planned investment will be profitable if you can borrow the needed funds at five percent interest. The going interest rate on loans is six percent, so you don't make the investment. But if inflation is two percent, then the real interest rate you could have borrowed at was only four percent, and your investment would have been profitable.

Inflation distorts savings decisions. If you don't take likely inflation into account when planning and saving for a future expense, then you probably will put aside too little. For example:

- Parents decide to put aside money for their child's future college education. Looking at current costs, they determine they will need to save $30,000—and they do so. But when their child reaches college age, inflation has increased costs and they find they haven't saved enough.

Another example: A couple determines that they will need an annual income of $50,000 to live comfortably in retirement, and they save enough to generate that income. But when they retire, they discover that inflation has increased prices, and their retirement income is no longer enough for the way they wanted to live.

Because inflation can be very costly if you haven't prepared for it, businesses and individuals both expend real resources to attempt to predict future levels of inflation. Persons who can accurately predict future inflation will probably end up winners in the inflation game.

- Home buyers seeking a mortgage must research and decide between getting a fixed rate or a variable rate mortgage. A variable rate mortgage provides a lower initial interest rate, but carries the risk of higher costs in the future if inflation increases.
- Major corporations employ economists whose main job is to attempt to predict future economic trends, inflation being one of the most important.
- Much time and effort is expended parsing statements from the Federal Reserve, and tracking other economic indicators thought to influence future inflation.

Whether you can predict future inflation or not, you still must adjust to it when it occurs.

- When inflation occurs, businesses must revalue their inventories for tax purposes.
- When prices change, it takes time and effort to relabel price tags, print new price sheets, and edit computerized price lists.
- Good shoppers remember the prices of items they regularly buy—a task that becomes much harder when those prices frequently change.

All of the time and effort, all of the resources, invested in predicting future inflation or in adjusting to inflation when it occurs, would be lower or completely unnecessary if the price level did not change. A stable price level would free up real resources that could then be applied to more productive activities.

8. HYPERINFLATION

A very large and rapid rise in the price level is called hyperinflation. This can lead to a general breakdown in economic and social institutions. The most infamous example of hyperinflation was in Weimar Germany after the first World War.

A very large and rapid rise in the price level is called hyperinflation. A hyperinflation is characterized by inflation of at least fifty percent per month, lasting for a year or more.

The twentieth century saw many examples of hyperinflation.
- Austria, between 1914 and 1921, inflation peaked at 1,426%
- Brazil, between 1989 and 1994, inflation peaked at 2,075%
- Greece, between 1942 and 1945, inflation peaked at 13,800%
- Hungary, between 1945 and 1946, at its peak prices doubled every 15 hours
- Zimbabwe, between 2007 and 2008, inflation peaked at 8 billion percent

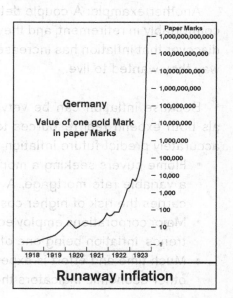

Runaway inflation

The United States almost experienced hyperinflation twice in its history.
- During the Revolutionary War, monthly inflation for the continental currency peaked at 47%—this is the origin of the phrase "not worth a continental."
- During the Civil War, Confederate currency lost almost all value by the last months of the war, while monthly inflation in the Union greenback peaked at 40%.

Hyperinflation can lead to a general breakdown in a country's economic and social institutions.
- As hyperinflation destroys the purchasing power of money, people stop using it, resorting to highly inefficient barter instead.
- Savings are wiped out and investment dries up.
- Banks and other financial institutions fail.
- Anyone who can remove their assets does, while those who can't are reduced to poverty.
- Governments are unable to collect tax revenues, and public services collapse.
- Strong and widespread distrust of economic and political authorities and institutions develops.

Put simply, hyperinflation dissolves the glue that holds modern societies together.

At the end of World War I, the victorious Allied powers imposed crippling reparations on Germany. Germany, the Allies declared, had been responsible for the war, and now had to repay the Allies for the damages caused by the war. Germany could not meet these demands, and so, starting in 1921, they simply printed ever increasing amounts of German currency to buy foreign currency to pay the reparation demands.

For the next three years inflation raged out of control in Germany. By November 1923, prices were doubling every two days. The Weimar government issued ever larger denominations of currency in an attempt to keep up with rising prices—culminating in a 100,000,000,000,000 Mark note.

A 5 billion Mark note

The German economy effectively collapsed. Workers refused to accept payment in currency. Anyone who did receive currency rushed to spend it before it lost all value. Interest rates rose to astronomical levels. Real assets were hoarded or spirited out of the country. France and Britain seized military control of the Ruhr region to exact reparations payments in coal and other real goods. The German government was helpless in the face of this calamity.

The Weimar Republic was discredited and fatally weakened by the three years of economic chaos caused by the hyperinflation. Discontent and distrust of the government paved the way for the takeover of Germany by the Nazi party under Adolf Hitler in the 1930s.

All of this was predicted in 1919 by the economist John Maynard Keynes, in his book *The Economic Consequences of the Peace*. Hear his prophetic description of what would happen in Germany three years later:

"Lenin is said to have declared that the best way to destroy the Capitalist System was to debauch the currency. By a continuing process of inflation, governments can confiscate, secretly and unobserved, an important part of the wealth of their citizens. By this method they not only confiscate, but they confiscate arbitrarily; and, while the process impover- ishes many, it actually enriches some … Lenin was certainly right. There is no subtler, no surer means of overturning the existing basis of society than to debauch the currency. The process engages all the hidden forces of economic law on the side of destruction, and does it in a manner which not one man in a million is able to diagnose."

SUMMARY OF CHAPTER 6

Inflation is a general increase in the price level. Inflation is measured using a price index.
- A price index is a way to combine the prices of a mix of different goods and services into a single number.

There are four basic steps to constructing a price index:
1. Select a market basket of goods and services.
2. Assign appropriate weights to each item in the market basket.
3. Measure the prices of each good in two different time periods.
4. Multiply the price of each good by its weight, and sum the products.

The price index is the ratio of the summed total in the second period to the summed total in the first period.

The most common price indexes used in the United States are:
- The CPI (Consumer Price Index): measures change in prices paid by consumers
- The PPI (Producer Price Index): measures change in prices received by producers
- The GDP Deflator: measures change in prices of major sectors of the economy

The CPI is a broad-based index that well represents the typical purchases of urban consumers. The CPI is not a true cost-of-living index, as it does have some known, relatively small, biases.

Price indexes are used to convert nominal values to real values. Multiply the nominal value by a ratio of price indexes to get the real value.
- With a price index, we can calculate the purchasing power of the dollar, the real wage rate, and the real interest rate.

Inflation reduces the value of fixed income and fixed assets. Protection against inflation is provided by COLA (cost of living adjustment) clauses and by TIPS (Treasury inflation protected security).

Inflation redistributes income in unexpected ways. It distorts investment saving decisions. Real resources must be expended to predict and adjust for inflation.

Hyperinflation is a very large and rapid rise in the price level. It can lead to a general breakdown in economic and social institutions.

CH SEVEN

AGGREGATE DEMAND/ AGGREGATE SUPPLY

AD/AS is a model of the macro economy. It combines the real and financial sides of the economy by graphing the level of real GDP against the aggregate price level.

Macroeconomic equilibrium is where the AD and AS curves intersect. Any equilibrium away from potential GDP is short-run only. In the long-run, disequilibrium in resource markets will shift the AS curve back to potential GDP.

The AD/AS model is a concise and intuitive way to characterize the macro economy at a point in time. The AD/AS model is basically static—it is not well suited to illustrating dynamic change over time.

1. BUSINESS CYCLES

Business cycles are alternating periods of economic growth and decline. When real GDP falls for two consecutive quarters, the economy is in a recession. The most recent recession ran from December 2007 to June 2009.

The U.S. economy does not grow at a steady rate. Rather it experiences alternating periods of economic growth and decline. These periodic ups and downs in economic activity are called the business cycle.

There are four parts to every business cycle:
1. The Peak is the top of the business cycle. It is the highest value reached by real GDP.
2. After the peak comes the contraction. This is the period when real GDP is falling. When real GDP falls for two consecutive quarters, the contraction is termed a recession.
3. The period of contraction ends with the Trough. This is the low point of the business cycle.
4. After the trough comes the expansion. This is the period when real GDP is rising again. The expansion that comes after a recession is termed a recovery.

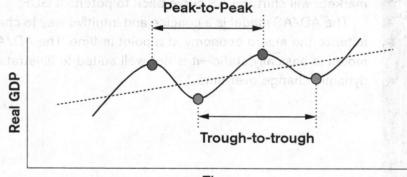

The length of a business cycle can be measured from peak to peak, or from trough to trough.

The dashed line represents the average rate of growth of real GDP. The economy seldom grows at exactly that average rate.

Start and end dates for recessions are determined by the National Bureau of Economic Research. The NBER defines a recession as "a significant decline in economic activity spread across the economy, lasting more than a few months, normally visible in real GDP, real income, employment, industrial production, and wholesale-retail sales."

This definition is both more detailed and fuzzier than "two consecutive quarters of decline in real GDP." It reflects the reality that there is more to an economic recession than simply falling real GDP, and that it can be difficult at times to tell if an economy is in a recession or not.

The most recent U.S. recession started in December 2007 and ended in June 2009. Lasting 18 months, it was the longest contraction in over 70 years. It was also the most severe recession since the end of World War II, with real GDP falling by 4.3%.

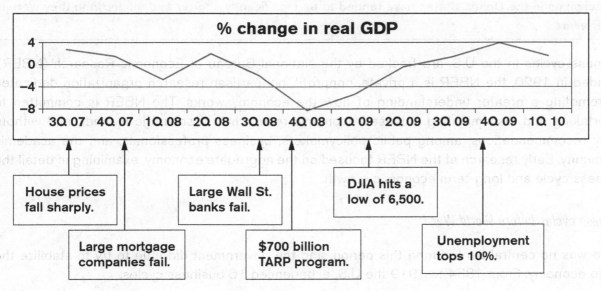

Portrait of the recession		Unemployment rate	Stock market (DJIA)	Average house price	Consumer confidence
Before	Jan. 2007	4.6%	12,657	$314,000	110.20
After	Jan. 2010	9.7%	10,730	$273,000	56.50

What causes these swings in economic activity? Why don't we experience steady growth?
- One reason is that the economy regularly experiences external shocks. These can be natural events (like hurricanes and floods), political events (like wars and terrorism), or price events (like the spike in oil prices in the 1970s). External shocks can be negative (like the destruction caused by Hurricane Sandy or the terror attacks on 9/11), or positive (like the changes resulting from the invention of the personal computer). External shocks cause a sudden and unexpected shift in either the aggregate supply or aggregate demand curve, with a resulting change in real GDP.
- A second reason is the role of expectations in the economy. Expectations of what the economy will be like in the future can change suddenly and dramatically, and can affect both demand and supply decisions. An example was the house price bubble in the past decade, and the huge changes in investor behavior that followed its bursting.

2. HISTORICAL DATA ON BUSINESS CYCLES

Business cycles are tracked by the National Bureau of Economic Research. Since the end of World War II, recessions in the United States have tended to be significantly shorter and milder than they were in earlier years.

Business cycles in the U.S. are tracked by the National Bureau of Economic Research (NBER). Founded in 1920, the NBER is a private, nonprofit, nonpartisan research organization dedicated to promoting a greater understanding of how the economy works. The NBER is committed to undertaking and disseminating unbiased economic research in a scientific manner, and without policy recommendations, among public policymakers, business professionals, and the academic community. Early research at the NBER focused on the aggregate economy, examining in detail the business cycle and long-term economic growth.

Business cycles before World War I:

There was no central bank during this period, and the government did little to try to stabilize the macro economy. From 1854 to 1919 the U.S. experienced 16 business cycles.

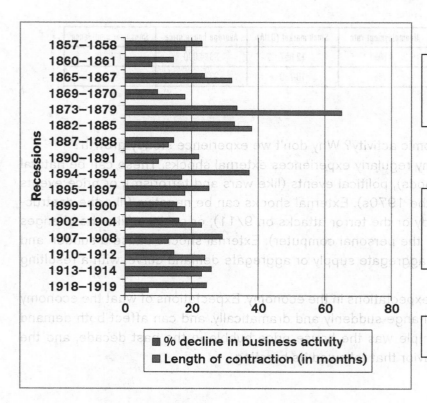

The dating of these recessions is controversial, as modern economic statistics were not gathered during this period.

Contractions lasted almost as long as expansions:

- Avg. contraction = 22 months
- Avg. expansion = 27 months

Average decline in business activity = 22.7%

Business cycles between the world wars:

Government began to take a more active role in stabilizing the macro economy. The Federal Reserve System was founded in 1913. Government stimulus policies grew dramatically in the 1930s.

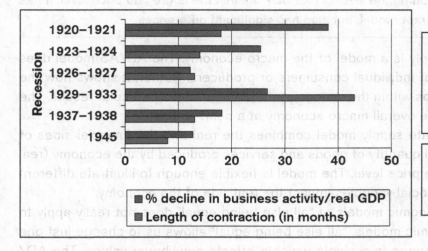

Except for the Great Depression, contractions were only half as long as expansions:

- Avg. contraction = 18 months
- Avg. expansion = 35 months

Modern economic statistics began in 1929. Earlier info on business activity is not directly comparable to GDP.

Business cycles since World War II:

Stabilization policy has become much more effective: shorter and milder contractions, longer expansions. Major cause is the growth in the use of automatic stabilizers.

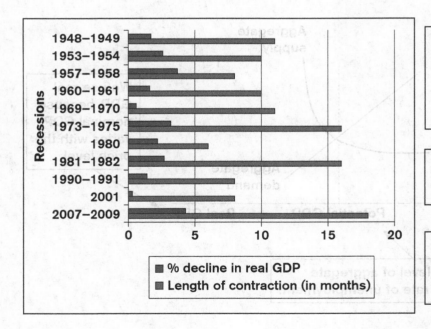

Short contractions and lengthy expansions have become the norm:

- Avg. contraction = 11 months
- Avg. expansion = 59 months

Declines in real GDP have been tiny compared to recessions from 1929 to 1945.

The most recent recession was the longest and the most severe in the post-WWII era.

3. AGGREGATE DEMAND/AGGREGATE SUPPLY MODEL

Aggregate demand/aggregate supply is a model of the macro economy. It combines the real and the financial sides of the economy by graphing the level of real GDP against the aggregate price level. It has similarities to the demand/supply market model, but also has significant differences.

Aggregate demand/aggregate supply is a model of the macro economy. The AD/AS model does not attempt to show the behavior of individual consumers or producers. Rather, it shows how the behavior of highly aggregated groups within the economy interact to produce particular results. The AD/AS graph paints a picture of the overall macro economy at a point in time.

The aggregate demand/aggregate supply model combines the real and the financial sides of the economy. It shows how the total quantity of goods and services produced by the economy (real GDP) is affected by changes in the price level. The model is flexible enough to illustrate different theories about how changes in financial variables impact the real side of the economy.

The standard assumption in economic models of "all else being equal" does not really apply to the AD/AS model. For most economic models, "all else being equal" allows us to change just one variable, and then see how that change in a single variable affects equilibrium values. The AD/AS model, however, is showing the interactions between highly aggregated groups. A change in a single factor is likely to affect more than just one group, causing more than just one effect. In addition, a change in one factor can set off secondary changes in other factors. This can make it impossible to hold all else equal, and very difficult to isolate the influence of a single variable.

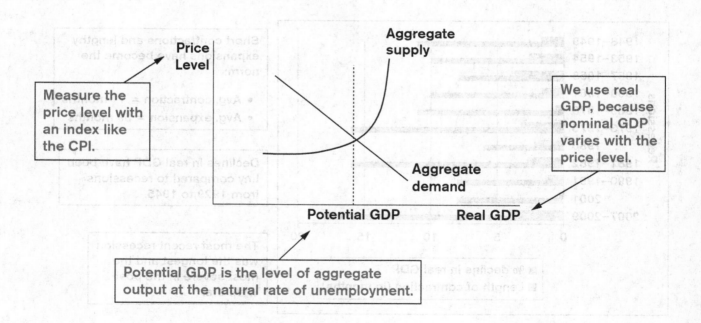

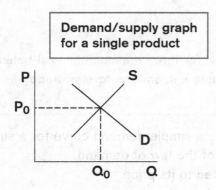

Demand/supply graph for a single product

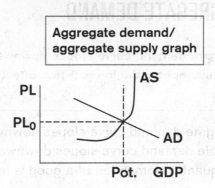

Aggregate demand/ aggregate supply graph

On the surface, the aggregate demand/aggregate supply model has many similarities to the demand/supply model for a single product market.

- The demand curve for a single product slopes downward, and the aggregate demand curve slopes downward.
- The supply curve for a single product slopes upward, and the aggregate supply curve slopes upward.
- The simple demand/supply graph records the quantity of a single product on the horizontal axis, while the AD/AS graph aggregates the quantities of all goods into real GDP on the horizontal axis.
- The simple demand/supply graph records the price of a single product on the vertical axis, while the AD/AS graph aggregates the prices of all goods into the price level on the vertical axis.
- The intersection of the simple demand and supply curves yields the equilibrium price and quantity in a single product market, and the intersection of the aggregate demand and aggregate supply curves yields the equilibrium GDP and equilibrium price level for the economy as a whole.

However, this surface similarity between simple demand/supply and aggregate demand/ aggregate supply hides highly significant differences between the two models.

- A simple demand curve slopes downward because of the law of demand. But the law of demand does not apply to aggregate demand at all. The AD curve slopes downward for very different and much more complex reasons.
- A simple supply curve slopes upward because of the law of supply. But the law of supply does not apply to aggregate supply at all. The AS curve slopes upward for very different and much more complex reasons. This also is why the AS curve actually does curve—it can't be drawn as a straight line.
- The AD/AS model must include the level of potential GDP. Potential GDP serves as an anchor point around which the AD and AS curves are drawn. The simple demand/supply model has nothing equivalent to it.

3.1. AGGREGATE DEMAND

The aggregate demand curve slopes downward. It does so for three reasons: the real-balances effect impacts consumption, the interest-rate effect impacts investment, and the foreign-trade effect impacts net exports.

The aggregate demand curve slopes downward, as does a simple demand curve for a single product. A simple demand curve slopes downward because of the law of demand.

- The quantity demanded of a good is inversely related to its price.

The main reason why the law of demand works is that the relative prices of goods change as you move along a good's demand curve. When the price of a good rises, other goods have become relatively less expensive, so some consumers substitute with goods whose relative prices have fallen. When the price of a good falls, other goods have become relatively more expensive, so some consumers use substitutes for those goods whose relative prices have risen.

The aggregate demand curve slopes downward, but not because of the law of demand. Relative prices do not change with movement along the aggregate demand curve—a change in the price level by itself says nothing about the relationship between prices. Even if relative prices did change, substitution between goods would change the composition of GDP, but would not change the level of GDP.

The aggregate demand curve slopes downward for three reasons:
- Real-balances effect
- Interest-rate effect
- Foreign-trade effect

Real balances effect:

When the price level rises (when there is inflation), this reduces the purchasing power of the dollar.
- Purchasing power of the dollar = $100/CPI

With the dollar now worth less, the real value of a consumer's cash savings and all fixed assets will also fall. This decline in consumer wealth leads to a reduction in consumer spending (because consumer wealth is one factor determining the level of demand).
- Less consumer spending means a lower GDP.

Interest rate effect:

When the price level rises, this increases the demand for borrowing by businesses (any planned investment now costs more dollars than it did before). Increased demand for borrowing causes interest rates to rise (the interest rate being the price of borrowing money). Higher interest rates reduce the expected profitability of investment projects, so some businesses either cancel or reduce their investment activity.
- Less business investment means a lower GDP.

Foreign trade effect:

When the price level rises, domestically produced goods become more expensive for foreigners. As a result, foreigners buy fewer American-made goods—U.S. exports fall. At the same time, foreign-produced goods become relatively less expensive for American consumers. As a result, Americans buy more foreign-made goods—U.S. imports rise. With imports rising and exports falling, net exports also fall.

- Net Exports = Exports − Imports
- Lower net exports means a lower GDP.

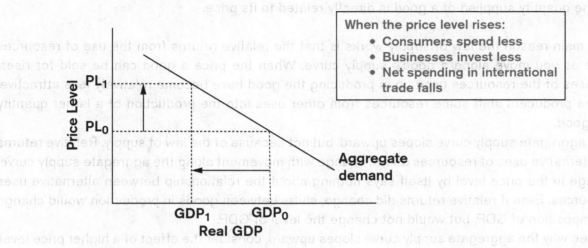

When the price level rises:
- **Consumers spend less**
- **Businesses invest less**
- **Net spending in international trade falls**

Remember that we define GDP by its expenditure components.

GDP = Consumption + Investment + Government expenditures + Net Exports
GDP = C + I + G + NE

The real-balances effect impacts Consumption.
The interest-rate effect impacts Investment.
The foreign-trade effect impacts Net Exports.

The three effects work equally well in the opposite direction. If the price level falls:

- Purchasing power of dollar rises, increasing consumer wealth, leading to higher consumption.
- Demand for business borrowing falls, lowering interest rates, improving profitability of investment projects, leading to higher investment.
- U.S.-made goods become relatively less expensive, so exports increase and imports decrease, leading to higher net exports.

3.2. AGGREGATE SUPPLY

The aggregate supply curve slopes upward. The steepness of the curve depends on the relationship of the economy to potential GDP. At outputs well below potential GDP, the aggregate supply curve is quite flat. At outputs above potential GDP, the aggregate supply curve is quite steep.

The aggregate supply curve slopes upward, as does a simple supply curve for a single product. A simple supply curve slopes upward because of the law of supply.

- The quantity supplied of a good is directly related to its price.

The main reason the law of supply works is that the relative returns from the use of resources change as you move along a good's supply curve. When the price a good can be sold for rises, other uses of the resources used up in producing the good have become relatively less attractive, so some producers shift some resources from other uses into the production of a larger quantity of the good.

The aggregate supply curve slopes upward, but not because of the law of supply. Relative returns from alternative uses of resources do not change with movement along the aggregate supply curve. A change in the price level by itself says nothing about the relationship between alternative uses of resources. Even if relative returns did change, shifts between goods in production would change the composition of GDP, but would not change the level of GDP.

To see why the aggregate supply curve slopes upward, consider the effect of a higher price level.

1. Higher prices for final goods (which is what we measure when we use the CPI for the price level) means rising profits for producers.
   - Since only the prices of final goods have risen, producers' costs stay the same while their revenue goes up.
2. Rising profits encourages businesses to expand production.
3. In order to increase production, businesses must employ more resources, so demand for resources rises.
4. Increased demand for resources causes a rise in the price of those resources.
5. Higher resource prices means higher production costs, which means (all else being equal) lower profits.
6. Rising resource prices and production costs leading to lower profits chokes off part of the increase in production.

The key question in this entire process is:
- How much of the increase in production gets choked off by higher resource prices?

The answer is: It depends on where the economy stands relative to potential GDP when the initial price increase occurs.

If the economy is operating well below potential GDP:

GDP well below potential means that the unemployment rate is well above the natural rate. This means that there are lots of unemployed workers who would be happy to take a job at the going wage rate. When GDP is well below potential there are factories standing idle and many other unused (or under-used) resources. A business wanting to expand can hire additional workers and purchase additional resources without bidding up wage rates or resource prices.

- The aggregate supply curve is nearly horizontal under these conditions.

If the economy is operating near potential GDP:

Unemployment is near the natural rate, so there are some unemployed workers, and some unused resources, but not a whole lot. A business wanting to expand is going to have to offer somewhat higher wages to attract additional workers, and is going to face somewhat higher prices for other resources.

- The aggregate supply curve slopes upward ever steeper as GDP approaches potential.

If the economy is operating above potential GDP:

Unemployment is below the natural rate. There are very few unemployed workers, and few unused resources. A business wanting to expand is going to have to offer much higher wages to attract additional workers, and is going to face significantly higher prices for other resources.

- The aggregate supply curve is nearly vertical under these conditions.

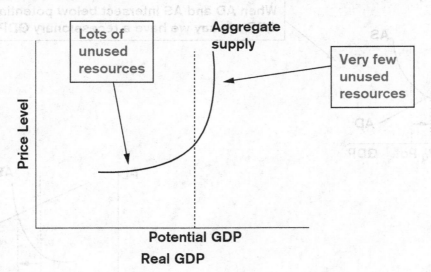

This is why the aggregate supply curve actually does curve around the level of potential GDP.

3.3. MACROECONOMIC EQUILIBRIUM

Macroeconomic equilibrium is where the AD and AS curves intersect. If equilibrium output is below potential GDP, there is a recessionary GDP gap. Any equilibrium away from potential GDP is short-run only. In the long-run, disequilibrium in resource markets will shift the AS curve back to potential GDP.

In a simple demand/supply model of a single product market, equilibrium is reached at the price and quantity where the demand and supply curves intersect. This is the point at which the plans of the buyers in the market exactly match the plans of the sellers in the market. At any price other than the equilibrium price, excess demand or excess supply will fuel discontent which will push the price back toward equilibrium. Once equilibrium is reached, there is no force at work to cause the price to change any further.

Macroeconomic equilibrium is reached at the price level and level of GDP where the aggregate demand curve and the aggregate supply curves intersect. However, this macroeconomic equilibrium is very different from equilibrium in a single product market.

- First, the aggregate demand and aggregate supply curves do not directly represent the plans of buyers and sellers. Rather, the curves show how the behavior of highly aggregated groups within the economy interact to produce particular results. There is no implication that these results are desirable for society, nor that the plans of individual economic actors are in fact being met.
- Second, there is no guarantee that any particular macroeconomic equilibrium is stable. In fact, there will usually be forces at work to shift the equilibrium positions. It is better to think of the intersection of AD and AS as being the initial impact on the macro economy of a demand or supply shock. Or perhaps as the first step in a dynamic adjustment process.

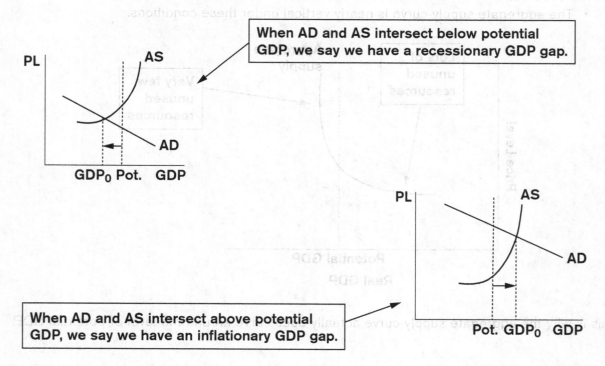

When AD and AS intersect below potential GDP, we say we have a recessionary GDP gap.

When AD and AS intersect above potential GDP, we say we have an inflationary GDP gap.

Any macroeconomic equilibrium away from the level of potential GDP is a short-run equilibrium only. This is because any level of unemployment different from the natural rate of unemployment creates disequilibrium in labor markets. Equilibrium in labor markets is restored by changes in the price of labor (the wage rate). These changes in the price of labor resources cause the aggregate supply curve to shift, and the economy moves to a new macroeconomic equilibrium.

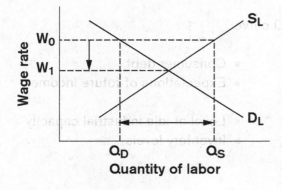

Labor market when there is a recessionary GDP gap

The excess supply of labor (unemployment higher than the natural rate) puts downward pressure on wage rates.

Falling wage rates reduce production costs for businesses, shifting the AS curve downward.

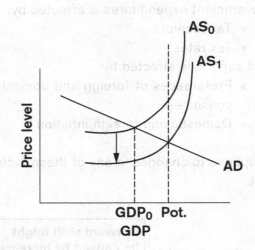

The excess supply of labor is eliminated only when the aggregate demand curve intersects the new lower aggregate supply curve at the level of potential GDP. Long-run macroeconomic equilibrium must be at the level of potential GDP.

4. SHIFTS IN AD AND AS

Changes in any of the expenditure components of GDP cause the AD curve to shift in or out. Changes in the quantity or quality of resources cause the AS curve to shift in or out. Changes in the prices of resources cause the AS curve to shift up or down.

Many underlying factors can cause a shift in the aggregate demand curve. Basically, anything that can affect one of the expenditure components of GDP can cause a shift in the aggregate demand curve.

Here are some of the factors that can shift the AD curve:
- Consumption is affected by:
  - » Consumer income
  - » Consumer wealth
  - » Consumer debt
  - » Expectations of future income
- Investment is affected by:
  - » Real interest rate
  - » Expectations of future business conditions
  - » Level of idle industrial capacity
  - » Inventory levels
- Government expenditures is affected by:
  - » Tax receipts
  - » Tax rates
  - » Transfer payments
  - » Perceived needs (political pressure)
- Net exports is affected by:
  - » Preferences of foreign and domestic consumers
  - » Domestic and foreign inflation
  - » Income of foreign consumers
  - » Trade barriers

In response to changes in any of these factors, the aggregate demand curve shifts horizontally in or out.

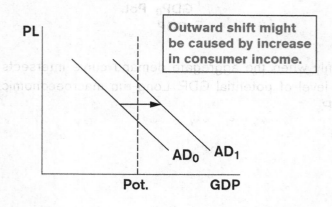

Outward shift might be caused by increase in consumer income.

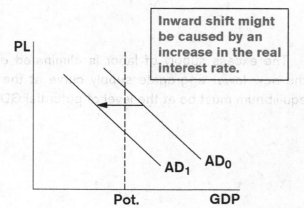

Inward shift might be caused by an increase in the real interest rate.

In contrast to the multitude of factors that can shift the AD curve, there are only three factors that can shift the aggregate supply curve: the quantity of available resources, the quality of the resources, and the price of the resources.

Changes in the quantity or quality of the resources available to an economy cause the aggregate supply curve to shift horizontally in or out. Because real resources have changed, the level of potential GDP also shifts in or out.

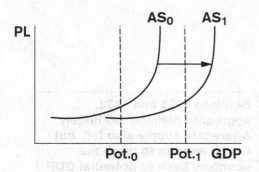

Outward shift might be caused by improvements in technology.

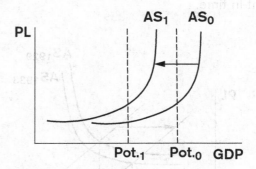

Inward shift might be caused by a major earthquake in California.

Changes in the price of resources cause the aggregate supply curve to shift vertically up or down. Because the quantity and quality of resources available to the economy have not changed (only their prices changed), the level of potential GDP stays the same.

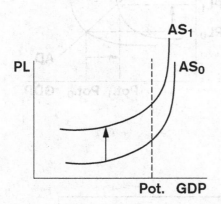

Upward shift might be caused by a big increase in the minimum wage.

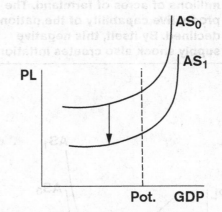

Downward shift might be caused by a big drop in the price of oil.

5. POWER OF AD/AS ANALYSIS

The AD/AS model is useful for describing the macro economy. It is a concise and intuitive way to characterize the macro economy at a point in time, and can be used to illustrate the differences between various schools of macroeconomic thought.

The AD/AS model is a concise and intuitive way to characterize the macro economy at a single point in time.

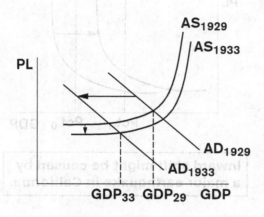

Between 1929 and 1933, aggregate demand fell hugely. Aggregate supply also fell, but not by enough to bring the economy back to potential GDP. A large recessionary GDP gap still remained.

The Dust Bowl of the 1930s was an environmental disaster that ruined millions of acres of farmland. The productive capability of the nation declined. By itself, this negative supply shock also creates inflation.

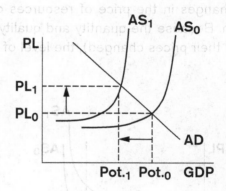

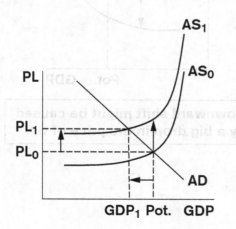

The OPEC (Organization of Petroleum Exporting Countries) oil cartel formed in the early 1970s and raised crude oil prices dramatically. The upward shift in AS created both inflation and a recessionary GDP gap.

The aggregate demand/aggregate supply model is also a useful tool for illustrating the differences between various schools of macroeconomic thought.

Consider the question: "What effect will a large increase in the money supply have on the level of GDP?"

One school of economic thought argues that an increase in the money supply will lower interest rates and lead to an increase in investment.

• This means that the aggregate demand curve shifts outward.

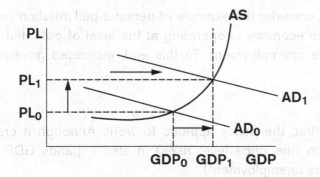

> The increase in AD will cause some inflation, but will also cause growth in real GDP.

If the economy started at a point below potential GDP, then increasing the money supply might return us to potential GDP.

Another school of economic thought argues that an increase in the money supply will have no effect on real output, but will merely push up the price level, raising prices for both final goods and input resources.

• This means that the aggregate supply curve shifts upward to match the outward shift in aggregate demand.

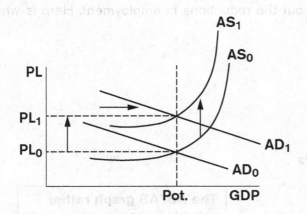

> There is no increase in real GDP, because the shift in AS returns us to potential GDP.

The only effect of more money is to cause inflation—to push the economy to a higher price level.

6. WEAKNESS OF AD/AS ANALYSIS

The AD/AS model is basically static—it is not as well suited to illustrating dynamic change over time. The normal "all else being equal" assumption of economic models often does not work well with AD/AS, since there can be multiple changes in response to a single initial change.

The aggregate demand/aggregate supply model is basically static; it provides a picture of the economy at a single point in time. The model is not well suited to illustrate dynamic change over time.

To illustrate the idea of static vs. dynamic, consider the example of demand-pull inflation caused by excessive government spending when the economy is operating at the level of potential GDP. The goal of government policy is to reduce unemployment. To this end, increased government spending shifts the AD curve outward.

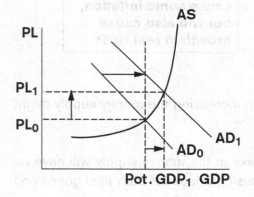

At first, the policy appears to work. Although it creates inflation (the price level rises), it also expands GDP (and reduces unemployment).

However, excess demand for labor soon pushes up wage rates, shifts up the aggregate supply curve, and returns the economy to potential GDP; unemployment rises back to the natural rate.

To hold unemployment below the natural rate, the government must repeatedly increase government spending to drive the aggregate demand curve ever further outward, only to see the subsequent rise in aggregate supply cancel out the reductions in employment. Here is what this dynamic change over time looks like:

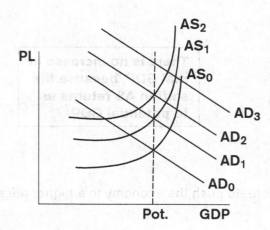

> **The AD/AS graph rather quickly becomes very messy and difficult to read.**

More seriously, the normal "all else being equal" assumption of economic models often does not work well with the AD/AS model. This is because a single initial change in an underlying factor can cause multiple changes in the aggregate demand and aggregate supply curves.

The main effect of devaluation of the dollar is that U.S. goods are now less expensive to foreigners, and foreign goods are now more expensive to Americans. As a result, exports increase and imports decrease; so net exports increase.

To illustrate this, consider the question: "What is the effect on the macro economy of devaluation of the dollar?"

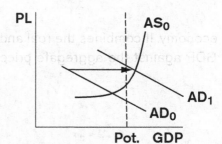

The increase in net exports shifts the AD curve outward.

However, devaluing the dollar also makes foreign resources more expensive for U.S. producers.

Higher resource prices shifts the AS curve upward.

Both the outward shift in AD and the upward shift in AS cause the price level to rise. This inflation causes interest rates to rise, thereby increasing the cost of borrowing.

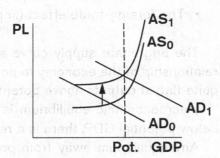

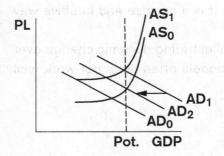

Higher borrowing costs lead to reduced investment. The AD curve shifts inward.

Where does the macro economy end up after all of this? Who can tell?

The AD/AS model is unable to predict where the economy will end up as a result of the single initial change.

SUMMARY OF CHAPTER 7

Business cycles are alternating periods of economic growth and decline.

> When real GDP falls for two consecutive quarters, the economy is in a recession.
>
> Business cycles are tracked by the National Bureau of Economic Research.
>
> • The most recent U.S. recession was December 2007 to June 2009.

Since the end of World War II, recessions in the United States have tended to be significantly shorter and milder than they were in earlier years.

Aggregate demand/aggregate supply is a model of the macro economy. It combines the real and the financial sides of the economy by graphing the level of real GDP against the aggregate price level.

> The aggregate demand curve slopes downward because of:
>
> • The real-balances effect (impacts consumption)
> • The interest-rate effect (impacts investment)
> • The foreign-trade effect (impacts net exports)

The aggregate supply curve slopes upward. The steepness of the AS curve depends on the relationship of the economy to potential GDP. At outputs well below potential GDP, the AS curve is quite flat; at outputs above potential GDP, the AS curve is quite steep.

> Macroeconomic equilibrium is where the AD and AS curves intersect. If equilibrium output is below potential GDP, there is a recessionary GDP gap.

> Any equilibrium away from potential GDP is short-run only. In the long-run, disequilibrium in resource markets will shift the AS curve back to potential GDP.

> The AD/AS model is useful for describing the macro economy. It is a concise and intuitive way to characterize the macro economy at a point in time.

> The AD/AS model is basically static—it is not as well suited to illustrating dynamic change over time. The normal "all else being equal" assumption of economic models often does not work well with AD/AS.

CH EIGHT

KEYNES AND THE CLASSICISTS

The classical model of the macro economy stresses the self-correcting nature of the economy. Keynes overthrew the classical model with his 1936 book, *The General Theory of Employment, Interest and Money*. Keynes argued that wages are sticky downward, so that it is possible for the economy to stay in a recessionary equilibrium.

Keynesian macro models concentrate on changes to aggregate demand, and the relationship of aggregate demand to aggregate expenditures. The distinction between planned investment and actual investment is critical. In a Keynesian model, recessions are the result of insufficient aggregate demand. The remedy is for the government to increase spending.

Milton Friedman

1. OVERVIEW OF COMPETING MACRO THEORIES

The major macroeconomic schools of thought all have their roots in the twentieth century. They tend to disagree on the extent and type of interaction between the real and financial sides of the economy, on the extent and speed with which the economy self-adjusts back to potential GDP, and on what the government can and should do to influence macroeconomic equilibrium.

There are three broad schools of macroeconomic thought:
- Classical macroeconomics
- Keynesian macroeconomics
- Monetarism

All three of these major macroeconomic schools of thought have roots in the twentieth century.

Adam Smith

Classical macroeconomics reaches all the way back to Adam Smith and the formation of economics as a distinct discipline in the 1800s. Early classical economists studied the macro issues of economic growth and development, but applied much more effort to the development of microeconomic issues.

His 1776 book, *The Wealth of Nations*, is the start of modern economics.

The mature version of classical macroeconomics was developed in the early twentieth century when classical economists such as Irving Fisher combined business cycle theory with monetary theory.

Keynesian macroeconomics began in 1936 with the publication of *The General Theory of Employment, Interest and Money*, by John Maynard Keynes. Writing during the depths of the great depression, Keynes strove to understand why economies were behaving so differently (and so badly) from the way classical theory predicted. Keynes shifted the focus of macroeconomics from aggregate supply to aggregate demand. His policy prescriptions were implemented by many governments, and his macro theory became the standard form for analysis. Within a very few years, Keynes' ideas effectively ended classical macroeconomics.

Milton Friedman

Monetarism began in the mid-1950s as a reaction against Keynesian macro theory. The principal founder of monetarism is Milton Friedman. Friedman reformulated many of the ideas of the classical school in light of Keynes' criticisms. Monetarism (as its name implies) concentrates on the financial side of the economy. Its ideas have influenced government monetary authorities in many nations.

Debate between proponents of these three schools of macroeconomic thought (and numerous off-shoots from them) continues today.

The three schools of macroeconomic thought disagree in three important ways.

1. **On the extent and type of interaction between the real and the financial sides of the economy**

- Classical school says that financial variables cannot affect the real side of the economy. Increasing the money supply only causes inflation.
- Keynesian school says that financial variables always affect the real side of the economy. Increasing the money supply leads to an increase in aggregate demand.
- Monetarist school says that financial variables can sometimes affect the real side of the economy. While increasing the money supply can cause inflation, decreasing the money supply can cause a recession.

2. **On the extent and speed with which the economy self-adjusts back to potential GDP**

- Classical school says that the economy quickly and reliably self-adjusts back to potential GDP.
- Keynesian school says that self-adjustment back to potential GDP, if it occurs at all, is very slow.
- Monetarist school says that the economy will quickly adjust back to potential GDP, unless there is an insufficient supply of money.

3. **On what the government can and should do to influence macroeconomic equilibrium**

- Classical school says that the government cannot influence macroeconomic equilibrium. The economy always returns to potential GDP. If the government tries to change this, all they do is create inflation.
- Keynesian school says the government must act to influence macroeconomic equilibrium, because the economy can't do it by itself.
- Monetarist school says that the government should not try to influence macroeconomic equilibrium. Attempts to do so are likely to backfire and make things worse.

2. CLASSICAL MODEL

The classical model of the macro economy was the first developed. It stresses the self-correcting nature of the economy and argues that financial variables have little impact on real variables, and that the government should do little to try to manage macroeconomic equilibrium. The main problem with the classical model was that the real world persisted in acting differently than the model predicted it would.

The classical model of the macro economy was the first developed. In the early twentieth century it owed much to the work of neo-classical microeconomists such as Alfred Marshall, who stressed the importance of equilibrium positions and the interaction between supply and demand. Classical macro theorists extended these micro ideas to the economy as a whole.

In the classical model, financial variables (such as the money supply) have little impact on real variables (such as GDP).

- The price level is determined solely by financial variables (by the size of the money supply relative to GDP).
- Real GDP is determined solely by real variables (quantity and quality of resources, and the available technology).

In effect, the classical model places a wall between the real and financial sides of the economy—events on one side of the wall do not affect variables on the other side of the wall.

The classical model stresses the self-correcting nature of the economy. Classical economists believed that, unless the government interferes, both resource and product markets adjust quickly back to equilibrium. This means that the aggregate supply curve will quickly adjust to any movement of the economy away from potential GDP, shifting up or down as a result of changes in the price of input resources.

It was believed that there could be no large (or lasting) discrepancy between aggregate demand and aggregate supply, because, as the circular flow showed, the value of the goods and services produced (aggregate supply) had to be equal to the income generated by their production (aggregate demand).

Recessions were viewed as a normal part of the adjustment back to equilibrium. When good times lasted too long, businesses and individuals threw caution to the winds and behaved badly. Recessions were when businesses and households unwound past excesses, wrote off bad investments, and behaved with restraint once again. Recessions, though painful, were necessary medicine to purge the economy of past unhealthy practices and prepare the way for renewed economic vitality and growth.

Classical macroeconomists argued that the government should do little to try to manage macroeconomic equilibrium. Since the economy would self-adjust, government intervention could only slow the inevitable process and make things worse. The best thing the government could do was to keep its hands off and allow the economy to run itself.

The problem with the classical macro model was that the real world persisted in behaving differently than the classical model predicted. During the classical period:
- The economy routinely experienced strong swings in economic activity: high rates of growth in boom times, deep recessions.
- Self-adjustment back to potential GDP often was not quick at all: recessions would last for years.
- Shifts from boom to bust tended to be sudden rather than gradual: banking "panics" repeatedly threw the economy into turmoil.
- The cost of such economic instability was very high: businesses bankrupt, households thrown into destitution, serious social unrest.

And then in 1929 came the Great Depression. This was the worst economic downturn in American history, and it just went on and on, year after year. Classical theory seemed unable to either explain or to remedy this disaster.

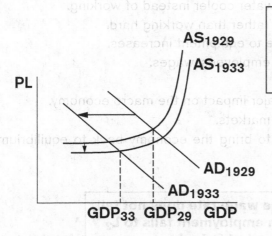

Four years after the start of the Great Depression, there was still a very large recessionary GDP gap, and it would remain for the rest of the decade.

Classical macro-economic theory could not explain why the economy was not self-correcting. Why was there still disequilibrium in labor markets? Why hadn't aggregate supply fallen further?

The best advice of the classical macroeconomists (which was to stay the course and wait for the economy to fix itself) seemed totally inadequate in the face of the Great Depression."

Something had to change.

3. KEYNES' NEW IDEAS

Keynes started a revolution in macroeconomics with his 1936 book, *The General Theory of Employment, Interest, and Money*. Keynes argued that wages are sticky downward, so that it is possible for the economy to stay in a recessionary equilibrium.

John Maynard Keynes was the most influential economist of the twentieth century. His 1936 book, *The General Theory of Employment, Interest and Money,* started a revolution in macroeconomics. The existing classical theory of macroeconomics was swept away, replaced wholesale by an entirely new analytical approach.

John Maynard Keynes

What were Keynes' new ideas, and how did they affect our view of the macro economy?

Most basically, Keynes observed that wages are sticky downward. When there is slack demand in labor markets, the demand/supply model predicts that wage rates will fall to restore equilibrium in labor markets. However, employers are reluctant to reduce wage rates, often choosing to lay off some employees rather than cut wages for all employees. The reason for this is clear: cuts in wages make employees unhappy, and unhappy employees are not very productive.

- Picture disgruntled workers griping around the water cooler instead of working.
- Disgruntled workers are more likely to slack off rather than working hard.
- When workers are unhappy, "accidental" damage to equipment increases.

It can be very expensive to a business to cut their employees' wages.

The fact that wages are sticky downward has a major impact on the macro economy.

- It means that disequilibrium can persist in labor markets.
- It means that aggregate supply will not adjust to bring the economy back to equilibrium at potential GDP.

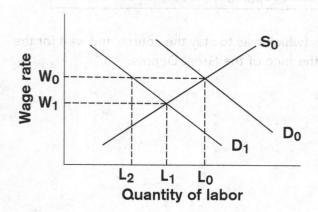

If the wage rate does not fall, then employment falls to L_2 instead of to L_1.

The difference between L_0 and L_2 is persistent unemployment — persons willing to work at the going wage rate, but unable to find jobs.

Is a recessionary equilibrium possible?

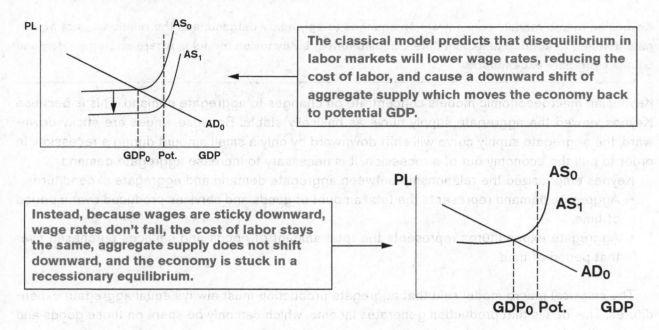

The classical model predicts that disequilibrium in labor markets will lower wage rates, reducing the cost of labor, and cause a downward shift of aggregate supply which moves the economy back to potential GDP.

Instead, because wages are sticky downward, wage rates don't fall, the cost of labor stays the same, aggregate supply does not shift downward, and the economy is stuck in a recessionary equilibrium.

Classical macroeconomists argued that the recessionary equilibrium only happens in the short-run. In the long-run, wage rates will fall, aggregate supply will shift downward, and the economy will self-adjust back to potential GDP.

- Keynes responded: "In the long-run we are all dead."

Keynes was saying that, when we are in the midst of a deep recession, with all of the human suffering and economic loss that entails, the long-run is not the appropriate time frame for our concern. We need to take short-run actions to improve things now!

Prior to Keynes, the prevailing view was that governments, like businesses, should be fiscally prudent and balance their budgets. Deficit spending and running up debt were seen as a moral failing for business and government both.

- Keynes argued forcefully that government deficit spending during a recession is a good thing. Fiscal prudence at such a time is foolish and destructive.

Keynes' arguments won the day. Classical macroeconomic theory was discredited. Keynes and his followers became the conventional wisdom. The victory of Keynes' new ideas was so complete that by 1965 it was widely reported that "We are all Keynesians now."

4. KEYNESIAN MODEL

Keynesian macro models concentrate on changes to aggregate demand, and the relationship of aggregate demand to aggregate expenditures. Equilibrium in a Keynesian model is where aggregate demand equals aggregate expenditures.

Keynesian macroeconomic models concentrate on changes to aggregate demand. This is because Keynes viewed the aggregate supply curve as basically stable. Because wages are sticky downward, the aggregate supply curve will shift downward by only a small amount during a recession. In order to pull the economy out of a recession, it is necessary to increase aggregate demand.

Keynes emphasized the relationship between aggregate demand and aggregate expenditures.
- Aggregate demand represents the total amount of goods and services produced over a period of time.
- Aggregate expenditures represents the total amount of goods and services purchased over that period of time.

The classical macro model said that aggregate production must always equal aggregate expenditures. The idea is that production generates income, which can only be spent on those goods and services that have been produced.

> This is known as Say's Law, and is commonly stated as: Supply creates its own demand.

Think of a circular flow diagram: income to workers finances expenditures by households, which is revenue to businesses financing their purchases of resources used to produce the goods and services that are bought by households.

> In the words of the Scottish economist John Mill, "Production of commodities creates a market for the commodities produced."

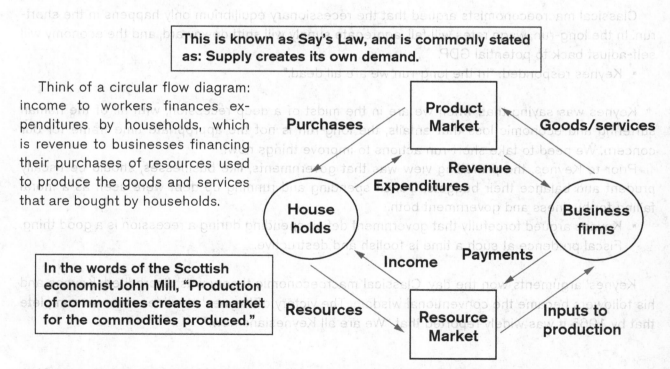

Keynes disputed this theory of classical macroeconomics. He argued that supply can be out of sync with demand. What he was saying is that the circular flow is not a closed system—there can be leakages from the flow, so that expenditures do not cover all production. And this causes real problems.

A high-level Keynesian model of the macro economy looks a lot like the definition of GDP.

$$AE = C + I_p + G + NE$$

Keynes said that:
- Consumption depends upon the level of disposable income available to households (the more income households have at their disposal, the more they will spend).
- Planned Investment depends upon the real interest rate (the lower the opportunity cost of borrowing, the more businesses will want to invest).
- Government Expenditures depend upon the decisions of government policy makers (government can spend whatever it chooses, irrespective of other economic factors).
- Exports depend upon the decisions of foreign consumers (they are not directly affected by changes in the domestic economy), while Imports depend upon the level of disposable income (when households have more to spend, they will increase spending on foreign goods and domestic goods both).

The Keynesian model is in equilibrium when aggregate expenditures equals aggregate demand.

Keynesian macro models can be (and often are) much more detailed than this. The basic technique for expanding a Keynesian macro model is to break down one or more of the components into smaller sub-components. For example:
- Labor markets could be broken down into skilled and unskilled labor.
- Business firms could be broken down to agriculture, manufacturing, and services.
- Government activity could be broken down to expenditures on goods and services, taxes, and transfer payments.
- Imports and Exports could be broken down between final goods and input resources.

Use of Commodities by Industry					
Name	Agriculture, forestry, fishing, and hunting	Mining	Utilities	Construction	Manufacturing
Agriculture, forestry, fishing, and hunting	94325	160	0	1939	275162
Mining	2473	54705	33987	10292	568596
Utilities	4168	3563	2191	2192	55702
Construction	2657	5770	3257	154	14645
Manufacturing	83010	48039	23886	269116	1948788

A detailed Keynesian model then specifies what each of the sub-components depends upon, and how the various sub-components interact with each other. Such models can become so large and complicated that they can only be analyzed with the help of computers.

For example, here is a portion of an input-output table for a more detailed macro model.

4.1. CONSUMPTION AND SAVING

Keynes models the consumption component of aggregate expenditures as a function of disposable income. Total consumption is the sum of some base level (autonomous consumption) plus some percentage (marginal propensity to consume) of disposable income.

Keynes models the consumption component of aggregate expenditures as being dependent upon the level of disposable income.

- In the National Income and Product Accounts, disposable income is defined as personal income minus personal taxes.
- For Keynes, disposable income is simply the total income available to households.

It makes sense to have consumption depend upon disposable income, because income is largely what households have to spend. The more income you receive, the more you are able to spend. Given the unlimited nature of human wants, when folks have more, they tend to spend more.

Total consumption is the sum of some base level of spending (termed autonomous consumption) plus some percentage (termed the marginal propensity to consume) of disposable income.

- Total consumption = Autonomous consumption + Induced consumption

Autonomous consumption is the amount that would be spent if there were zero disposable income. Even if one has no income at all, there must still be spending on basic necessities and prior debt obligations. Without an income, one spends by borrowing or by using up previous savings.

Induced consumption is the amount spent out of received income. The level of induced consumption changes as one's income changes.

The marginal propensity to consume is the percentage of any increase in disposable income that gets spent. For example, if, when your income rises by $100, you spend $80 more, then your MPC = 80%.

The relationship between disposable income and consumption is summarized by the consumption function.

> Total consumption = Autonomous consumption + Marginal propensity to consume x
> Disposable income
>
> TC = AC + MPC x DI

It is important to note that the consumption function does NOT describe the behavior of individual consumers. Rather, it describes the result of behavior of consumers in the aggregate.

This table shows total consumption at various levels of disposable income.

Disposable income (DI)	Autonomous consumption (AC)	Induced consumption (IC)	Total consumption (TC)	Savings (S)
1000	500	800	1300	-300
2000	500	1600	2100	-100
3000	500	2400	2900	100
4000	500	3200	3700	300

Autonomous consumption is a constant. It does not change as income increases.

The marginal propensity to consume is also a constant. In this example the MPC is 80%. Induced consumption is always 80% of disposable income.

Savings equals Disposable Income minus Total consumption. (S = DI – TC)

The savings decisions of individuals are influenced by many factors.

- Planned future expenditures, expectations of future changes in income, interest rates, level of prior debt, and so on.

But savings in the aggregate is determined solely by the level of disposable income.

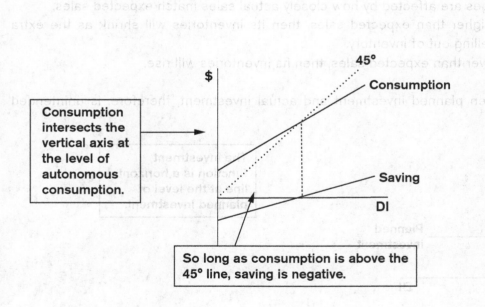

Consumption intersects the vertical axis at the level of autonomous consumption.

The dashed 45° line is a useful addition to the graph. It shows the points where the amount on the vertical axis is equal to disposable income on the horizontal axis.

So long as consumption is above the 45° line, saving is negative.

Saving is zero when consumption equals disposable income.

4.2. INVESTMENT

Keynes models the investment component of aggregate expenditures as a function of the interest rate. Keynes makes an important distinction between planned investment and actual investment.

Investment expenditures consists of:
- New construction and improvements to existing structures
- Purchases of new production machinery, equipment, furniture, vehicles, computer software
- Changes in private inventories

Keynes models the investment component of aggregate expenditures as depending upon the interest rate. This is because the interest rate represents the cost of borrowing funds to invest (and the opportunity cost of investing out of retained earnings). When the cost of investing goes up, the quantity of investment demanded goes down. This is simply the law of demand in action.

Keynes draws an important distinction between planned investment and actual investment.
- Planned investment is spending on structures and equipment, plus intended changes in business inventories.
- Actual investment is spending on structures and equipment, plus actual changes in inventories.

Actual inventory changes are affected by how closely actual sales match expected sales.
- If a business has higher than expected sales, then its inventories will shrink as the extra demand is met by selling out of inventory.
- If a business has lower than expected sales, then its inventories will rise.

The difference between planned investment and actual investment, therefore, is unintended inventory changes.

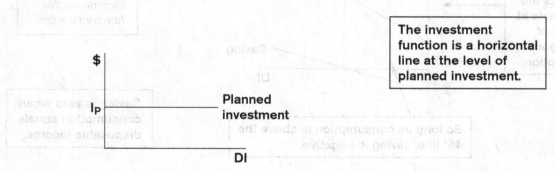

> The investment function is a horizontal line at the level of planned investment.

> Planned investment depends on the interest rate; it does not depend on the level of disposable income.

4.3. GOVERNMENT PURCHASES

Keynes models the government component of aggregate expenditures as something determined by factors outside of his model. That is, government expenditures, taxes, and transfers are simply whatever the government decides they will be, rather than being determined by income or interest rate or any other economic variable.

Government activity directly affects aggregate expenditures in three ways:
- Government purchases of goods and services is one of the components of aggregate expenditures.
- Government taxes reduce the level of disposable income available to households, thereby reducing the consumption component of aggregate expenditures.
- Government transfer payments increase the level of disposable income available to households, thereby increasing the consumption component of aggregate expenditures.

When we graph the consumption function, we assume that both taxes and transfer payments are constant (they are covered under the standard "all else being equal" assumption).

Keynes models the government component of aggregate demand as being exogenous. This means that government expenditures are determined by factors outside of Keynes' macro model. Government expenditures, taxes, and transfer payments are simply whatever government policy makers decide they will be. They are not affected by changes in disposable income, interest rates, or any other economic variable in the model.
- Why did Keynes do this? It does not seem unreasonable that government policy makers might be influenced by all sorts of economic variables that Keynes does include in his model.
- The reason Keynes assumed that government expenditures are exogenous is because he wanted government to be an active agent in his model. Government policy makers in a Keynesian model do not simply react to changes in economic variables in predictable ways (as do consumers and businesses)—rather, they have the ability to choose their behavior independent of those economic variables.

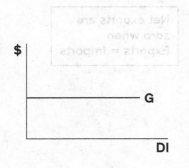

The government expenditures function is a horizontal line.

Government expenditures is whatever policy makers decide it will be; it does not depend on the level of disposable income.

4.4. NET EXPORTS

Keynes models exports as a constant not influenced by any other variable in the model. Imports, on the other hand, are a function of disposable income. That means that net exports (exports minus imports) are also a function of disposable income.

The Net Exports component of aggregate expenditures is defined as Exports minus Imports. Spending on exports adds funds to the domestic economy, while spending on imports removes funds from the domestic economy. That means that net exports is the net contribution to aggregate expenditures from the international trade sector of the economy.

Keynes models exports as exogenous. That is, he models exports as a constant not influenced by any other variable in his model. Keynes was well aware that exports depend upon the level of disposable income available to foreign consumers. But, since his macro model was of the domestic economy only, foreign income is not a variable he included.

Keynes does model imports as being determined by disposable income. This is because, when the income available to domestic consumers increases, they not only purchase more domestically produced goods, but also purchase more foreign-produced goods.

Thus, net exports are also determined by disposable income. The table below demonstrates this.

Disposable income	Exports	Imports	Net Exports
1000	300	200	100
2000	300	300	0
3000	300	400	- 100

Imports increases as disposable income increases, but exports stay constant.

Net exports decreases as disposable income increases.

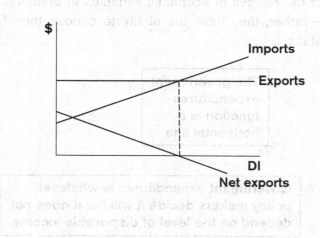

Net exports are zero when Exports = Imports

4.5. AGGREGATE EXPENDITURES

In a Keynesian model, aggregate expenditures is the sum of consumption, planned investment, government expenditures, and net exports. Aggregate demand (or aggregate production) is very similar, but includes actual investment instead of planned investment.

In a Keynesian macro model, aggregate expenditures is the sum of consumption, planned investment, government purchases, and net exports.

$$AE = C + I_P + G + NE$$

Aggregate demand (or perhaps better, aggregate production) is very similar to this, but includes actual investment in place of planned investment.

$$AP = C + I_A + G + NE$$

The difference between planned investment and actual investment is that actual investment includes unintended changes in business inventories.

To see the distinction between AE and AP, assume that businesses are happy with their existing level of inventories, and so plan to keep their inventory level unchanged.

- If sales are better than expected, then inventories will unexpectedly be drawn down. This means that unintended inventory change is negative, actual investment is less than planned investment, and aggregate expenditures is greater than aggregate production.
- If sales are slower than expected, then inventories will unexpectedly rise. This means that unintended inventory change is positive, actual investment is greater than planned investment, and aggregate expenditures is less than aggregate production.

The independent variables in a Keynesian macro model are disposable income and interest rates.
- Disposable income affects consumption and imports.
- Interest rates affect investment.
- Government purchases and exports are exogenous (unaffected by any variable in the model).

Keynes was concerned with an economy in recession. During a recession, investment is likely to be quite unresponsive to changes in interest rates (because investor pessimism is high). This means that disposable income is the most important variable in a Keynesian macro model.

5. THE MULTIPLIER

A Keynesian model is dynamic—that is, it explicitly models change over time. A one-time change in any component of aggregate expenditures is not the end of the story. Rather, it sets off a chain reaction that multiplies the effect of the original change.

A Keynesian model is dynamic—that is, it explicitly models change over time. Adjustments in a Keynesian model do not occur instantaneously; it takes time for the consequences of a change to work their way through the macro model.

This is very different from the analysis process with a static model. A static macro model (like the aggregate demand/aggregate supply model) provides a snapshot of the economy at a particular point in time. When some significant event occurs, the static model shifts from its original position to a new position. The emphasis in the static model is on the differences between the starting point and the ending point. Little attention is paid to precisely how the economy moves from the starting point to the ending point.

In contrast, a dynamic macro model walks you step by step through the process by which the economy shifts between its starting and ending points. This dynamic process highlights the inter-relationships between economic variables. Each step in the adjustment process can be examined to see if there are any weak points in the chain of cause and effect. A dynamic analysis, though more complicated than a static analysis, is also potentially much richer.

In a Keynesian model, the ultimate size of the impact of an event on the economy is larger than the initial event. A one-time change in any component of aggregate expenditures is not the end of the story. Rather, it sets off a chain reaction that multiplies the effect of the original change.

This process is called the multiplier.

Here is an example of how the multiplier works.

Assume a simple two-sector economy (households and business firms).
- Note that the multiplier process works equally well in a more complex economy that also includes government and international trade sectors; it simply is easier to demonstrate the process in a two-sector economy.

Starting conditions	Disposable income	Consumption	Investment	Aggregate expenditures
	4000	3500	500	4000

Now let investment increase by 200.

DI	C	I	AE
4000	3500	500 → 700	4000 → 4200

But the new investment is also disposable income to whoever receives it, and as disposable income increases, so does consumption.

DI	C	I	AE
4000 → 4200	3500 →3660	700	4200 → 4360

Now the new consumption increases disposable income again, which increases consumption again.

DI	C	I	AE
4200 → 4360	3660 → 3788	700	4360 → 4488

And the process repeats itself, as this new consumption itself increases disposable income again, which in turn increases consumption yet again.

DI	C	I	AE
4360 → 4488	3788 → 3890	700	4488 → 4590

And the multiplier continues—around and around the circular flow of the economy

Ending conditions	Disposable income	Consumption	Investment	Aggregate expenditures
	5000	4300	700	5000

The initial increase of 200 in investment is multiplied as it circulates around the economy, repeatedly generating new disposable income and new consumption, until ultimately aggregate expenditures expands by 1000. This is five times as large a final effect as the original change.

The size of the multiplier in this simple economy is: Multiplier = 1 / (1 – MPC)

In this example, the marginal propensity to consume is 80%, so the value of the multiplier is:

$$1 / (1 - 0.8) = 1 / 0.2 = 5$$

Note that the increase in aggregate expenditures is smaller in each successive round of the multiplier process. This is because part of each increase in disposable income leaks out of the process in the form of savings. Income that is saved is not spent, and income that is not spent does not become additional income to someone else.

6. EQUILIBRIUM IN A KEYNESIAN MODEL

A Keynesian model is in equilibrium when Aggregate Production = Aggregate Expenditures. Disequilibrium is shown by there being unintended changes in business inventories. Producer actions to restore inventories to their desired level is the force that drives a Keynesian model back to equilibrium.

A Keynesian model is in equilibrium when aggregate production equals aggregate expenditures. That is, when the aggregate amount produced is equal to the aggregate amount purchased.

- This doesn't mean that every single good produced gets purchased. Nor does it mean that there is a perfect match between the quantity supplied and quantity demanded in every product market. It is quite possible that there is excess demand for some products (leading to shortages) and excess supply for some products (leading to unwanted surpluses).
- What it does mean is that there is no overall glut or shortage of production. The aggregate value of the goods purchased is equal to the aggregate value of the goods produced.

There are a number of ways to state this equilibrium condition:

- Aggregate production = Aggregate expenditures
- Planned investment = Actual investment
- Unintended inventory changes are zero
- Injections into the economy equal leakages out of the economy

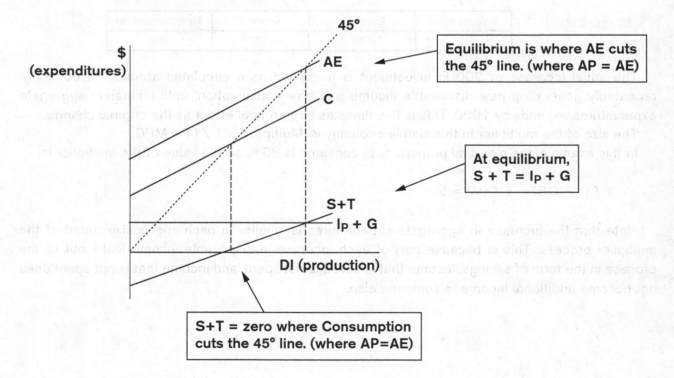

Equilibrium is where AE cuts the 45° line. (where AP = AE)

At equilibrium, $S + T = I_P + G$

S+T = zero where Consumption cuts the 45° line. (where AP=AE)

When a Keynesian macro model is in disequilibrium, there are unintended changes in business inventories. The dissatisfaction investors experience because of these unintended inventory changes is the force which drives the model back to equilibrium. Let's use an example to see how this works. The table below shows aggregate values for a three-sector economy (there is no international trade sector).

Disposable income (aggregate production)	Consumption	Planned investment + Government spending	Saving + Taxes	Aggregate expenditures $(C + I_p + G)$	Unintended changes to inventories
1000	900	500	100	1400	-400
2000	1700	500	300	2200	-200
3000	2500	500	500	3000	0
4000	3300	500	700	3800	+200
5000	4100	500	900	4600	+400

In the table, when aggregate production = 1000 or 2000, it is lower than aggregate expenditures.
- More is being bought than was produced; the extra sales come out of existing inventories.
- Business inventories are being drawn down unexpectedly.
- Planned investment is greater than actual investment.
- Injections to the economy (I_p+G) are larger than leakages (S+T).
- Businesses respond by increasing production to build inventories back up to their desired level.

In the table, when aggregate production = 5000 or 4000, it is higher than aggregate expenditures.
- More was produced than is being bought; the unbought goods become part of existing inventories.
- Business inventories are building up unexpectedly.
- Planned investment is smaller than actual investment.
- Leakages from the economy are larger than injections.
- Businesses react by decreasing production; to draw inventories back down to their desired level.

In the table, when aggregate production = 3000, it is equal to aggregate expenditures.
- The amount being bought matches the amount that was produced.
- Business inventories hold steady at their desired level.
- Planned investment is the same as actual investment.
- Injections to the economy just equal leakages from the economy.
- Since inventories are at their desired level, there are no further changes in production. This is equilibrium.

7. WHAT CAUSES RECESSIONS?

According to a Keynesian macro model, recessions are the result of a fall in any of the components of aggregate expenditures, which sets off a downward multiplier process. Keynes' prescription for getting out of a recession is for government spending to increase.

According to a Keynesian macro model, recessions are the result of a fall in any of the components of aggregate expenditures. The initial fall in aggregate expenditures, whatever its source, sets off a downward multiplier process.

For example, say that investors become pessimistic about business conditions in the future. Their new attitude concerning the future means that it is less attractive for them to invest in the present: planned investment falls. Current production that would have been purchased by investors goes into growing inventories instead. With inventories now higher than what businesses desire to hold, businesses cut back on production to reduce their excess inventories. Less production requires fewer workers, so unemployment rises and disposable income falls. The fall in disposable income causes a fall in consumption, which further reduces aggregate expenditures. A downward spiral sends the economy into recession.

Consider another example; the government decides to balance its budget by raising taxes and reducing transfer payments. Both of these actions reduce disposable income, and households respond by reducing consumption. Those items that consumers fail to buy add to business inventories, pushing those inventories higher than businesses desire. Businesses cut back on production to reduce their excess inventories. Less production requires fewer workers, so unemployment rises and disposable income falls. The fall in disposable income causes a fall in consumption, which further reduces aggregate expenditures. A downward spiral sends the economy into recession.

The resulting recessionary GDP gap is not likely to be eliminated by a downward shift in the aggregate supply curve. Wages are sticky downward, so any shift in aggregate supply will be too small to move the economy back to potential GDP. In addition, cutting wages has the immediate effect of further reducing disposable income and thus further reducing consumption and aggregate expenditures.

For a recession to end, we need an increase in one or more of the components of aggregate expenditures.

From what component of aggregate expenditures is an increase likely to come?

From consumption? Not likely.

- Disposable income falls in a recession when unemployment rises. Consumption is unlikely to rise until the economy begins to recover.

From planned investment? Not likely.

- The level of investment is strongly influenced by investor expectations of future business conditions. When the economy is in a recession, future business prospects look bleak—it appears to be a bad time to invest. Planned investment is unlikely to rise until the economy begins to recover.

From net exports? Not likely.

- Though it is true that spending on imports will decline in a recession, so that net exports will rise, the international trade sector in the U.S. is too small for the tick upward in net exports to have a significant impact on the economy as a whole.

All that is left is the government sector. Keynes' prescription for getting out of a recession is for government to increase its own spending. Once increased government spending gets the recovery started, consumption and investment will then also start to rise.

- The increased government expenditures will increase disposable income to households, which will increase their consumption spending in response.
- As production expands to satisfy the new higher spending by the government, unemployment will fall and household disposable income will rise, leading to additional consumption and an upward spiral of the multiplier process.
- With the economy recovering, future business conditions look brighter to investors, and planned investment increases, adding further to the upward movement in aggregate expenditures.

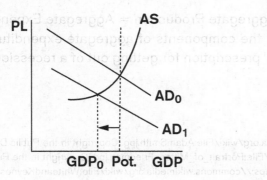

A decline in aggregate demand (from AD_0 to AD_1) creates a recessionary GDP gap.

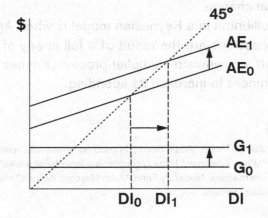

The rise in government spending increases aggregate expenditures, leading to increased production.

SUMMARY OF CHAPTER 8

There are 3 broad schools of macroeconomic thought:
- Classical, Keynesian, and Monetarist

The classical model stresses the self-correcting nature of the economy, argues that financial variable have little impact on real variables, and that the government should do little to try to manage macroeconomic equilibrium. The main problem with the classical model was that the real world persisted in acting different than the model predicted it would.

Keynes overthrew the classical model with his 1936 book, *The General Theory of Employment, Interest and Money*. Keynes argued that wages are sticky downward, so that it is possible for the economy to stay in a recessionary equilibrium.

Keynesian macro models concentrate on changes to aggregate demand and the relationship of aggregate demand to aggregate expenditures.

Keynes models:
- Consumption as a function of disposable income
- Investment as a function of the interest rate
- Government spending as exogenous
- Net exports as a function of disposable income

The distinction between planned investment and actual investment is critical. The difference between them is unintended changes to inventories, and unintended inventory changes is the force that drives the Keynesian model to equilibrium.

A Keynesian model is dynamic—it explicitly models change over time. A one-time change in any component of aggregate expenditures sets off a chain reaction that multiplies the effect of the original change.

Equilibrium in a Keynesian model is when Aggregate Production = Aggregate Expenditures.

Recessions are the result of a fall in any of the components of aggregate expenditures, which sets off a downward multiplier process. Keynes' prescription for getting out of a recession is for the government to increase its spending.

Credits

CH NINE

FISCAL POLICY

Fiscal policy is government action taken to counteract the business cycle. It involves changing government expenditures, changing tax receipts, or changing government transfer payments.

During a recession, an expansionary fiscal policy is appropriate. To be effective, a fiscal policy must be applied at the right time, in the right amount, and in the right direction.

The proper timing of fiscal policy is particularly difficult, as there are three lags inherent in the process: recognition lag, administrative lag, and operational lag. Automatic stabilizers are fiscal policy tools which are not subject to the lags that afflict discretionary fiscal policy.

1. HOW FISCAL POLICY WORKS

Fiscal policy is government action taken to counteract the business cycle. It involves changing government expenditures, changing tax receipts, or changing government transfer payments. During a recession, an expansionary fiscal policy is appropriate.

Fiscal policy is government action taken to counteract the business cycle. It is designed to give a boost to a faltering economy and to restrain a booming economy. By moderating the up and down swings of the business cycle, fiscal policy helps keep the economy operating closer to potential GDP. Fiscal policy involves changing government expenditures, changing tax receipts, or changing government transfer payments.

Government expenditures are the goods and services purchased by the government. These could be:
- Items the government purchases from the private sector. For example, guns from Colt, submarines from General Dynamics, computers from Dell, email service from Google.
- Workers (and other resources) the government hires itself. For example, economists by the Bureau of Labor Statistics, rangers by the National Park Service, or the thousands of workers hired by the Civilian Conservation Corp during the depression years.
- Infrastructure built by the government itself. For example, dams along the Tennessee River, rural electrification, or the interstate highway system.

Tax receipts come from income taxes, Social Security taxes, excise taxes (like those on gasoline, cigarettes, and alcohol), import tariffs (taxes on foreign-produced goods), and from fees (for example, entrance fees at National Parks, or charges for grazing rights on public lands).

Transfer payments are funds simply given by the government to individuals or groups (not in exchange for any good or service). These include unemployment insurance, various means-tested welfare programs, agricultural price support, and the like.

During a recession, an expansionary fiscal policy is appropriate. This involves some combination of increasing government expenditures, reducing tax receipts, and increasing transfer payments. With an overheated economy, a contractionary fiscal policy is appropriate. This involves some combination of decreasing government expenditures, increasing tax receipts, and decreasing transfer payments.

Fiscal policy works by changing aggregate expenditures in a straightforward way. For example, with an expansionary fiscal policy:
- Increased government expenditures directly increases aggregate expenditures, since G is one of the components of AE.
- Decreased taxes or increased transfer payments both increase households' disposable income, which leads to increased consumption, which is one of the components of AE.

Once fiscal policy makes its initial impact on aggregate expenditures, then the multiplier process kicks in.

- For an expansionary fiscal policy, the initial increase in aggregate expenditures spurs production and hiring, which increases disposable income, which increases consumption, which spurs additional production and hiring, which creates more disposable income and more consumption, and so on, round and round the circular flow.

One interesting aspect of fiscal policy is that it can be used to expand the economy without increasing federal debt. This is called the balanced budget multiplier. It involves an equal increase in government expenditures and tax receipts.

- For example, consider the impact of a $100 million increase in government expenditures, along with a $100 million increase in taxes, on an economy where the marginal propensity to consume is 75%.
- The $100 million increase in expenditures leads to a $400 million increase in aggregate expenditures after the multiplier works. (With MPC = 75%, the multiplier = 4)
- The $100 million increase in taxes leads to a $300 million decrease in aggregate expenditures after the multiplier works. The first step in the downward multiplier process is a fall of $75 million (not $100 million) because the $100 million increase in taxes is offset by a fall of $75 million in consumption and a fall of $25 million in savings.
- The combined effect is an increase of $100 million in aggregate expenditures, even though the government budget is still balanced.

The effect of a balanced budget expansionary fiscal policy is to increase the size of the government sector relative to the sizes of the other sectors of the economy.

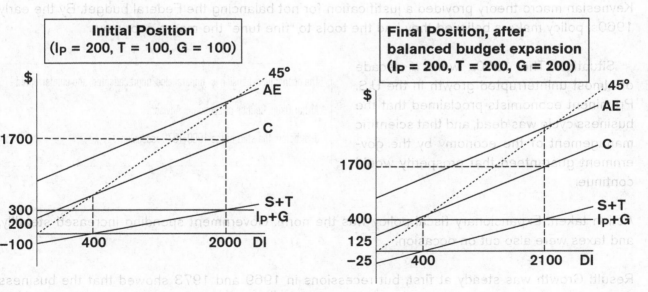

2. HISTORICAL EXAMPLES OF FISCAL POLICY

The United States first practiced fiscal policy during the Great Depression. After World War II, U.S. fiscal policy actions became both larger and more frequent.

The U.S. first practiced fiscal policy during the Great Depression.

Situation: It was the worst economic downturn in American history. Real GDP fell by nearly fifty percent between 1929 and 1933, while the unemployment rate rose to over twenty-five percent. In 1932, President Hoover proposed to cut spending and raise taxes in order to balance the federal budget. He lost the 1932 election to Franklin Roosevelt.

Action taken: President Roosevelt at first opposed deficit spending. But as the depression continued, he expanded government spending in many ways. The government increased direct support programs for the needy, invested in infrastructure, and itself hired thousands of unemployed workers. There had never before been a larger peacetime increase in government spending.

> Roosevelt's "New Deal" included:
> - Works Progress Administration
> - Tennessee Valley Authority
> - Social Security
> - Federal Deposit Insurance Corporation
> - Civilian Conservation Corp
> - National Labor Relations Board

Result: There was a weak economic recovery between 1933 and 1937, but unemployment still remained at historically high levels, and real GDP was still lower than it had been in 1929. The Great Depression did not end until the start of World War II.

After the end of World War II, U.S. fiscal policy actions became both larger and more frequent. Keynesian macro theory provided a justification for not balancing the Federal budget. By the early 1960s, policy makers believed they had the tools to "fine tune" the macro economy.

Situation: The 1960s were a decade of almost uninterrupted growth in the U.S. Prominent economists proclaimed that the business cycle was dead, and that scientific management of the economy by the government guaranteed that prosperity would continue.

> The economic expansion is "unparalleled, unprecedented, and uninterrupted."
>
> Arthur Okun, Council of Economic Advisors
>
> Just before the start of the 1969-1970 recession

Action taken: Expansionary fiscal policy was the norm. Government spending increased steadily, and taxes were also cut on occasion.

Result: Growth was steady at first, but recessions in 1969 and 1973 showed that the business cycle was still with us. Inflation began to creep up, and became a serious problem in the 1970s.

Supply-side fiscal policies had been tried before—most notably the Kennedy tax cuts of 1961. They received their biggest test with the Reagan tax cuts of 1981–1982.

Situation: Inflation reached double digits in the late 1970s. Highly contractionary monetary actions by the Federal Reserve brought inflation down, but put the country into a serious recession.

Action taken: Marginal income tax rates were cut dramatically. Government regulation of business practices in many industries were eliminated.

Result: A long period of economic growth, with only one relatively mild recession over the next 20 years. Federal budget deficits remained historically high for peacetime over the entire period.

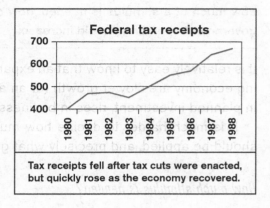

Tax receipts fell after tax cuts were enacted, but quickly rose as the economy recovered.

The Great Recession started in 2007. One of President Obama's first acts in office was to propose the largest fiscal stimulus in U.S. history.

Situation: The bursting of the house price bubble in 2007 led to chaos in financial markets. Private sources of credit dried up, and planned investment fell sharply. The U.S. experienced its worst economic performance since the end of World War II.

Action taken: Traditional expansionary fiscal policy, but of unprecedented size. The 2009 stimulus package was the largest in American history—over $800 billion.

Result: Recovery started in the second half of 2009, but sluggishly. Growth remains low; unemployment remains high. Federal budget deficits exceeded all previous levels in 2009, 2010, and 2011.

All in all, a mixed record of achievement from fiscal policy. Fiscal policy actions have gotten progressively larger, but not progressively more successful. One constant is that expansionary fiscal policy has been used much more frequently than contractionary fiscal policy. This bias toward expansionary fiscal policy is inherent to our form of government.

- Voters like to receive increases in government spending and reductions in their taxes. Voters don't like cuts in government spending programs they benefit from, and don't like to have their taxes go up.
- So politicians, seeking to please voters, are more likely to support expansionary policies than contractionary policies.

3. DESIGNING A STIMULUS POLICY

It is one thing to know that government economic stimulus is called for. It is quite another to decide how much of a stimulus is needed, how quickly and how long it should be applied, and precisely what government spending should increase.

It is relatively easy to know that an expansionary fiscal policy is needed. The indicators of a weakening economy are slower growth (or an actual fall) in real GDP, rising unemployment rates, declines in planned investment, rises in business inventories, and declines in consumer confidence.

It is much harder to decide how much fiscal stimulus is needed, how quickly and how long it should be applied, and precisely what government spending should increase.

How much stimulus is needed?

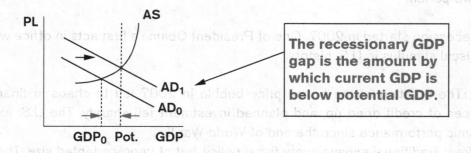

The recessionary GDP gap is the amount by which current GDP is below potential GDP.

The aim of fiscal stimulus is to shift out aggregate demand until the economy reaches equilibrium at potential GDP. To do this, the government policy makers must know both the size of the GDP gap and the size of the multiplier.

For example, assume that the recessionary GDP gap is $1000 billion.
- If the MPC = 80%, then we need $200 billion in stimulus to eliminate the GDP gap.
  » ($200 billion / (1 − MPC = $200 billion / 0.2 = $1000 billion)
- If the MPC is higher (say 90%), then less stimulus is needed to eliminate the GDP gap.
  » $100 billion / 0.1 = $1000 billion
- If the MPC is lower (say 75%), then more stimulus is needed to eliminate the GDP gap.
  » $250 billion / 0.25 = $1000 billion

How long should the stimulus be applied?

The caution here is that we do not want the effect of the stimulus to continue to be felt even after the economy reaches potential GDP. If the stimulus is still being applied when the economy reaches potential GDP, then the stimulus will begin to overheat the economy.

- It will become pro-cyclical instead of counter-cyclical.

To get the proper timing of the stimulus, we need to know the length of the multiplier process. Part of this is knowing how quickly consumer and business expectations will change, since expectations of future conditions influences present consumption and planned investment.

Precisely what government spending should increase?

In theory it doesn't matter what the stimulus is spent on. The point when the economy is in a recession is to increase aggregate expenditures; the increase itself is what is important, not where the increase comes from. Keynes famously said that the government could hire one set of workers to dig holes, and a second set of workers to fill the holes in again, and still have the desired effect on the macro economy. This is because any increase in aggregate expenditures sets off the multiplier process.

In practice, of course, it matters greatly just what the stimulus is spent on. For example, digging holes and filling them in again does not increase potential GDP, while the same level of spending on repairing/building infrastructure will increase future production possibilities.

The stimulus is also likely to have distributional effects. The providers of the new goods and services purchased by the stimulus will enjoy the greatest benefits. Expanding the military most benefits military contractors, repairing/building roads/dams/airports/other structures most benefits building contractors, and so on.

> **Here is what Keynes actually said:**
>
> *"If the Treasury were to fill old bottles with banknotes, bury them at suitable depths in disused coalmines which are then filled up to the surface with town rubbish, and leave it to private enterprise on well-tried principles of laissez-faire to dig the notes up again ... there need be no more unemployment and, with the help of the repercussions, the real income of the community, and its capital wealth also, would probably become a good deal greater than it actually is."*

An additional consideration is that the marginal propensity to consume varies between groups. Stimulus spending that goes largely to lower-income groups (who typically have higher MPCs), will pack a bigger punch than stimulus spending that goes largely to higher-income groups (who typically have lower MPCs).

4. TIMING OF FISCAL POLICY

The proper timing of fiscal policy is particularly difficult, as there are three types of lags inherent in the process: a recognition lag, an administrative lag, and an operational lag.

The proper timing of fiscal policy is particularly difficult. There are three types of lags inherent to the process of forming and carrying out fiscal policy: a recognition lag, an administrative lag, and an operational lag. The inevitable delays resulting from these lags can seriously throw off the timing of fiscal policy.

The **recognition lag** is the time it takes for policy makers to identify that a fiscal policy action is needed. This lag is partly because the relevant economic indicators are not continually and instantaneously available—it takes time to gather, calculate, and publish economic statistics. And it is partly because economic indicators, when available, do not always paint a clear picture of the state of the economy.

The **administrative lag** is the time it takes for policy makers to devise an appropriate fiscal policy and to hammer out the details of that policy. This lag is partly because reasonable people can disagree on the best course of action, but mostly because the re-distributional aspects of any fiscal policy action guarantees a political fight between potential winners and losers.

The **operational lag** is the time it takes for an approved fiscal policy action to be implemented and to take effect. This lag is partly because most projects need time for planning and preparation before they can really get going. In addition, the full effect of any fiscal policy action is only felt after the multiplier process has had time to work its way through the economy.

The timing problem caused by lags.

These three lags are inherent to the process of discretionary fiscal policy—they can (perhaps) be reduced, but they can never be eliminated.

4.1. RECOGNITION LAG

The recognition lag is the time required for government officials to identify that a fiscal policy action is needed. The basic data on GDP is available only once every three months. Leading economic indicators can help.

The recognition lag is the time required for government policy makers to identify that a fiscal policy action is needed.

This lag occurs partly because the relevant economic indicators are not continually and instantaneously available. It takes time to gather, calculate, and publish economic statistics.
- Most relevant for identifying recessions is GDP, since the definition of a recession is two consecutive quarters of decline in real GDP.
- GDP statistics are available once every three months, and then with a two-month lag. So, for example, GDP statistics for October to December will not be available until February of the following year.
- It will be a minimum of eight months after the start of a recession that we can officially know that a recession has begun. There have been recessions that had actually ended before it was officially announced that they had begun!

We don't have to wait for an official announcement to know that the economy is faltering and an expansionary fiscal policy is appropriate. Clues about the future short-term condition of the economy are provided by leading economic indicators. These are indicators that usually change before the economy as a whole changes. For example:
- Manufacturers' new orders: A decline in new orders is usually soon followed by a decline in production.
- New building permits: A decline in new building permits usually precedes a decline in construction.
- Consumer confidence: Falling consumer confidence usually indicates a decline in consumption in the future.

If several leading economic indicators point to a weakening economy, an expansionary fiscal policy can be started without waiting for the official notification of the recession.

The main problem with basing fiscal policy actions on leading economic indicators is that those indicators do not always paint a clear picture of the economy. What should you do when some indicators point to a coming downturn in the economy, but other indicators do not? The Conference Board combines ten indicators into a single index of leading economic indicators. This index has fallen before every recession in the last fifty years—but has also fallen several times when no recession followed. When attempting to predict the future, errors are not only possible, they are inevitable.

> It is said that the LEI index has successfully predicted 12 of the last 6 recessions.

4.2. ADMINISTRATIVE LAG

The administrative lag is the time required for the government to decide how much fiscal stimulus (or restraint) is needed, and precisely what government spending should change. This is an intensely political process, and disagreement is inevitable.

Once it has been seen that a fiscal policy action is needed, the administrative lag is the time required for government policy makers to devise an appropriate policy: how much fiscal stimulus (or restraint) is needed, and precisely what government spending should change.

Fiscal policy requires cooperation between the executive and legislative branches of the government.

- A typical process will start with economists in the executive branch (perhaps in the Treasury Department, Office of Management and Budget, or Council of Economic Advisors) preparing an expert analysis of economic conditions and government policy options. They are likely to receive a great deal of advice (both solicited and not) from the media, special interest groups, and the academic world.
- Eventually one or more bills will be submitted in Congress. Both the House and the Senate will vigorously (often acrimoniously) debate both the need for action and details of the proposed policy. Amendments to the bills will be submitted, debated, and voted on.
- If the House and Senate bills differ (as they almost certainly will), they then go to a joint committee for reconciliation. If the bill that finally emerges is too different from what the president wants, he might veto it—and then it is back to Congress for more argument and negotiation.

All of this takes time—potentially a lot of time.

Disagreement in Congress over any proposed fiscal policy is more than just the simple fact that reasonable people can disagree on issues and on details. Fiscal policy actions have distributional effects. There will be winners and losers depending on the details of which government spending programs are increased or cut back.

- Infrastructure projects to build highways in West Virginia are of most benefit to folks in West Virginia.
- Expanded job training programs in California are of most benefit to workers in California.
- Buying new ships for the Coast Guard is of most benefit to the companies that will build these new ships.

Every representative and senator wants a fiscal stimulus to benefit their district and their state. Every representative and senator wants fiscal restraint to be borne by someone else's district or state. Every member of Congress seeks those changes in government spending that will most benefit their own constituents and supporters.

4.3. OPERATIONAL LAG

The operational lag is the time required for the fiscal policy action to be implemented and to take effect. Government agencies tend to work slowly, and the full effect of a fiscal policy action isn't felt until the multiplier process has had time to work.

Once a specific fiscal policy program is agreed upon, then the operational lag sets in. The operational lag is the time required for the approved policy action to be implemented and to take effect. Delay at this point is again inevitable.

Changes in government spending are implemented by the various government agencies spelled out in the details of the fiscal policy program. These agencies tend to work slowly. They operate on annual budgets passed by Congress, and tend to spread their spending relatively equally over the year. When a government agency receives extra funds as part of a fiscal stimulus program, they typically won't even attempt to spend most of it until six months or so later.

There are practical problems in spending a lot of money quickly. Significant preparatory work may be needed before spending can occur at all. A lot of advance work is often necessary before a project is truly "shovel-ready." Even then, opponents of a particular project usually have effective means to slow it down. Preparation of an environmental impact study can take months, and its findings can later be challenged in court—a tactic good for many more months of delay.

Even after the stimulus money is spent, the full effect of a fiscal policy action is not felt until the multiplier process has had time to work. The impact of the initial increase in aggregate expenditures is multiplied as the stimulus goes around and around in the circular flow. This process takes time. Estimates of the length of the multiplier process vary widely, though it is generally agreed that it is likely to take one to two years for the full effect of a fiscal policy action to be felt.

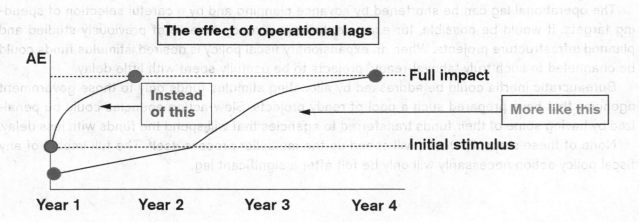

5. EFFECT OF LAGS

The lags in fiscal policy are not things that can be "fixed"—they are inherent to the process. As a result of these lags, discretionary fiscal policy is as likely to be pro-cyclical as it is to be counter-cyclical.

The lags in the application of discretionary fiscal policy are not things that can be "fixed"—they are inherent to the process. There are some things that can be done to shorten the lags, but it is not possible to eliminate them. Any attempt to assess the potential usefulness of a fiscal policy action must take these inevitable lags into account. An action that would be useful if it could take effect immediately, will not necessarily be useful when it will only take effect with lags.

What can be done to shorten the three lags in discretionary fiscal policy?

The recognition lag can be shortened by using leading economic indicators to make predictions about future economic conditions. Such predictions are less reliable the further out into the future they go, and they sometimes make mistakes even in the short-run. Nevertheless, leading economic indicators clearly can provide some advance warning of significant economic downturns.

The administrative lag can be shorted by congressional agreement to "fast-track" fiscal policy legislation. Such agreement is more likely to be reached when all parties avoid pushing for overtly partisan provisions. However, the likelihood of such restraint is pretty low in anything other than the most extraordinary situations. Politicians, after all, are by definition "political." It is in the individual interest of a politician to push for partisan provisions. The U.S. system of government is designed to work slowly and to encourage disagreement—it is the price we pay for avoiding the abuses of a dictator.

The operational lag can be shortened by advance planning and by a careful selection of spending targets. It would be possible, for example, to have a ready reserve of previously studied and planned infrastructure projects. When an expansionary fiscal policy is desired, stimulus funds could be channeled to such truly "shovel-ready" projects to be usefully spent with little delay.

Bureaucratic inertia could be addressed by allocating stimulus funds only to those government agencies that have prepared such a pool of ready projects. Slow-acting agencies could be penalized by having some of their funds transferred to agencies that will spend the funds with less delay.

None of these steps, however, will speed up the multiplier process itself. The full impact of any fiscal policy action necessarily will only be felt after a significant lag.

The likely effect of lags is to cause discretionary fiscal policy to be pro-cyclical rather than counter-cyclical.

- A pro-cyclical policy will cause business cycle swings to be larger; it will increase instability in the economy.

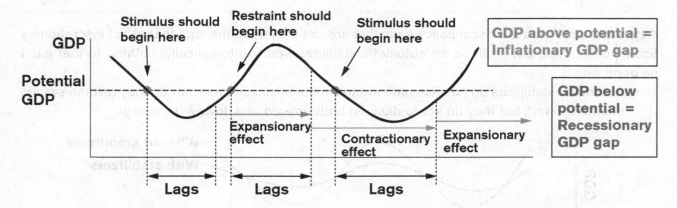

- Because of the lags, the expansionary effect is mostly felt when fiscal restraint is called for. The effect of fiscal policy is to further overheat the economy.
- Because of the lags, the contractionary effect is mostly felt when fiscal stimulus is called for. The effect of fiscal policy is to worsen the downturn.

If we know we are likely to apply any fiscal policy too late, why not simply start to apply it sooner? Since the end of World War II, the average length of expansions is about five years, while the average length of contractions is about one year. If lags add about a year to fiscal policy, why not start an expansionary policy four years into an expansion? With the lags delaying things by a year, the effect of the stimulus would start to be felt just when the expansion was starting to end—just when the stimulus is needed.

- If expansions and contractions were all of the same length, we could do this. However, the business cycle is highly variable in length. A fixed schedule for fiscal policy would work badly.

Here is what would have happened over the last forty years if we had used a five-year schedule for stimulus:

Start of expansion	Start stimulus	Contraction occurred	Result of policy
1971	1974	1973	Too late: recession is over before stimulus is felt
1976	1979	1980	Good timing: stimulus moderates the recession
1983	1986	1990	Too soon: stimulus overheats the economy
1992	1995	2001	Too soon: stimulus overheats the economy
2002	2005	2008	Too soon: stimulus overheats the economy

Any other schedule will show similarly poor results.

6. AUTOMATIC STABILIZERS

Automatic stabilizers are fiscal policy tools that are not subject to the lags that afflict discretionary fiscal policy. They are things such as federal income taxes and unemployment insurance that act promptly, appropriately, and without anyone needing to pay attention, to dampen swings in the business cycle.

Automatic stabilizers are fiscal policy tools that are not subject to the lags that afflict discretionary fiscal policy. Once put in place, an automatic stabilizer works automatically; nothing further must be done with it.

- Automatic stabilizers do not eliminate swings in the business cycle, nor do they reverse swings once they start, but they do act to dampen both upward and downward swings.

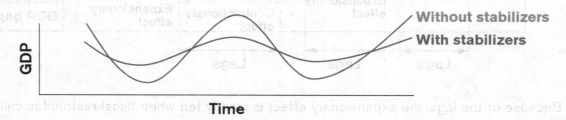

The most important automatic stabilizers are income and social insurance taxes, unemployment insurance, and means-tested welfare programs. Consider how these programs react to swings in the business cycle.

When a contraction starts, businesses cut back on production and lay off some workers. Household income falls as unemployment rises. Consumption declines because of the fall in income, and this further reduces aggregate expenditures in the familiar multiplier process.

- Those workers who are no longer receiving a paycheck are also no longer having withholdings for income tax and Social Security tax taken out of their paychecks. Lower household income means lower income tax liability. The decline in income tax offsets part of the fall in income, so that disposable income does not fall as far as it otherwise would.
- Newly unemployed workers are likely to be eligible to receive state unemployment insurance payments. These benefits vary from state to state, but can replace up to fifty percent of lost earnings.
- Households which lose a wage earner to unemployment might then qualify for food stamps or other government transfer programs designed to aid low-income families. Receipt of such benefits offsets part of the loss in income.

As a result of the automatic stabilizers offsetting part of the decline in household disposable income, aggregate expenditures do not fall as far as they otherwise would. This means that the multiplier effect is also proportionately smaller. The business cycle contraction is not ended, but it is not as severe as it would have been in the absence of the automatic stabilizers.

When an expansion starts, businesses ramp up production and hire additional workers. Household income rises as unemployment falls. Consumption rises because of the increase in income, and this further increases aggregate expenditures in the familiar multiplier process.

- Those newly hired workers who now receive a paycheck also now have withholdings taken out of that paycheck for income tax and Social Security tax. Higher household income means higher income tax liability. The rise in income tax offsets part of the rise in income, so that disposable income does not increase as much as it otherwise would.
- Rehired workers are no longer eligible to receive state unemployment insurance payments.
- Households that gain a wage earner might no longer qualify for food stamps or other government transfer programs designed to aid low-income families. The loss of such benefits offsets part of the increase in income.

As a result of the automatic stabilizers offsetting part of the increase in household disposable income, aggregate expenditures do not rise as far as they otherwise would. This means that the multiplier effect is also proportionately smaller. The business cycle expansion is not ended, but it is not as pronounced as it would have been in the absence of the automatic stabilizers.

The genius of automatic stabilizers is that they act promptly, appropriately, and without anyone needing to pay attention.

- Promptly: The impact on a worker's disposable income is felt as soon as they receive (or miss) a paycheck. There is bureaucratic hassle involved in applying for unemployment insurance, food stamps, and other support programs, but little delay in receiving the benefits.
- Appropriately: Automatic stabilizers cushion any fall in income (what should happen in downturns), and dampen any rise in income (what should happen in an overheating economy).
- Without anyone paying attention: Tax withholding rises and falls along with income according to preset formulas. The government employees who administer support programs have established eligibility rules to follow. For payments to increase, the only person who has to notice anything is the worker who has lost their job—and that is hard for them to overlook!

Business cycles in the U.S. since the end of World War II have been much improved over previous periods. Expansions have tended to last much longer, while recessions have tended to be much shorter and milder.

- This improvement is probably the result of the growth in automatic stabilizers.
- Individual income and social insurance taxes were only 15.2% of federal government receipts in 1934, but had grown to 69.9% in 1970, and 81.6% in 2013.
- State unemployment insurance programs began during the great depression in the 1930s.
- The Food Stamp program began in 1939. It, and other means-tested support programs, expanded greatly in the 1960s.

7. IS DISCRETIONARY FISCAL POLICY EFFECTIVE?

Fiscal policy is effective if it is applied at the right time, in the right amount, and in the right direction. There are good reasons for doubting that discretionary fiscal policy will be effective, and the historical record supports this.

What is necessary for discretionary fiscal policy to be effective? It must be applied:
- In the right direction: Expansionary policy during a recession, and contractionary policy when the economy is overheated.
- In the right amount: The size of the fiscal policy action is commensurate to the size of the recessionary or inflationary GDP gap.
- At the right time: So that the expansionary (contractionary) impact of the fiscal policy action is felt most strongly when it is most needed, and fades away when it is no longer needed.

If these three conditions are not met, then discretionary fiscal policy, rather than damping down the swings in the business cycle, might actually make them worse.

There are good reasons for doubting that discretionary fiscal policy will be effective.
- The government bias in favor of increased government spending means that expansionary fiscal policies are much more likely to be applied than contractionary policies, regardless of what economic conditions call for.
- Conceptual difficulties in measuring the size of recessionary or inflationary GDP gaps, or the size of the multiplier, means that we can only guess at the right amount of stimulus or restraint.
- The lags that are inherent in the process of designing and implementing fiscal policy mean that discretionary fiscal policy actions are unlikely to ever be applied at precisely the right time.

A further impediment is that fiscal policy is an intensely political process. There are substantive philosophical differences between the major political parties on the appropriate role of the government in stabilizing the macro economy (reflected in the differing policy prescriptions of the various schools of economic thought). The distributional effects of fiscal policy (there are always winners and losers) guarantees acrimony.

It is even hard to tell if a fiscal policy action "worked" or not. If, after a stimulus action, the economy does not strongly recover, does this mean:
- The policy failed because it was bad policy?
- The policy failed, but only because the stimulus wasn't strong enough?
- The policy succeeded because it prevented the recession from being even worse?

The lessons of history do not end the arguments about the effectiveness of fiscal policy; they merely give each side something else to argue about.

If discretionary fiscal policy were well-timed, there should in general be a negative relationship between growth in government spending and growth in real GDP. When GDP growth is slow, we should see a speedup in government spending (a stimulus). When GDP growth is fast, we should see a slowdown in government spending (fiscal restraint).

- It is difficult to see any particular relationship in the chart below.
- Either fiscal policy is poorly timed, or government spending is driven by goals other than stabilizing the macro economy.

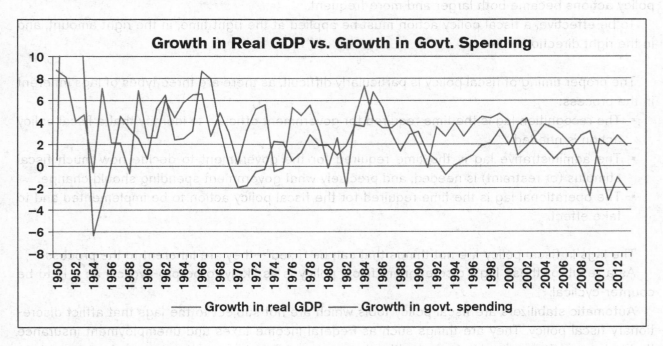

The historical record supports this view of discretionary fiscal policy. Consider, for example:

- **Buildup at the start of World War II:** There was a huge expansion in government spending from 1941–1943. This finally ended the Great Depression, as unemployment virtually vanished. A triumph for fiscal policy? Hardly. The purpose of the expansion was to meet the demands of war. Macroeconomic stabilization was a happy by-product, not the goal.
- **Vietnam War:** Government spending increased significantly in the late 1960s, even though the economy was growing robustly. The inappropriate fiscal stimulus contributed to the economy overheating and set off serious inflation. Political considerations overrode the goal of economic stabilization.
- **The roaring 90s:** The decade of the 1990s started with a recession, but then saw almost uninterrupted economic growth. Again, stabilization was secondary. The primary goal in the 1990s was reducing the federal budget deficit. Fiscal policy was actually contractionary during the recession at the start of the decade.

SUMMARY OF CHAPTER 9

Fiscal policy is government action taken to counteract the business cycle. It involves changing government expenditures, changing tax receipts, or changing government transfer payments.

During a recession, an expansionary fiscal policy is appropriate. When the economy is over-heated, a contractionary fiscal policy is appropriate.

The U.S. first practiced fiscal policy during the Great Depression. After World War II, U.S. fiscal policy actions became both larger and more frequent.

To be effective, a fiscal policy action must be applied at the right time, in the right amount, and in the right direction.

The proper timing of fiscal policy is particularly difficult, as there are three types of lags inherent in the process:

- The recognition lag is the time required for government officials to identify that a fiscal policy action is needed.
- The administrative lag is the time required for the government to decide how much fiscal stimulus (or restraint) is needed, and precisely what government spending should change.
- The operational lag is the time required for the fiscal policy action to be implemented and to take effect.

The lags in fiscal policy are not things that can be "fixed"—they are inherent to the process.

As a result of these lags, discretionary fiscal policy is as likely to be pro-cyclical as it is to be counter-cyclical.

Automatic stabilizers are fiscal policy tools which are not subject to the lags that afflict discretionary fiscal policy. They are things such as Federal income taxes and unemployment insurance that act promptly, appropriately, and without anyone needing to pay attention, to dampen swings in the business cycle.

There are good reasons for doubting that discretionary fiscal policy will be effective, and the historical record supports this.

CH[...] TEN

FEDERAL BUDGET

The federal budget can be viewed online at: **www.gpo.gov/ fdsys/browse/collectionGDP.action?collectionCode= BUDGET**

The federal government runs a deficit any year that government expenditures exceed tax receipts. The U.S. debt is the aggregated total of the yearly deficits and surpluses.

The main argument against balancing the federal budget is that it would weaken the government's ability to counteract the business cycle. The main argument for balancing the federal budget is to counteract government bias toward ever-increasing spending.

1. COMPARISON OF FEDERAL BUDGET TO HOUSEHOLD BUDGET

As compared to an individual household's budget, the federal budget is huge, complex, involves many people and much time, and is massively documented. Nevertheless, both must balance income and expenditures, and both have a large "unavoidable" component.

The federal budget of the United States is very large and complex. Nevertheless, it shares some important characteristics with the much smaller and simpler budget for an individual household.

Creating a household budget involves balancing income and expenses. Your spending is ultimately limited by your available income. A household budget is a tool to assist in purchasing the optimal combination of goods and services, subject to an income constraint.

Some items in a household's budget will be unavoidable. Certain types of expenditures must be made.

1. Payments promised for prior spending. For example:
   - If you borrowed when you bought a car, you must make your monthly payment on that loan.
   - If you took out a mortgage when you bought a house, or signed a contract when you rented an apartment, you must make your monthly payments.
   - If you keep a balance on a credit card, you must make a minimum monthly payment.

2. Payments necessary to support life. For example:
   - One must eat, so some expenditures on food are unavoidable.
   - One can't go about naked, so some expenditures on clothing are unavoidable.
   - Likewise for housing, medical care, and other essentials.

It's not that one can't skip an "unavoidable" expense, but rather that it is costly to do so. For example:
- If you stop paying on your auto loan, the title holder will repossess your car.
- If you miss a payment on a credit card, the company may raise your interest rate to a punishingly high level.

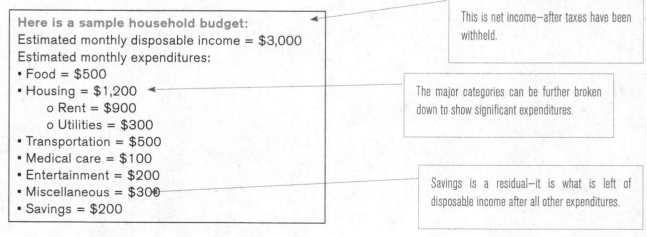

Here is a sample household budget:
Estimated monthly disposable income = $3,000
Estimated monthly expenditures:
- Food = $500
- Housing = $1,200
  - Rent = $900
  - Utilities = $300
- Transportation = $500
- Medical care = $100
- Entertainment = $200
- Miscellaneous = $300
- Savings = $200

This is net income—after taxes have been withheld.

The major categories can be further broken down to show significant expenditures.

Savings is a residual—it is what is left of disposable income after all other expenditures.

There are several ways in which an individual household's budget differs from the federal budget.

A. The number of persons involved in preparing the budget

Household budget: Only a few persons are involved—the head of the household, perhaps their spouse or parents, perhaps some major creditors.

Federal budget: Tens of thousands of persons are involved—budget offices of every federal agency, Office of Management and Budget, Congress, the president, an army of lobbyists.

B. The time required to prepare the budget

Household budget: Very little—couple of hours to sketch it out, maybe a couple of hours a week thereafter keeping track of how you're doing.

Federal budget: Millions of hours—the annual federal budget process actually takes at least eighteen months, so the budget offices of federal agencies are typically working on more than one year's budget at any point in time.

C. The size of the budget

Household budget: Seldom covers more than $100,000.

Federal budget: Over $3 trillion, and getting bigger all the time.

D. Formality of the budget process

Household budget: Pretty informal—might be written down, might not be; perhaps uses a software package like Quicken or Microsoft Money. Drafted and modified at need.

Federal budget: Highly structured, and massively documented—a mountain of paper and electronic files every year. Specific products expected on specific dates.

There are also several important ways in which a household's budget is similar to the federal budget.

E. Both must balance income and expenditures.

If a household spends more than their disposable income, they must go into debt (borrow) to make up the difference.

If the government spends more than it collects in tax revenue, it must go into debt (borrow) to make up the difference.

F. Both have large unavoidable components

For a household: payments for past spending (loans, credit card debt) and items essential to life.

For the government: Interest payment on the debt, legal obligations (Social Security, employee pensions, means-tested welfare programs), and items inherent to government (national defense, money supply).

G. Both are the source of numerous headaches, fights, tension, and hard feelings.

2. THE FEDERAL BUDGET PROCESS

There are four major steps in the federal budget process:
1. **The president develops a proposed budget.**
2. **Congress modifies the proposed budget.**
3. **The President signs or vetoes each budget bill.**
4. **Federal agencies then spend money and collect taxes.**

These are the four major steps in the federal budget process.

Step #1: The president develops a proposed budget

All of the activity takes place within the executive branch of the government. Each government agency develops its own budget document. This budget document includes:
- A description of the funding structure for the agency
- Funding from the previous year as a starting level for this budget
- Description of incremental changes from the previous year's budget, with reasons for changes
- Description of new program initiatives, with justifications for the new programs

The budget document is largely prepared by the agency's budget office, but relies on input from managers across the agency.

Each agency's proposed budget is reviewed at a higher level within the executive branch (usually at a departmental level). There is back and forth negotiation between agency and department until a departmentally approved document is ready. This then goes for review at the Office of Management and Budget. Again there is back and forth negotiation until the department-level document is approved for inclusion in the President's budget.

The entire process takes about a year and a half. Work on the Fiscal Year 2015 budget (which went into effect on October 1, 2014) started in July 2012. The president traditionally sends his budget to Congress in February.

Step #2: Congress modifies the president's proposed budget

Heads of the individual government agencies appear before Congress to testify and answer questions about their agency's proposed budget. There are separate hearings in both the House of Representatives and in the Senate. Congressional committees propose changes to specific items in the budget, vote on the changes in committee, then pass the modified budget to the full chamber for debate and vote.

If the House and the Senate each pass a different version of a budget bill, then the two bills go to a joint House/Senate conference committee. The joint committee reconciles differences in the bills, and then sends the reconciled bill back to both chambers for another vote. This process repeats until both sides of Congress have passed the identical bill.

The legislative budget process is intended to take no more than eight months. It is intended that each agency's budget be passed before the start of the fiscal year in October. When (as often happens) the budget bills are not passed by October, Federal agencies either shut down or operate under a continuing resolution which allows them to spend money at the same rate as in the previous year.

To illustrate the impact of the legislative review, the following table shows part of the budget for one government agency (the U.S. Geological Survey) for fiscal year 2010.

	FY2009 budget	Proposed FY2010	House version	Senate version	Enacted FY2010
Geographic Research					
Remote sensing	61,718	62,057	63,707	62,057	63,707
Geographic analysis	10,598	11,135	44,135	11,135	11,135
Geospatial program		70,748	70,748	70,748	70,748
Geologic Hazards					
Earthquake	55,760	56,201	57,021	56,021	57,021
Volcano	23,901	24,171	24,171	24,421	24,421
Landslide	3,350	3,405	3,405	3,405	3,405

Proposed budget amounts generally increase somewhat.

House and Senate changes generally are small.

Here is a budget item new for 2010.

Conference committees generally go with the higher option.

Step #3: The president either signs or vetoes each budget bill in its entirety.

If the President vetoes a bill, it goes back to Congress. Congress then either modifies the bill until it meets with the president's approval or votes to override the veto and enact the budget bill over the president's disapproval.

At one point Congress voted to allow the president to veto individual portions of a budget bill (the line-item veto), but the Supreme Court ruled that this violated the Constitution.

Step #4: Federal agencies actually spend money and collect taxes

A Federal agency must have either an approved budget or a continuing resolution in order to operate.

Budget Timeline for Fiscal Year 2015

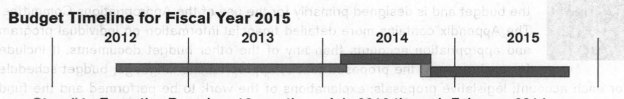

| 2012 | 2013 | 2014 | 2015 |

Step #1: Executive Branch : 18 months : July 2012 through February 2014
Step #2: Legislative Branch : 8 months : February 2014 through September 2014
Step #3: President signs : 1 month : September 2014
Step #4: Federal agencies : 12 months : October 2014 through September 2015

3. FEDERAL BUDGET DOCUMENTS

The federal budget can be viewed online at: www.whitehouse.gov/omb/budget/ and at www.gpo.gov/fdsys/browse/collectionGDP.action?collectionCode=BUDGET.

The Federal budget is published by the Government Printing Office. It can be viewed online at:
- **www.whitehouse.gov/omb/budget/ or**
- **www.gpo.gov/fdsys/browse/collectionGDP.action?collectionCode=BUDGET**

- Fiscal Year 2015
  ± Budget of the U. S. Government
     Barack H. Obama. Tuesday, March 4, 2014

Contains the Budget Message of the President, information on the President's priorities, budget overviews organized by agency, and summary tables.
These are the 4 main components of the budget.

> These are the 4 main components of the budget.

± Analytical Perspectives
Barack H. Obama. Monday, March 10, 2014.

Contains analyses that are designed to highlight specified subject areas or provide other significant presentations of budget data that place the budget in perspective. This volume includes economic and accounting analyses; information on Federal receipts and collections; analyses of Federal spending; information on Federal borrowing and debt: baseline or current services estimates, and other technical presentations. The Analytical Perspectives volume also contains supplemental material with several detailed tables, including tables showing the budget by agency and account and by function, subfunction, and program that is available on the Internet and as a CD-ROM in the printed document.

± Appendix
Tuesday, March 4, 2014.

Contains detailed information on the various appropriations and funds that constitute the budget and is designed primarily for the use of the Appropriations Committees. The Appendix contains more detailed financial information on individual programs and appropriation accounts than any of the other budget documents. It includes for each agency: the proposed text of appropriations language; budget schedules for each account; legislative proposals; explanations of the work to be performed and the funds needed and proposed general provisions applicable to the appropriations of entire agencies or group of agencies. Information is also provided on certain activities whose transactions are not part of the budget totals.

± Historical Tables

Barack H. Obama. Monday. March 10, 2014.

Provides data on budget receipts, outlays, surpluses or deficits. Federal debt, and Federal employment over an extended time period generally from 1940 or earlier to 2015 or 2019. To the extent feasible, the data have been adjusted to provide consistency with the 2015 Budget and to provide comparability over time.

Here is budget detail from the Appendix. It is for the Agricultural Research Service, an agency of the Department of Agriculture.

Program and Financing (in millions of dollars)

Identification code 12–1400–0–1–352	2013 actual	2014 est.	2015 est.
Obligations by program activity:			
0001 Product quality/value added	93	99	95
0002 Livestock production	70	87	82
0003 Crop production	211	216	218
0004 Food safety	89	102	97
0005 Livestock protection	54	74	71
0006 Crop protection	171	181	174
0007 Human nutrition research	79	86	86
0008 Environmental stewardship	175	200	199
0009 National Agricultural Library	21	24	24
0010 Repair and maintenance of facilities	18	20	20
0011 Decentralized GSA and Security Payments			5
0012 Homeland security	33	33	33
0014 Miscellaneous Fees/Supplementals		9	
0799 Total direct obligations	1,014	1,131	1,104
0881 Reimbursable program activity	137	137	137
0889 Reimbursable program activities, subtotal	137	137	137
0900 Total new obligations	1,151	1,268	1,241

Enacted total from last year

Request in president's budget this year

Selected economic assumptions used in 2014 federal budget:

	Actual	Projections			
	2012	2013	2014	2015	2016
Growth rate, nominal GDP	4.6	3.2	4.6	5.2	5.3
Inflation rate, CPI	2.1	1.4	1.6	2.0	2.1
Unemployment rate	8.1	7.5	6.9	6.4	6.0
3-month interest rate	0.1	0.1	0.1	0.3	1.2

Some of the more valuable historical tables:

Table 1.1: Summary of Receipts, Outlays, and Surpluses or Deficits

Table 2.1: Receipts by Source: 1934–2019

Table 2.4: Composition of Social Insurance and Retirement Receipts and of Excise Taxes: 1940–2019

Table 4.1: Outlays by Agency: 1962–2019

Table 6.1: Composition of Outlays: 1940–2019

Table 7.1: Federal Debt at the End of Year: 1940–2019

Table 8.5: Outlays for Mandatory and Related Programs: 1962–2019

Table 8.7: Outlays for Discretionary Programs: 1962–2019

Table 9.1: Total Investment Outlays for Major Public Physical Capital, Research and Development

4. DEFICIT AND DEBT

The federal government runs a deficit any year that government expenditures exceed tax receipts. It runs a surplus any year that tax receipts exceed government expenditures. The U.S. debt is the aggregated total of the yearly deficits and surpluses.

The federal government runs a deficit any year that it spends more than it collects in taxes. It runs a surplus any year that it spends less than it collects in taxes.

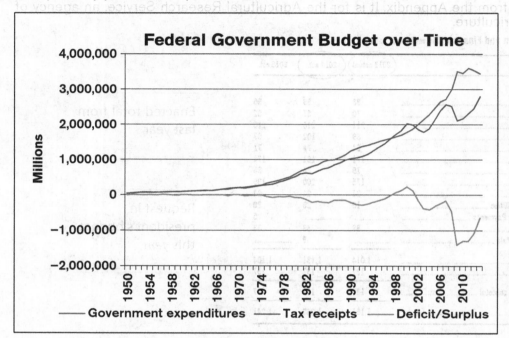

Both government expenditures and tax receipts have grown rapidly over the past 50 years.

Federal deficits have grown greatly since the 2007-2008 economic crisis.

The U.S. debt is the aggregated total of the yearly deficits and surpluses.

The U.S. debt first exceeded $1 trillion in 1982.

The current U.S. debt just exceeded $17 trillion.

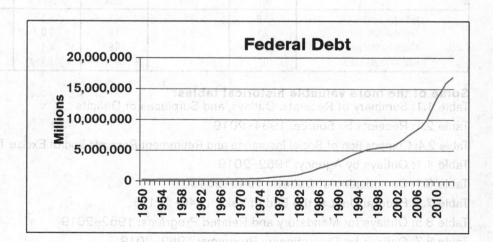

When a household spends more than its disposable income, it has to borrow to make up the difference. When a household borrows, it goes into debt—that is, someone else now has a claim on the household's future income.

It is the same with government. When the government spends more than it collects in taxes, it must borrow to make up the difference. The government borrows by selling government securities (Treasury bills). When an investor buys a Treasury bill, they are loaning their money to the government—and they will expect to get that money back, with interest.

Government debt differs from household debt in three important ways.

1. Household debt must someday be repaid. Fixed length loans must be repaid in sixty months or thirty years—whatever the length of the loan. Revolving loans (like a credit card) do not have a fixed repayment date, but must be settled at least upon the death of the card holder.
   - Government debt can be rolled over forever. Government need never settle up its debt. When securities come due, they can be paid off by the sale of new securities.

2. Household debt is almost exclusively owed to persons outside the household. When that debt is repaid, it is income leaving the household. The household becomes poorer when its debt is repaid.
   - Government debt is largely owed to ourselves (to Americans). When that debt is repaid, it is income moving within the nation—income is redistributed,

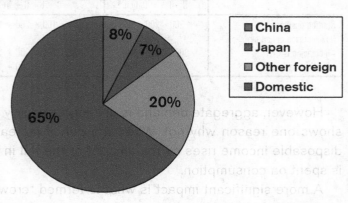

Distribution of U.S. Debt

- China
- Japan
- Other foreign
- Domestic

8%
7%
20%
65%

not lost. At present, almost two-thirds of U.S. debt is owed to ourselves rather than to foreigners.

3. Federal debt can be monetized. The government can reduce the real value of its debt simply by causing inflation. Inflation reduces the purchasing power of the dollar, so the government then can pay off its creditors with dollars that are worth less in real terms.
   - A household does not have this option for reducing the real value of its debt.

5. IMPACT OF DEFICIT ON AGGREGATE DEMAND

For any given level of government spending, a larger deficit means a greater net increase in aggregate demand. This is because tax receipts reduce disposable income, and thereby reduce consumption. However, aggregate demand is unlikely to rise by the full amount of the deficit.

All else being equal, a larger federal budget deficit means a greater increase in aggregate demand. There are two ways the deficit can get larger.

1. For any given level of tax receipts, higher government spending will increase the size of the deficit.

   - Government expenditures are one component of aggregate demand, so AD rises.

2. For any given level of government spending, lower tax receipts will increase the size of the deficit.

   - Lower taxes increases disposable income for households, which leads to increased consumption; since consumption is a component of aggregate demand, AD rises.

Here is a numerical example demonstrating the increase in aggregate demand:

	G – Tax = Deficit	C + I + G + NE = AD	
Starting position	200 – 200 = 0	600 + 100 + 200 + 100 = 1000	
Now increase deficit by:			
Increasing G	300 – 200 = 100	600 + 100 + 300 + 100 = 1100	
Decreasing Taxes	200 – 100 = 100	680 + 100 + 200 + 100 = 1080	← **MPC = 80%**

However, aggregate demand is unlikely to rise by the full amount of the deficit. The table above shows one reason why not. When the deficit increases as a result of a fall in taxes, consumers' disposable income rises by the amount of the fall in tax; but not all of the new disposable income is spent on consumption.

A more significant impact is what is termed "crowding out." Crowding out occurs in the market for loanable funds. When the government runs a deficit, it must borrow funds to cover the deficit. The government does this by selling securities. The funds that go to government are no longer available to fund business investment. Some private investment is "crowded out" by the government borrowing.

Market for Loanable Funds

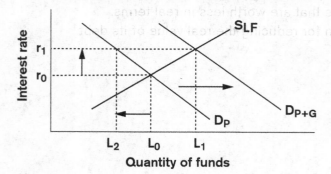

$L_1 - L_2$ = **Deficit**
$L_1 - L_0$ = **Increase in investment funds**
$L_0 - L_2$ = **Decrease in business investment**

Explanation of the graph:

The government enters the market to borrow funds to cover the deficit.

- This increases the demand for funds from D_P to D_{P+G}.

There is now excess demand at the original interest rate r_0.

- This causes interest rates to rise from r_0 to r_1.

Higher interest rates make investment more expensive for business firms.

- They reduce their investment from L_0 to L_2.

Part of the increase in aggregate demand caused by the government running a deficit is offset by the decreased investment by business firms.

The government budget deficit also has an impact on the foreign trade sector. This happens in two ways.

1. When consumers' disposable income rises, they purchase more goods, both domestic and foreign. A rise in imports, while exports are constant, leads to a fall in net exports.

2. The rise in interest rates makes U.S. securities more attractive to foreigners. This increases the value of the dollar in foreign markets (in effect, foreign goods become cheaper for Americans, and American goods become more expensive for foreigners). This reduces exports, increases imports, and decreases the net exports component of aggregate demand.

There is one other way in which a government budget deficit might affect consumers. Consumers see the government running a deficit today, and realize this means that taxes are likely to be raised in the future to pay off this deficit. Anticipating higher future taxes, some consumers increase their savings now in order to be ready for the expected higher future taxes. The idea that households will reduce consumption now to support higher taxes in the future is called Ricardian equivalence. The effect is theoretically possible, but there is little empirical evidence that it actually occurs.

Here is how the previous numerical example changes because of the various offsets:

	G – Tax = Deficit	C + I + G + NE = AD
Starting position	200 – 200 = 0	600 + 100 + 200 + 100 = 1000
Increase govt. spending:	300 – 200 = 100	
Without offsets		600 + 100 + 300 + 100 = 1100
With offsets		580 + 50 + 300 + 80 = 1010

Consumption offset by increase in imports and Ricardian equivalence.
Investment offset by crowding out.
Net exports offset by rising imports and falling exports.

6. HIGH EMPLOYMENT DEFICIT

All else being equal, the federal deficit will vary along with the business cycle—deficits will grow during recessions and shrink during expansions. The "high employment" deficit is how large the deficit would be if the economy were at the level of potential GDP.

All else being equal, the federal budget deficit will vary along with the business cycle.
- Deficits will grow during recessions.
- Deficits will shrink during expansions.

This happens because of the activity of automatic stabilizers. The most important of these are the federal income tax and state unemployment insurance programs. During a recession, workers get laid off and household income falls.
- Household tax liabilities automatically fall along with income.
- Unemployment insurance programs replace some of the workers' lost income.
- Both of these actions (increased government spending and reduced tax receipts) increase the federal deficit.

During an expansion, the process works in the opposite direction.

The "high employment" deficit is what the Federal deficit would be if the economy were operating at the level of potential GDP.

During a recession, the high employment deficit is lower than the measured deficit.

The value of the "high employment" deficit concept is that it identifies the extent to which the existing federal deficit might be a long-term problem. When the high employment deficit is small, this indicates that the current budget imbalance is temporary, caused by a short-run swing in the business cycle. When the high employment deficit is large, this indicates a fundamental imbalance between government spending and tax receipts—the problem will not go away on its own.

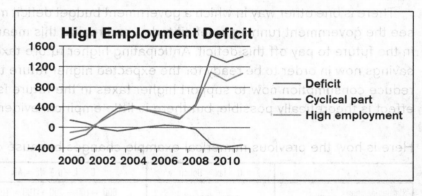

The difficulty with using the high employment deficit is the familiar problem that we can't accurately measure the level of potential GDP.
- If we estimate potential GDP to be higher than it actually is, then we downplay the long-term problems of a large current deficit.
- If we estimate potential GDP to be lower than it actually is, then we get unduly concerned with the long-term problems of a relatively small current deficit.

7. SHOULD WE BALANCE THE FEDERAL BUDGET?

One of the most controversial questions in macroeconomics is whether we should balance the federal budget. Different schools of economic thought give very different answers to this question, and to the wisdom of a balanced budget amendment to the Constitution.

One of the most controversial questions in macroeconomics is whether we should balance the federal budget. Different schools of economic thought give very different answers to this question.

- Classical: Yes—just as it is for households and businesses, it is fiscally irresponsible for the government not to live within its means.
- Keynesian: No—fiscal policy is the government's main tool for stabilizing the macro economy; it would be irresponsible to balance the budget during a recession.
- Monetarist: Yes in theory, but No in practice—government is biased toward increased spending; without the constraint of balancing the budget, government is all too likely to act irresponsibly.

Hear what different folks say about balancing the federal budget, and about the wisdom of a balanced budget amendment to the Constitution.

Thomas Jefferson: *"I wish it were possible to obtain a single amendment to our Constitution; an article taking from the Federal Government the power of borrowing."*

Thomas Sowell: *"Balanced budget requirements seem more likely to produce accounting ingenuity than genuinely balanced budgets."*

Ross Perot: *"The budget should be balanced, the treasury should be refilled, the public debt should be reduced and the arrogance of public officials should be controlled."*

William Feather: *"A budget tells us what we can't afford, but it doesn't keep us from buying it."*

Herman Cain: *"I believe we should cut the salaries of senators and congressmen 10 percent until they balance the budget."*

Jacob Lew: *"The budget is not just a collection of numbers, but an expression of our values and aspirations."*

Dilbert: *"Never base your budget requests on realistic assumptions, as this could lead to a decrease in your funding."*

What explains these wildly divergent opinions? At heart, they represent two fundamentally different world views.

World View #1: A market economy is basically robust and stable. External shocks are adjusted to quickly and efficiently. Market participants act rationally and are generally well informed. The main function of government is to provide a secure legal framework for the economy. Government intervention in markets usually causes problems.

World view #2: Market economies are fragile and volatile. External shocks can cause serious disruptions with long-lasting repercussions. Investors are driven by animal passions and the herd instinct, and market participants in general are woefully uninformed. The main function of government is to direct and stabilize the economy. Government intervention is needed in many areas to correct market imperfections.

It is not surprising that persons with one world view will disagree with those who hold the other world view.

7.1. INVESTMENT VS. CONSUMPTION SPENDING

There are both wise and foolish reasons for going into debt. Debt that finances productive investment can be repaid from increased future income. Debt that finances current consumption makes us poorer in the future.

There are both wise and foolish reasons for going into debt. Debt that finances productive investment can be repaid from increased future earnings. Debt that finances current consumption makes us poorer in the future when the debt is repaid.

Examples of wise household debt:

Student loan: This is wise debt because it is an investment in an individual's human capital. The college degree financed by student loan debt increases a person's future earnings potential. The more education you have, the more likely you are to find a job, and the higher the salary you are likely to earn. The student loan debt can be repaid from the higher future earnings, and you are left better off than if you hadn't taken on that debt.

Home mortgage: This could be wise debt. Real estate usually increases in value over time. If you intend to live in the house for a number of years, you will probably enjoy capital gains from it. You can pay off the mortgage debt when you later sell the house.

Auto loan: This could be wise debt. Owning a car gives you more flexibility than relying on public transportation. Improved mobility could open up opportunities to find a better paying job. Then the loan could be repaid from your higher earnings.

Examples of wise government debt:

Wartime spending: This is wise debt simply because the downside risk is so great—losing a war can be very expensive. The economies of the losing sides in the two world wars were literally shattered. Avoiding such a loss is a wise reason for going into debt.

European kings often went into debt to finance aggression against their neighbors. The expectation being that they would pay off the debt out of the spoils of a successful war. This proved a risky policy, as their wars were not always successful.

Investment in infrastructure: This is wise debt because a buildup of infrastructure increases a nation's productive capacity and encourages growth. The debt incurred to make the initial investment can be repaid out of the higher tax receipts generated by a wealthier economy.

U.S. history is filled with examples of debt-financed public infrastructure investment.
- In the nineteenth century, the Erie Canal and the railroad network
- In the twentieth century, rural electrification and the interstate highway system

These contributed greatly to the economic growth of the country.

Examples of foolish household debt:

Credit card debt to pay for non-essential current consumption: "Non-essential" means you can do without it. "Current consumption" means here today and gone tomorrow. It is foolish to build up credit card debt to finance a lifestyle beyond your current means. Current consumption does not increase your earnings potential. When you pay off that debt, as eventually you must, you will be poorer for it. "Play today, pay tomorrow" can be attractive in the short run, but is a poor long-term strategy.

Borrowing for risky investments: The classic example is a gambler who goes to a loan shark to get $1000 to put on a long shot at the race track. But qualitatively this is no different from someone who invested in stocks on the margin in the 1920s, or someone who took out a big sub-prime mortgage in 2007. This is not foolish debt because there is no possibility of gain, but rather because there is such a significant risk of loss. Foolish to wager money you can't afford to lose.

Examples of foolish government debt:

Deficit funding of current consumption: As with a household, current consumption merely maintains the status quo. It is foolish for a government to spend more on its routine operations than it collects in tax revenue, because this is not sustainable in the long run. When a government routinely spends beyond its means, eventually its citizens lose confidence in it, and it is overthrown.

Deficit financing of current consumption is a recipe for disaster. It will become more and more tempting for the government to either monetize the debt through heavy inflation, or to repudiate the debt outright. Either action is very bad for the economy.

Politically driven redistribution: This involves taking money from a less-favored group and giving it to a more-favored group. This behavior is toxic to a democracy (and tends to be highly inefficient economically) under any circumstances, but is particularly so when deficit financed. With a balanced budget there is a limit to how much can be redistributed. There is no limit with deficit financing; to get more to redistribute, simply run a larger deficit!

Is the debt the U.S. is currently racking up, wise or foolish debt?

2013 Federal Budget	
Outlays	3682
Defense	652
Non-defense	611
Mandatory	2193
Interest	222
Receipts	2712
Deficit	919

Most current Federal outlays are for mandatory programs. This is largely Social Security and Medicare. These are redistributive programs, taking money from the young and giving it to the old.

Though not politically driven, this redistribution is pretty clearly for current consumption, not for investment. As such, this is probably foolish debt, and not sustainable in the long run.

7.2. EFFORTS TO CONTROL THE BUDGET

The Federal budget was generally balanced up until the 1930s, but the government has run persistent (and growing) deficits ever since. Numerous efforts have been made to control the budget, most unsuccessful. The basic problem is that the government does not like the only truly effective approach—reducing government spending.

The Federal budget was generally balanced up until the 1930s. The budget was not balanced every year, but was balanced over time. The typical pattern was for the government to run large deficits during wartime, and then to pay off the wartime debt by running surpluses during the peacetime years that followed. The chart below shows this pattern for the period of World War I and the peacetime decade that followed.

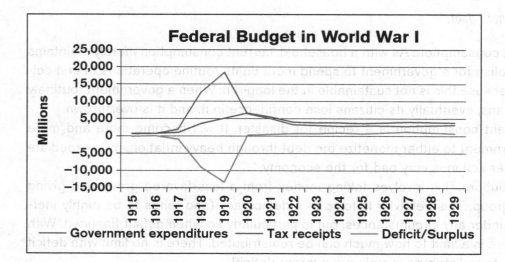

> Taxes did go up during the war years, but WWI was mostly financed by incurring debt.

> After the war, government spending dropped significantly, and there was a budget surplus every year for the next decade.

There was a widely held belief (both outside government and within it) that government officials have a moral responsibility to balance the federal budget. If households or businesses did not balance their budgets, they went bankrupt, and the responsible parties went to the poor house or to prison. The same standard held for government; for the government to fail to practice fiscal responsibility was a betrayal of the public trust.

This all ended in the 1930s. The U.S. government has run persistent (and growing) budget deficits ever since. What changed in the 1930s was the Great Depression and John Maynard Keynes. Keynes argued that the economy would not recover from the Great Depression on its own, but would only recover if the government increased aggregate demand by increasing government expenditures (and thereby running a deficit). Deficit spending during a recession was not fiscal irresponsibility, but was in fact just what the doctor ordered. The government's budget was fundamentally different from a household or business budget—recovery from a recession was a much higher priority than the old-fashioned desire to balance the budget.

Keynesian analysis provided politicians with a powerful moral rationale for doing something they were naturally inclined to want to do anyway—spend. Voters like to have the government provide services, and don't like to pay for those services with taxes. So politicians (who depend on voters to return them to office) like to spend and don't like to tax. This is a prescription for persistent federal budget deficits. Politicians' preference for spending was held in check until the 1930s by the belief that balancing the budget was fiscally responsible. Keynes destroyed that belief; with the restraint removed, budget deficits took over.

In the thirty years prior to 1930, the government ran budget surpluses in nineteen years. In the forty years after 1950, the government ran budget surpluses in only five years. It took over 200 years for the U.S. to accumulate $1 trillion in debt, but only four years (from 1982 to 1986) to double that to $2 trillion. Congress and the president both acknowledged that the federal budget was out of control, and began a thirty-year struggle to rein in deficits.

On the surface it appears that this should not be difficult. All that is needed to eliminate a budget deficit is either spending cuts or increased taxes. However, deciding precisely which programs to cut proved to be politically impossible. Congress could not agree.

- In 1985 the Gramm-Rudman Act, rather than cutting particular programs, enacted across-the-board cuts to all government programs. Congress quickly passed exemptions to this, and deficits continued.
- Having failed to cut spending, the 1990 tax increase was touted as the solution to deficits; tax revenues rose, but government spending rose also, and deficits continued.
- In 1996 both political parties joined in a bipartisan pledge to eliminate the deficit over the next seven years. Since the government had, at that point, run deficits for twenty-seven years running, the pledge was met with widespread skepticism.

Yet, only two years later (1998) the budget was in surplus, and remained in surplus through 2001. Something that had seemed politically impossible, was achieved. What happened? Strong economic growth in the 1990s increased tax receipts, and Congress refrained from passing large new spending bills—the country grew itself out of deficits.

This did not last long. Budget deficits returned in 2002, bigger than ever. In 2009–2011, the deficit exceeded $1 trillion every year. Again unable to decide which spending programs to cut, Congress in 2012 created sequestration, a new requirement for across-the-board spending cuts. And the following year they passed exemptions to this. As Yogi Berra said, "It's déjà vu all over again."

The basic problem is that government officials do not like the only truly effective approach to controlling the deficit, which is to reduce government spending. Government officials, whether elected or appointed, have a bias toward ever-increasing spending.

7.3. REASONS TO BALANCE OR NOT BALANCE

The main argument against balancing the federal budget is that it would weaken the government's ability to counteract the business cycle. The main argument for balancing the federal budget is to counteract government bias toward ever-increasing spending.

The main argument against balancing the federal budget is that it would weaken the government's ability to counteract the business cycle. Given that the principal task of macroeconomic policy makers is to stabilize the economy, this is a serious concern.

What does history tell us?

First, that stable economic growth is a valuable goal. The boom and bust is painful! Banking panics (recessions) ruin lives and destroy wealth.

Second, that without government intervention, there won't be stable growth. Prior to World War I, when the government first began trying to stabilize the macro economy, business cycles came fast and strong.

Third, that government stabilization policies actually help. Since the end of World War II, U.S. business cycles have been longer and milder. Much of the credit for this probably goes to automatic stabilizers.

How would balancing the budget every year affect this?

Balancing the federal budget every year would destroy the effectiveness of automatic stabilizers.

- During a recession, automatic stabilizers cause government spending to increase and tax receipts to fall. These actions offset part of the loss in disposable income that follows falling production and job layoffs, but also put the federal budget into deficit. To balance the budget the government would have to cut spending and increase taxes. These steps would further reduce disposable income and make the downturn worse.

- During an expansion, automatic stabilizers cause a reduction in government expenditures and an increase in tax receipts. These actions offset part of the rise in disposable income, and help to curb over exuberance, but also push the federal budget into surplus. To balance the budget, the government would have to increase spending and cut taxes. These steps would further increase disposable income and fuel an overheated economy.

These fears are not idle. In 1930, at the start of the Great Depression, the Hoover administration cut government spending in order to balance the federal budget. This made the economy worse.

- Ironically, in the presidential election of 1932, Franklin Roosevelt criticized Hoover for not balancing the budget in 1931 and 1932.

The main argument for balancing the federal budget is that this is the only way to counteract the government bias toward ever-increasing spending.

- Elected officials believe that voters send them to Washington to "do something"—new programs, new benefits, means more spending.
- Appointed officials believe in the value of what their agencies do, and argue always that they could do even more good if they only had more funding.

Given that the government bias toward spending is demonstrably true, this is a serious concern.

What does history tell us?

First, that when government balances its budget, government spending stays relatively small. By 1930, government spending accounted for only 3.4% of GDP.

Second, that when budget restraint is removed, government spending grows rapidly. Since 1930, government spending has grown to account for 20.8% of GDP.

Third, that the government, acting on its own, will not control its spending. Government officials, both those elected and those appointed, have strong incentives not to cut spending—they simply won't do it unless they are forced to do it.

How would balancing the budget every year affect this?

The requirement to balance the budget every year would change the incentives for elected officials. Politicians could no longer curry favor with voters by providing new government benefits and avoiding new taxes, because new spending could only be done if there were also new tax receipts to offset it.

Could we not combine the best features of both approaches, by balancing the federal budget, not every year, but over the course of the business cycle? That is, run deficits during downturns in the business cycle, and run surpluses during expansions, with the two offsetting each other.

- This would retain the desirable stabilization property of automatic stabilizers.
- But would also restrain the government bias toward spending.

This is equivalent to saying that we will keep the high employment deficit at zero.

As attractive as this proposal sounds, there are practical difficulties.

- We cannot directly measure the high employment deficit (because we can't directly measure potential GDP).
- Business cycle contractions/expansions are of variable length, and can't be known in advance.

What seems highly likely is that a policy of balancing the budget over the course of the business cycle would be too weak a restraint on government spending. Deficits would be run during downturns, but the surpluses during expansions would not.

SUMMARY OF CHAPTER 10

As compared to an individual household's budget, the federal budget is huge, complex, involves many people and much time, and is massively documented. Nevertheless, both the household budget and the federal budget must balance income and expenditures, and both have a large "unavoidable" component.

There are four major steps in the federal budget process:
1. The president develops a proposed budget.
2. Congress modifies the proposed budget.
3. The president signs or vetoes each budget bill.
4. Federal agencies then spend money and collect taxes.

The Federal budget can be viewed online at:
www.gpo.gov/fdsys/browse/collectionGDP.action:collecitonCode=BUDGET

The Federal government runs a deficit any year that government expenditures exceed tax receipts. It runs a surplus any year that tax receipts exceed government expenditures. The U.S. debt is the aggregated total of the yearly deficits and surpluses.

For any given level of government spending, a larger deficit means a greater net increase in aggregate demand. However, because of the crowding out effect on private investment, aggregate demand is unlikely to rise by the full amount of the deficit.

All else being equal, the federal deficit will vary along with the business cycle—deficits will grow during recessions and shrink during expansions. The "high employment" deficit is how large the deficit would be if the economy were at the level of potential GDP.

Different schools of economic thought have wildly divergent views on the wisdom of balancing the federal budget.

There are both wise and foolish reasons for going into debt. Debt which finances productive investment can be repaid from increased future income. Debt which finances current consumption makes us poorer in the future.

The main argument against balancing the federal budget is that it would weaken the government's ability to counteract the business cycle. The main argument for balancing the federal budget is to counteract government bias toward ever-increasing spending.

Credits

Fig 10.4: Office of Management and Budget, "Budget of the U.S. Government," www.whitehouse.gov/omb/budget/. Copyright in the Public Domain.

Fig 10.5: Office of Management and Budget, "Program and Financing," www.whitehouse.gov/omb/budget/. Copyright in the Public Domain.

CH ELEVEN
MONEY AND BANKS

The main function of money is to serve as a medium of exchange. In the U.S. the money supply is measured by the Federal Reserve System. M1 measures money used as a medium of exchange. The interest rate represents the price of money.

Major bank assets are reserves, loans, and securities. Major bank liabilities are deposits, borrowings, and bank capital. When a bank makes a loan, it creates money.

The Federal Reserve System regulates the banking sector and implements monetary policy.

1. FUNCTIONS OF MONEY

The main function of money is to serve as a medium of exchange. That is, transactions take place in terms of money. Other functions of money (serving as a store of value and as a unit of account) are incidental to its function as a medium of exchange.

The main function of money is to serve as a medium of exchange. Transactions take place in terms of money. We exchange goods and services for money rather than for other goods and services.

Barter is the direct exchange of one good or service for some other good or service (rather than for money). Barter does still occur in modern economies. For example:
- School children trading lunches (I'll trade you an apple for your bag of chips).
- Neighbors trading favors (We'll babysit your kids tonight, and you can babysit ours next week).
- Baseball card collectors (I'll give you a Roger Maris and a Yogi Berra for your Mickey Mantle).

As the examples suggest, barter is minor in a modern economy. This is because barter is a very inefficient way to exchange goods and services. Successful barter requires a double coincidence of wants.
- Say you have a chicken, but would rather have a pound of salt. In order to barter, you need to find someone who has a pound of salt, but would rather have a chicken.

Using money as a medium of exchange makes everything much easier.
- You sell your chicken for money (to anyone who wants a chicken—they don't need to have a pound of salt), then use the money you get to buy some salt (from anyone with salt to sell— they don't have to want a chicken).
- Although this requires two exchanges instead of barter's one exchange, both exchanges are vastly quicker and easier than satisfying that coincidence of wants.

Many different things have served as money throughout history. All share one critical feature: money is anything that you can take into a store and exchange for goods and services. To put this slightly differently, what defines money is people's willingness to accept it in exchange for goods and services.

The government generally declares what is used as money within a nation's boundaries, but it is people's willingness to accept it that actually makes it money. Something that had been money stops being money when people stop accepting it as money.
- In 1861, southern states seceded from the Union, and started issuing their own money— confederate dollars. The citizens of the Confederacy accepted confederate dollars in exchange for goods and services, so it was money. But by 1865, it was clear that the Confederacy was going to lose the war, and its citizens stopped accepting confederate dollars. At this point, confederate dollars were no longer used as a medium of exchange, and they stopped being money.

This works in the other direction as well; if people accept something as money, then it is money, even if the government says that it isn't.

- In towns along the border between the U.S. and Canada, store keepers are likely to accept payment in either U.S. dollars or Canadian dollars. (They will probably have a conversion table on hand.) According to the U.S. government, Canadian dollars are not legal tender in the United States. But that doesn't stop them from being money in U.S. border towns, where store owners accept Canadian dollars in exchange for goods and services.

Money does have functions other than as a medium of exchange. Money serves as a store of value and as a unit of account. However, these other functions of money are all incidental to its use as a medium of exchange.

Store of value

Money is a convenient way to store value over time. Say you slip a $100 bill between the pages of a book and leave it undisturbed for a year; when you retrieve it a year later, you can still exchange it for $100 worth of goods and services.

Saving is merely a way to transfer purchasing power from the present to the future. People can, and do, save things other than money.

- How many of us wish that we hadn't thrown out our childhood collections of comic books or trading cards? If we had kept them, we would now have to exchange them for money before we could purchase any other goods or services.

Money is a convenient way to save, because it is the medium of exchange. You know when you put aside money today, that you will be able to directly exchange it for your desired purchase in the future.

Unit of account

Money is the common denominator used to express the value (or price) of all goods and services. When going shopping for fruit, you don't have to remember that:

- 1 orange = 3 apples = 2 bananas = ¼ watermelon

Instead, the prices of all are expressed in terms of a common unit of account:

- Orange = $1.00; Apple = $0.33; Banana = $0.50; Watermelon = $4.00

Anything could be used as a common unit of account.

- You could, for example, express all prices in terms of their equivalent number of bottles of beer. (Orange = ½ bottle of beer; Apple = 1/6 bottle of beer; and so on.)

The dollar is simply the most convenient unit of account, because it is dollars that will actually be exchanged.

2. TYPES OF MONEY

Most money today is fiat money. Fiat money has little or no intrinsic value—it's good for nothing except to spend as money. In contrast, commodity money (for example, gold or silver coins) does have value in and of itself—commodity money has valued uses other than spending as money.

There are two general types of money: fiat money and commodity money. Until relatively recently almost all societies used commodity money. Today almost all societies use fiat money.

Dollar bill origami

Fiat money has little or no intrinsic value. That is, fiat money is good for nothing except to spend as money. Examples of modern fiat monies are the coins and folding paper money in your wallet or purse, and the electronic balances on your debit card. Coins and bills are not totally without other uses; for example:

- You can flip a coin to help you make a decision.
- Before circuit breakers, a copper penny could replace a fuse.
- Dollar bills can be folded into cute origami creations.
- During the 1890s, wealthy businessmen would light cigars with a $100 bill in an overt display of their wealth.

As the examples suggest, there is nothing of any import that can be done with today's coins and bills except to spend them as money. And electronic money is truly good for nothing else.

In contrast, commodity money does have value in and of itself. Commodity money has valued uses other than spending as money. The most common type of commodity money is gold or silver coins. Precious metal coins can be spent as money, but they can also be melted down and their gold or silver content used in jewelry, electronics, metallic thread, and so on. Some other examples of commodity money are:

- Cigarettes were used as money in German prisoner of war camps during World War II.
- Shells were used as money by Native Americans in the Pacific Northwest until the beginning of the twentieth century.
- Tobacco served as money in early Colonial Virginia.
- Salt was often used as money in ancient societies.

Whether fiat or commodity, an item chosen to serve as money must satisfy five criteria. Good money is:

1. Portable: Since you carry money with you in order to make purchases, good items to use as money will be small and light. Coins, bills, gems, and cigarettes all meet this criterion. Cotton bales would be a poor choice for use as money, because they are heavy and inconvenient to carry about.

2. Durable: If it is to be used as a store of value, money must last. Metal coins last for a very long time, paper bills less so. Poorer choices would be grains (which will rot), wine (easily spilled), or cigarettes (too flimsy).

3. Divisible: Because the items we buy have different prices, money needs to come in a variety of sizes. This is why there are different denominations of coins and bills. A debit card is fully divisible. Likewise, gold dust, salt, and wine are fully divisible. Precious gems, paintings, or rare books would not work well as money because they are not divisible at all.

4. Standardized: When all units of money come in the same shape, size, content, people can be confident in accepting it as face value. Wine would be a poor choice for use as money, since a gallon of wine can vary dramatically in quality.

5. Hard to counterfeit: If people can't tell fake money from real money, it won't be long before all money is fake. Merchants used to weigh gold coins to make sure they hadn't been clipped—that their content value matched their face value. The high-tech features in modern paper money are designed to foil counterfeiters.

Many of the coins that have been issued by the U.S. government are no longer found in circulation. Once the value of the metal content in a coin exceeds the coin's face value, people stop using that coin as money.

Value of metal content in selected U.S. coins (as of May 2014)	
Dime (1965–2014)	= 1.7 cents
Dime (1916–1964)	= $1.37
Quarter (1965–2014)	= 4.3 cents
Quarter (1916–1964)	= $3.42

← This is why the oldest dime or quarter you will find in circulation is from 1965.

Demand from coin collectors also causes some coins to disappear from circulation.

Value to collectors of selected U.S. coins (good quality)	
1909 Indian penny	= $8.05
1909 Lincoln penny	= $2.10
1938 Jefferson nickel	= $0.24
1967 Kennedy half dollar	= $4.00
2004 Wisconsin quarter (extra leaf)	= $24.20

Good idea to check your coins occasionally—you don't want to use older coins as money.

3. MEASURING THE MONEY SUPPLY

In the U.S., the money supply is measured by the Federal Reserve System. M1 measures money used as a medium of exchange. M2 is a broader measure that also includes near-monies.

In the United States, the money supply is measured by the Federal Reserve System. The Fed keeps track of the currency it has issued and collects information weekly from banks, credit unions, and other financial institutions on the sizes of the various accounts they hold.

There are two major measures of the money supply: M1 and M2. M1 corresponds to the stock of money immediately available for use as a medium of exchange. M1 money is what consumers can take into a store and exchange for goods and services.

There are four components of the M1 money supply measure.

- Currency in circulation: Coins and bills in the hands of the public. There are also bills and coins in bank vaults and in Federal Reserve Banks, but these are not included in M1.
- Traveler's checks: Fixed amount checks that are used in place of cash (mostly by persons on vacation—hence the name). They are safer than cash, because the issuer will replace them if they are stolen.
- Demand deposits: The amount of funds held in checking accounts issued by commercial banks.
- Other checkable deposits: The amount of funds held in checking accounts issued by financial institutions other than commercial banks. The main items here are Negotiable Order of Withdrawal (NOW) accounts and credit union share drafts. Other checkable accounts were developed to evade government regulatory restrictions on demand deposits—for all intents and purposes they are the same as demand deposits.

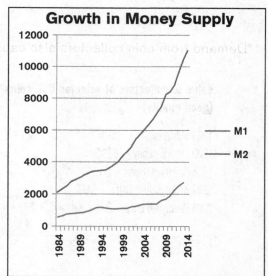

M2 is a broader measure of money. It includes both the medium of exchange money in M1 and also several near-monies. A near-money can't be directly used to make purchases, but it is relatively quick and easy to convert near-monies into money that can be directly used to make purchases.

The M2 measure of the money supply includes the four components of the M1 measure, plus:

- Savings deposits, Time deposits (CDs) under $100,000, Money-market deposits of individuals

The near-monies in M2 typically pay a higher interest rate to depositors. M1 monies typically pay no (or a very low) interest rate.

These screen shots all come from the Federal Reserve website.

Table 1
Money Stock Measures. Billions of dollars.

Date	Seasonally adjusted		Not seasonally adjusted	
	M1 [1]	M2 [2]	M1 [1]	M2 [2]
Dec. 2013	2,639.6	10,969.1	2,708.3	11,062.2
Jan. 2014	2,672.1	11,023.8	2,687.1	11,051.4
Feb. 2014	2,720.8	11,127.4	2,694.8	11,103.7
Mar. 2014	2,744.2	11,158.7	2,761.3	11,226.0

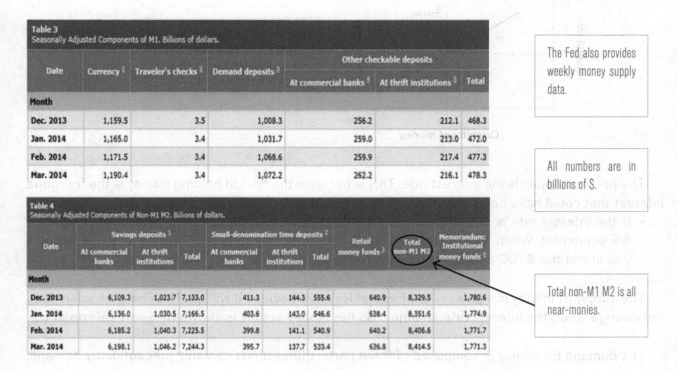

Table 3
Seasonally Adjusted Components of M1. Billions of dollars.

Date	Currency [1]	Traveler's checks [2]	Demand deposits [3]	Other checkable deposits		
				At commercial banks [4]	At thrift institutions [5]	Total
Month						
Dec. 2013	1,159.5	3.5	1,008.3	256.2	212.1	468.3
Jan. 2014	1,165.0	3.4	1,031.7	259.0	213.0	472.0
Feb. 2014	1,171.5	3.4	1,068.6	259.9	217.4	477.3
Mar. 2014	1,190.4	3.4	1,072.2	262.2	216.1	478.3

Table 4
Seasonally Adjusted Components of Non-M1 M2. Billions of dollars.

Date	Savings deposits [1]			Small-denomination time deposits [2]			Retail money funds [3]	Total non-M1 M2	Memorandum: Institutional money funds [4]
	At commercial banks	At thrift institutions	Total	At commercial banks	At thrift institutions	Total			
Month									
Dec. 2013	6,109.3	1,023.7	7,133.0	411.3	144.3	555.6	640.9	8,329.5	1,780.6
Jan. 2014	6,136.0	1,030.5	7,166.5	403.6	143.0	546.6	638.4	8,351.6	1,774.9
Feb. 2014	6,185.2	1,040.3	7,225.5	399.8	141.1	540.9	640.2	8,406.6	1,771.7
Mar. 2014	6,198.1	1,046.2	7,244.3	395.7	137.7	533.4	636.8	8,414.5	1,771.3

The Fed also provides weekly money supply data.

All numbers are in billions of $.

Total non-M1 M2 is all near-monies.

There are predictable seasonal variations in the money supply. Seasonal adjustment removes these variations and smooths out the monthly time series.

Currency		
2013	Seasonally adjusted	Not seasonally adjusted
Jan.	1096.7	1090.1
Feb.	1099.8	1100.6
June	1123.8	1125.0
July	1131.3	1130.3
Nov.	1153.2	1152.8
Dec.	1159.5	1162.0

Money supply is:
Higher than average in blue months
Lower than average in red months

4. THE MONEY MARKET

Money is a commodity (albeit a special one) and therefore is subject to the law of demand. The interest rate represents the price of money. The supply of money is set by the Federal Reserve.

Money is a commodity (albeit a special one) and therefore is subject to the law of demand. Here is a supply/demand model for the market for money.

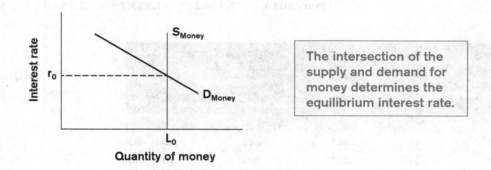

The intersection of the supply and demand for money determines the equilibrium interest rate.

The price of money is the interest rate. This is because the cost of holding money is the foregone interest that could have been earned if the money had been invested instead.

- If the interest rate is 5%, then holding $100 for a year costs you the opportunity of earning $5 in interest. When you simply hold the $100, in one year you will still have $100; while if you invest the $100 at 5%, in one year you will have $105.

The supply of money is whatever the Federal Reserve decides it will be. The Fed's decision does not change when the interest rate changes. So the money supply is shown by a vertical line at L_0.

The demand for money is composed of three parts: transactions demand, precautionary demand, and speculative demand.

- The transactions demand is the most important. People desire to hold money because they want to buy things, and money is the medium of exchange. The total amount of money people want to hold varies with changes in nominal GDP.
  - » Demand for money increases when there are more goods and services to buy (when real GDP rises).
  - » Demand for money increases when the price level rises (because now it takes more money to buy the same quantity of goods).
- The precautionary demand for money is closely related to the transactions demand. Since you never know when you might incur an unexpected expense, or come across a particularly good deal, you hold some extra money (above what you expect to spend) as a precaution.
- The speculative demand for money depends on peoples' expectations. If you expect interest rates to rise sharply in the future, you might not want to tie up your wealth in investments at the current low interest rate. You might speculate by holding more money now, in the hope of being able to invest at a higher interest rate in the future.

What happens in the money market if the demand for money changes?

- Assume that there is inflation, so nominal GDP rises.

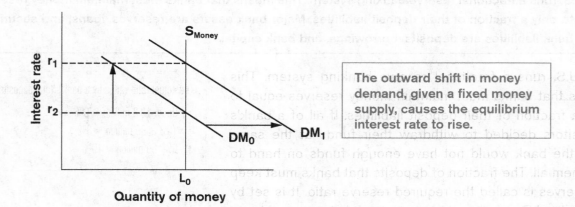

The outward shift in money demand, given a fixed money supply, causes the equilibrium interest rate to rise.

The higher interest rate will lead business firms to cut back on their investment spending. This is a movement up along the aggregate demand curve. This is the interest rate effect that helps explain why the aggregate demand curve slopes downward.

What happens if the Fed changes the supply of money?

- Assume that the Fed increases the money supply.

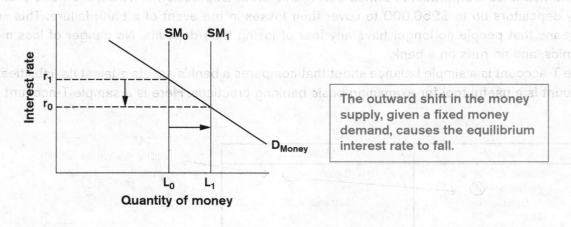

The outward shift in the money supply, given a fixed money demand, causes the equilibrium interest rate to fall.

There is one important qualification to these conclusions: does the "all else being equal" assumption hold? That is, if the Fed increases the money supply, will the demand for money remain unchanged?

- This will be explored in more detail in chapter 12.

5. THE BANKING SYSTEM

The U.S. runs a fractional reserve banking system. This means that banks must maintain money reserves equal to only a fraction of their deposit liabilities. Major bank assets are reserves, loans, and securities. Major bank liabilities are deposits, borrowings, and bank capital.

The U.S. runs a fractional reserve banking system. This means that banks must maintain money reserves equal to only a fraction of their deposit liabilities. If all of a bank's depositors decided to withdraw their funds at the same time, the bank would not have enough funds on hand to pay them all. The fraction of deposits that banks must keep in reserves is called the required reserve ratio. It is set by the Federal Reserve, and is approximately ten percent.

> The actual ratio varies by a bank's total deposits:
> - Under 13.3 million = 0%
> - 13.3 to 89 million = 3%
> - Over 89 million = 10%

Why do people put their money in banks, when the banks don't keep enough on hand to pay them all if everyone wants their money back at once? Quite simply, we all trust that only a few depositors will want their money at any one time, so that when we ourselves want to withdraw our money, the bank will have enough to pay us. When people stop believing this, there is a run on the bank. Depositors literally run to the bank to get their money. If they walk, they will be too late; other folks will beat them to it, and the bank won't have any money left to pay them.

Bank runs used to happen quite frequently. It is no coincidence that recessions used to be called "bank panics." Bank runs no longer occur in the United States. This is because of the Federal Deposit Insurance Corporation. Formed during the Great Depression in 1933, the FDIC promises to pay depositors up to $250,000 to cover their losses in the event of a bank failure. This safety net means that people no longer have any fear of losing their deposits. No danger of loss means no panics, and no runs on a bank.

The T-account is a simple balance sheet that compares a bank's assets against its liabilities. The T-account is a useful tool for examining basic banking practices. Here is a sample T-account for a bank.

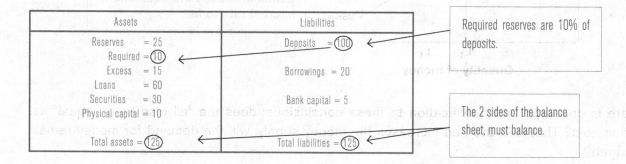

Bank liabilities are funds that the bank owes to someone else.

- Deposits are funds owed to the depositors. In effect, depositors have loaned their deposits to the bank, and they can get them back on demand.
- Borrowings are funds owed to other banks. A bank can borrow from other banks or from the Federal Reserve.
- Bank capital is the amount owed to the owners of the bank. The owners are residual claimants on the bank's revenue. Whatever assets remain after covering all other liabilities belong to the owners as bank capital.

Bank liabilities are also termed the source of funds for the bank.

Bank assets are the uses to which the bank puts its funds. Bank assets are funds that the bank owns, or that are owed to the bank by someone else.

- Reserves are funds that the bank keeps on hand in order to meet its daily obligations. Required reserves are the funds that the bank must (by Federal Reserve regulation) keep on hand. Excess reserves are any funds, over and above required reserves, that the bank chooses to keep on hand.
- Loans are funds that are owed to the bank by those who took out the loans. Interest that the bank charges on the loans it makes is the major source of revenue for the bank.
- Securities are financial instruments (typically U.S. Treasury bills) that the bank has purchased. The value of the securities are owed to the bank by the issuer of the security. Securities typically earn the bank less interest than a loan, but also are less risky than a loan.
- Physical capital are things that the bank owns. The bank might own the buildings it operates from, or the bank vault and computer equipment it uses. Banks also own titles to real estate, automobiles, and other items of collateral from defaulted loans.

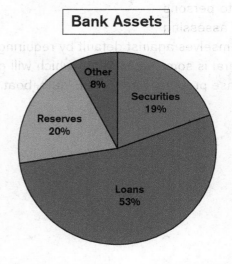

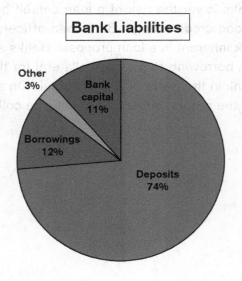

6. BANK LOANS

When a bank makes a loan, it converts one type of asset (reserves) into another type of asset (the loan). When a borrower defaults on a loan, this causes a loss of bank capital. Too large a loss of bank capital makes a bank insolvent.

The primary source of revenue for a bank is the interest earned on the money that the bank loans out.

When a bank makes a loan, they convert one type of asset (excess reserves) into another type of asset (the loan). For example, here is the effect on a bank's balance sheet when it makes a new loan of 10.

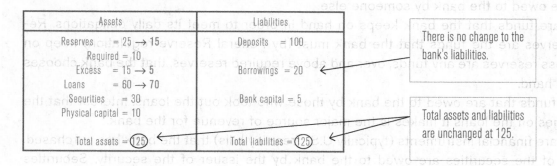

Assets	Liabilities
Reserves = 25 → 15	Deposits = 100
Required = 10	
Excess = 15 → 5	Borrowings = 20
Loans = 60 → 70	
Securities = 30	Bank capital = 5
Physical capital = 10	
Total assets = (125)	Total liabilities = (125)

> There is no change to the bank's liabilities.

> Total assets and liabilities are unchanged at 125.

The new loan comes out of the bank's excess reserves. (Excess reserves drop from 15 to 5.) The bank can't loan its required reserves, because Federal Reserve regulations require the bank to keep those funds on hand and available.

The bank earns revenue when the borrower pays back the loan, with interest. However, the bank benefits only if the borrower does in fact pay back the loan. There is a risk for the bank that the borrower will not pay back the loan, but will default on the loan instead.

> On a $20,000 60-month auto loan at 5% interest, the bank will receive back a total of $22,645.52.

Banks lower the risk of a loan default by only loaning to persons with good credit ratings. Bank loan officers are expert at assessing the risk inherent in a loan proposal. Banks also protect themselves against default by requiring the person borrowing to provide collateral for the loan. Collateral is some valued item which will go to the bank in the event of a loan default. On a loan to purchase property (real estate, auto, boat, and so on) the property itself is typically the collateral.

When a borrower defaults on a loan, three things happen to the bank's balance sheet.

1. The bank writes off the value of the loan.
   - Loan assets decrease by the amount of the defaulted loan.

2. The bank takes over the collateral on the loan.
   - Physical capital assets increase by the value of the collateral. The value of the collateral is certain to be less than the amount of the defaulted loan—if the collateral was worth more than the remaining amount on the loan, then the borrower would have kept paying on the loan.

3. Bank capital declines by the amount of the defaulted loan minus the value of the collateral.

For example, assume that a borrower defaults on a loan of 10, where the collateral is worth 6.

Assets	Liabilities
Reserves = 15	Deposits = 100
Required = 10	
Excess = 5	Borrowings = 20
Loans = 70 → 60	
Securities = 30	Bank capital = 5 → 1
Physical capital = 10 → 16	
Total assets = 125 → 121	Total liabilities = 125 → 121

Loans decrease by 10.

Physical capital increases by 6.

Bank capital falls by 10 − 6 = 4

The bank's total assets decline, because the loss of the loan asset is only partly offset by the gain of the collateral adding to physical capital assets. The two sides of the balance sheet have to balance, so total liabilities also fall—the fall coming out of bank capital.

When a bank suffers too large a loss of bank capital, the bank becomes insolvent. This means that the bank's assets are no longer sufficient to cover the bank's liabilities.
- An insolvent bank can be taken over by Federal regulators, who will liquidate the bank's remaining assets and pay off its creditors. The bank's officers at best will lose their jobs; at worst there could be fines or jail time for malfeasance.

Since the personal cost of a bank failure can be so high, bank officers tend to be quite conservative when it comes to their use of the bank's funds. They typically reduce risk by maintaining a diverse mix of loans and security investments.

7. MONEY CREATION

When a bank makes a loan, it creates money in the form of new demand deposits. As the new money circulates through the banking system, it creates new bank reserves and allows the making of new loans and additional money creation. This is called the money multiplier process.

When a bank makes a loan, it generally does not hand the borrower cash. Rather, the bank credits the borrower's checking account with the amount of the loan. When a bank makes a loan, it creates money in the form of new demand deposits. The bank literally creates the money out of thin air. Of course the borrower does not leave this new money in their checking account—they spend the money on whatever it was they took out the loan for.

Here is how a loan affects a bank's balance sheet. (Assume the bank makes a new loan of 10.)

Assets	Liabilities
Reserves = 25	
Required = 10 → 11	Deposits = 100 → 110
Excess = 15 → 14	
Loans = 60 → 70	

Assets	Liabilities
Reserves = 25 → 15	
Required = 11 → 10	Deposits = 110 → 100
Excess = 14 → 5	
Loans = 70	

The immediate effect is an equal increase in the bank's total assets and total liabilities.

Since deposits rise, required reserves also rise.

Once the borrower spends the loan, deposits fall back to their original level.

Excess reserves are now smaller—the bank has converted excess reserves to a new loan asset.

But the process doesn't stop there. Whoever the borrower bought from now has that new money, and they deposit it in their own bank. This increases that bank's excess reserves.

Here is the balance sheet for this second bank.

Assets	Liabilities
Reserves = 7	
Required = 7	Deposits = 70
Excess = 0	
Loans = 40	

Before the new deposit

Assets	Liabilities
Reserves = 7 → 17	
Required = 7 → 8	Deposits = 70 → 80
Excess = 0 → 9	
Loans = 40	

After the new deposit

The second bank now has 9 in excess reserves that they did not have before. This allows the second bank to make another loan. When the second bank makes a new loan, they create more money just like the first bank did.

As the newly created money circulates through the banking system, it repeatedly creates new excess reserves, allowing banks to make new loans and create more money.

Here is the balance sheet for the third bank in this process.

Assets	Liabilities		Assets	Liabilities
Reserves = 20	Deposits = 150		Reserves = 20 → 29	Deposits = 150 → 159
Required = 15			Req. = 15 → 15.9	
Excess = 5	Before the new deposit		Excess = 5 → 13.1	After the new deposit
Loans = 90			Loans = 90	

The new deposit of 9 in the third bank means that they now have 8.1 more in excess reserves than before. This allows the third bank to make a new loan and keep the process going.

This is called the money multiplier process. A small initial increase in excess reserves can lead to a much larger increase in the money supply. At each stage of the multiplier process, the increase in excess reserves is a little smaller. This is because part of the increase in reserves must be retained as required reserves to cover the growing amount of deposits.

The size of the money multiplier is determined by the size of the required reserve ratio.
- Money multiplier = 1 / Required Reserve Ratio
- When the required ratio is 10%, the money multiplier is 1 / 0.1, or 10.

In the example, the only leakage from the money multiplier process was the additional required reserves. In the real world other leakages are also possible.
- The recipients of new money at each stage do not have to deposit all of the new money in their checking accounts. They could decide to keep some of it as currency. Whatever portion they don't deposit in their bank does not create new reserves, and so can't support additional money creation.
- Likewise, banks do not have to loan out all of their new excess reserves. They could decide to increase their planned holdings of excess reserves. Whatever portion of excess reserves the bank does not loan out does not create any new money.

Therefore, the money multiplier in the real world will be less than 10. With a required reserve ratio of 10%, the money multiplier of 10 is the upper limit of new money creation possible for the banking system as a whole. For example, if there is currently a total of $10 billion in excess reserves in the banking system as a whole, then there is the potential for the creation of $100 billion in new money.

8. FEDERAL RESERVE SYSTEM

The Federal Reserve System regulates the banking sector and implements monetary policy. The Fed has three major components:
1. **Board of Governors**
2. **Twelve Federal Reserve Banks**
3. **Federal Open Market Committee**

Unlike many countries, the United States does not have a single central bank. Instead, the U.S. relies on the Federal Reserve System to regulate the banking sector and implement monetary policy. The Federal Reserve System has three major components:
1. Board of Governors
2. Twelve Federal Reserve banks
3. Federal Open Market Committee

The Board of Governors is the highest decision-making body of the Fed. It consists of seven members, called governors. The Fed governors are appointed by the president and confirmed by Congress. The governors serve a single fourteen-year term, and cannot be reappointed to a second term. The chairperson of the Board of Governors is one of the most powerful players in the U.S. macro economy. The chairperson is appointed by the president to a shorter two-year term, but can (and often does) serve for more than one term. The current chairperson of the Federal Reserve is Janet Yellen, whose term began in February 2014.

Janet Yellen

The Board of Governors of the Federal Reserve has many responsibilities. They establish the regulations under which the U.S. banking system operates. This includes:
- Record keeping and reporting requirements
- Standards to maintain bank solvency
- Restrictions on certain banking practices

The Board of Governors sets the required reserve ratio which determines the fraction of deposits that banks must maintain as reserves.

The Board of Governors determines monetary policy for the nation. Working within broad guidelines set by Congress, the Board of Governors decides if an expansionary or contractionary policy is needed, how much monetary stimulus or restraint is called for, when to start a particular policy, how long to maintain that policy, and when to end it. The Fed operates with a great deal of independence in planning and carrying out monetary policy.

The twelve Federal Reserve banks serve as bankers to the banking sector.

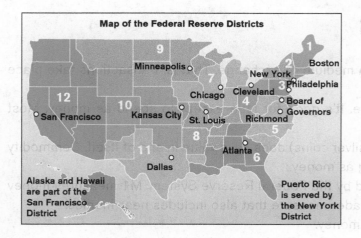

Map of the Federal Reserve Districts

Minneapolis 9
Boston 1
New York 2
Philadelphia 3
Chicago 7
Cleveland
Board of Governors
San Francisco 12
Kansas City 10
St. Louis
Richmond 5
Dallas 11
Atlanta 6
St. Louis 8

Alaska and Hawaii are part of the San Francisco District

Puerto Rico is served by the New York District

- The Federal Reserve banks accept deposits from member banks.
  - » Banks maintain most of their reserves as deposits at a Federal Reserve bank rather than as vault cash (currency on hand).
- The Federal Reserve banks make loans to member banks.
  - » These are called discount loans, and the interest rate that the Federal Reserve bank charges for these loans is called the discount rate.
- The Federal Reserve banks provide various services to member banks.
  - » They issue new currency.
  - » They retire damaged currency.
  - » They clear checks written on member banks' checking accounts.

The Federal Open Market Committee (FOMC) has twelve members:
- The seven governors of the Federal Reserve System
- The president of the New York Federal Reserve Bank
- Presidents of four other Federal Reserve banks, on a rotating basis

The FOMC is located at the New York Federal Reserve Bank.

The principal function of the Federal Open Market Committee is the day-to-day operation of monetary policy. The FOMC does this by buying and selling government securities on the open market (hence the name of the committee).
- This will be explained in more detail in chapter 12.

SUMMARY OF CHAPTER 11

The main function of money is to serve as a medium of exchange. That is, transactions take place in terms of money.

Fiat money has little or no intrinsic value. It's good for little except to spend as money. Most money today is fiat money.

Commodity money (for example, gold or silver coins) does have value in and of itself. Commodity money has valued uses other than spending as money.

In the U.S., the money supply is measured by the Federal Reserve System. M1 measures money used as a medium of exchange. M2 is a broader measure that also includes near-monies.

The interest rate represents the price of money.

The U.S. runs a fractional reserve banking system. This means that banks must maintain money reserves equal to only a fraction of their deposit liabilities.

Major bank assets are reserves, loans, and securities. Major bank liabilities are deposits, borrowings, and bank capital.

When a bank makes a loan, they convert one type of asset (reserves) into another type of asset (the loan). When a borrower defaults on a loan, this causes a loss of bank capital. Too large a loss of bank capital makes a bank insolvent.

When a bank makes a loan, it creates money in the form of new demand deposits. As the new money circulates through the banking system, it creates new bank reserves and allows the making of new loans and additional money creation. This is called the money multiplier.

The money multiplier is equal to 1/Required Reserve Ratio.

The Federal Reserve System regulates the banking sector and implements monetary policy. The Fed has three major components: Board of Governors, twelve Federal Reserve banks, and the Federal Open Market Committee.

The current chairperson of the Federal Reserve is Janet Yellen.

Credits

CH TWELVE
MONETARY POLICY

Monetary policy starts on the financial side of the economy, but then influences real variables. Monetary policy first impacts the money supply, which influences interest rates, which impacts investment and aggregate demand.

Keynes thought that monetary policy would be ineffective in ending a recession. Monetarists view monetary policy as too crude a tool to be useful in the short run. The Classical view of monetary policy is that it can't affect real values, it can only affect the price level.

Monetary policy affects real variables only indirectly, and there are serious operational problems in implementing it. The historical record of the past 100 years of monetary policy is not very good.

1. HOW MONETARY POLICY WORKS

Monetary policy starts on the financial side of the economy, but then influences real variables. Monetary policy first impacts the money supply, which influences interest rates, which impacts investment and aggregate demand.

Like fiscal policy, monetary policy is government action taken to counteract the business cycle. Monetary policy starts on the financial side of the economy, but then influences real variables.

- An expansionary monetary policy is appropriate during a recession. It aims to increase the money supply, reduce interest rates, and increase investment.
- A contractionary monetary policy is appropriate when the economy is overheating. It aims to reduce the money supply, increase interest rates, and decrease investment.

There are eight steps to an expansionary monetary policy.

Step #1: The Fed buys securities on the open market. This is handled by the Federal Open Market Committee.

Step #2: When the Fed buys securities, this increases the monetary base. The monetary base consists of currency in circulation plus bank reserves. When a bank sells securities to the Fed, a bank asset outside the monetary base is converted to an asset within the monetary base.

When the Fed buys 10 securities from the bank, the bank's reserves increase by 10.

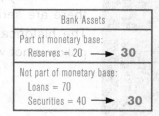

Step #3: When the Fed buys securities, bank excess reserves increase. Excess reserves are the difference between total reserves and required reserves. Since total reserves increase by the amount of securities purchased, and required reserves are unchanged (required reserves increase only if total bank deposits increase), then excess reserves also increase by the amount of securities purchases.

Step #4: The rise in excess reserves leads banks to make more loans. Excess reserves are idle funds for a bank. If kept as cash on hand, they earn no interest. If kept as deposits at a Federal Reserve bank, they earn very low interest. A bank can earn a higher interest rate if they loan out some of their excess reserves. All else being equal, when a bank's excess reserves increase, they will increase their loans.

Step #5: When banks make new loans, this increases the supply of money. When a bank makes a loan, they credit the loan amount to the borrower's checking account—this is newly created M1 money. Each new creation of money leads to new deposits in the banking system, which increases excess reserves and encourages new loans and more money creation in the money multiplier process. The initial expansionary monetary policy action here expands to have a much larger impact on the economy.

Step #6: The expanding money supply drives down the interest rate.

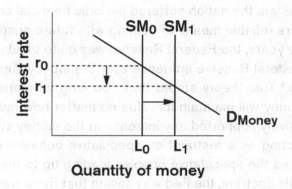

> If the demand for money stays the same, the only way to induce people to hold more money is to lower the interest rate.

Step #7: Lower interest rates lead businesses to increase investment. Since the interest rate is the cost of borrowing money, when interest rates fall it becomes less expensive for businesses to invest. All else being equal, they will invest more.

Step #8: When business investment increases, this increases aggregate demand. Investment is one of the components of aggregate demand: GDP = C + I + G + NE.

The expansionary monetary policy started on the financial side of the economy. At first it acted on financial variables—money supply and interest rate. But it ended up influencing real variables—raising output and lowering unemployment.

List of 8 steps to a contractionary monetary policy:	
Step #1 : Fed sells securities	Step #5 : Money supply shrinks
Step #2 : Monetary base shrinks	Step #6 : Interest rates rise
Step #3 : Excess reserves decline	Step #7 : Investment declines
Step #4 : Banks make fewer loans	Step #8 : Aggregate demand falls

2. HISTORICAL EXAMPLES OF MONETARY POLICY

Modern monetary policy started with the formation of the Federal Reserve in 1914. In early years monetary policy from the Fed was quite timid, but it has become much more aggressive over time.

Modern monetary policy in the United States started with the formation of the Federal Reserve System in 1914. From 1836, when President Andrew Jackson refused to renew the charter of the Second National Bank of the United States, the country had no central monetary authority. Creation and maintenance of the money supply was handled by private banks issuing national bank notes. Under this system the nation suffered periodic financial crises. The Federal Reserve was formed to provide a more reliable means of dealing with future crises.

In its early years, the Federal Reserve was quite timid in its practice of monetary policy.

At first, Federal Reserve influence over the money supply was limited by its holding to the "real bills doctrine." This theory stated that: "So long as money is only issued for assets of sufficient value, the money will maintain its value no matter how much is issued." In practice, this meant that the Fed passively supported any increase in the money supply for bank loans backed by collateral. Instead of acting as a restraint on speculative behavior driving up the "value" of assets, the Fed blithely ignored the speculative bubbles leading up to the stock market crash of 1929. By holding to the real bills doctrine, the Fed was saying that there was no connection between the money supply and the price level, so there was no reason for the Fed to even try to influence the money supply.

The early timidity of the Federal Reserve is seen most clearly by its deliberate inactivity during the first years of the Great Depression. Between 1929 and 1932, bank failures in the U.S. were widespread,

> **9,000 banks failed during the decade of the 1930s.**

with a resulting large fall in the money supply. The Federal Reserve allowed this to happen. Moreover, the Fed

> **The money supply fell by 25% between 1929 and 1932.**

argued that the ongoing liquidation of bad debt and the failure of weak financial institutions was a good thing, and that intervention to cushion the impact of the downturn would only delay the necessary adjustments and make things worse in the long run.

During World War II the Federal Reserve aided the war effort by keeping interest rates low so as to reduce the cost of government borrowing. After the war ended, the government pressured the Fed to continue to keep rates low. The Fed acquiesced, making other monetary policy goals subservient to keeping interest payments on the government debt low. It was only when rising inflationary pressures in the early 1950s became clear that the Fed broke away from this passive posture.

The Federal Reserve became much more aggressive in its application of monetary policy as time went by. By the last three decades of the twentieth century, the Fed had become a very powerful institution, and the Fed chair was one of the most influential players in the U.S. economy.

In 1979, the newly appointed Fed chair Paul Volcker undertook an aggressive contractionary monetary policy to combat persistent high inflation. The result was a short recession in 1980 and a longer and deeper recession in 1981–1982. The inflation rate was driven down from 13.3% in 1979 to 3.8% in 1983. Easy money policies in the face of rising inflation in the late 1960s and 1970s had led people to expect further expansionary policy from the Federal Reserve and higher inflation in the future. It took strong action from Volcker and the Fed to break these inflationary expectations.

Volcker's successor at the Federal Reserve was Alan Greenspan. Greenspan headed the Fed for twenty years (1987–2006) and presided over almost uninterrupted economic growth. His tenure was notable for repeated Fed intervention to offset short term fluctuations in financial markets.

- The stock market crash of 1987
- Bursting of the dot.com bubble in 1998
- Terrorist attacks of September 11, 2001

> An example of effective intervention by the Fed was its reaction to the stock market crash of 1987. The crash was over after the Fed very publicly "affirmed its readiness to serve as a source of liquidity to support the economic and financial system."

The successful balancing act by the Federal Reserve in avoiding significant recessions while also keeping inflation low, led to confident statements by many that "the business cycle is dead."

The Great Recession of 2008–2009 demonstrated that the business cycle was very much still alive and kicking. The new Fed chair Ben Bernanke responded with a massive expansionary monetary policy. Short term interest rates were driven to nearly zero. The money supply was increased significantly. When these traditional monetary policies did not have the desired effect, the Federal Reserve tried something new. Bernanke's policy of quantitative easing involved the Fed purchase of mortgage-backed securities, and pumped tens of billions of dollars every month into the financial sector. The unprecedented scale of Federal Reserve actions are widely credited with preventing the financial panic from turning into a second Great Depression.

> In November 2008, the Fed began buying $600 billion in mortgage-backed securities from banks.

3. KEYNES' VIEW OF MONETARY POLICY

Keynes thought that monetary policy would be ineffective in ending a recession. He argued that, during a recession, banks would be unlikely to make new loans, and that lower interest rates would not draw forth new business investment.

Keynes thought that monetary policy would be ineffective in ending a recession. He argued that an expansionary monetary policy would fail at two points in the eight-step process.

Keynes did not dispute that the Fed could start an expansionary monetary policy. The Fed indeed could buy securities on the open market. This would indeed increase the monetary base and increase excess reserves in the banking system.

However, Keynes argued, during a recession banks would be unlikely to use those additional excess reserves to make new loans. To see why not, consider what happens to the risk of loan default during a recession.

- Because unemployment rises in a recession, household disposable income falls.
- Consumption spending falls, so businesses receive less revenue.
- With lower disposable income, individuals are more likely to default on existing consumer loans.
- With lower revenue, businesses are more likely to default on their existing loans.
- All else being equal, both individuals and businesses seeking new loans will be less credit-worthy, and will pose a higher risk of default.
- Already stung by losses due to rising defaults on existing loans, banks will seek safer assets rather than riskier ones.

As a result of this, banks will likely increase their holdings of excess reserves during a recession. With banks not making many new loans, the money multiplier process never really gets going, and the expansionary monetary policy action fails to stimulate the economy.

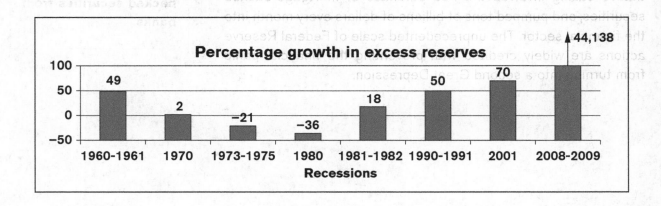

The historical record shows that Keynes was correct. Excess reserves in the banking system do tend to rise during recessions. This effect has been especially strong following the 2008–2009 recession.

Keynes further argued that, even if the Fed could lower interest rates, lower interest rates would not draw forth new business investment during a recession. To see why not, consider the expected profitability of investment during a recession.

- Businesses have lowered output, laid off employees, and idled machinery.
- New investment at this point would merely increase their unused capacity. If businesses want to increase output, they can do so without new investment, simply by bringing idle machinery back on line and calling back laid-off workers.
- Expectations of future business conditions tend to be bleak during a recession. Difficult to think about expansion when you're working hard simply to hold onto what you've got.
- Bottom line: a recession seems like a bad time to invest, and most businesses don't.

Given these factors, the business sector is likely to reduce investment during a recession, no matter how low the interest rate falls. In fact, a loss of investor confidence and a fall in planned investment may well be what starts the recession in the first place.

The historical record shows that Keynes was right again. Although interest rates tend to fall significantly during recessions, business investment, instead of rising, usually falls too.

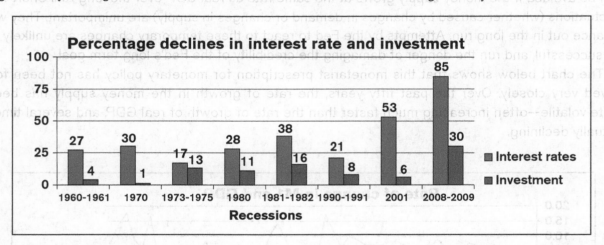

Keynes' belief in the ineffectiveness of expansionary monetary policy during a recession is why he argued for directly increasing aggregate demand by expansionary fiscal policy. Keynes thought that only the government sector of the economy could be relied upon to increase aggregate demand during a recession.

Keynes himself paid little attention to contractionary monetary policy. Writing during the Great Depression, he was concerned only with the downside of the business cycle.

4. MONETARIST VIEW OF MONETARY POLICY

Monetarists view monetary policy as too crude a tool to be useful in the short run. They argue that the only safe monetary policy is for steady growth in the money supply over the long run.

Monetarists view monetary policy as too crude a tool to be useful in the short run. Monetary policy can't be used to "fine-tune" the economy because:

- The reactions of banks, investors, and other market participants to a monetary policy action can't be precisely predicted. These reactions will vary depending on variables outside the control of (and perhaps not even known by) the Federal Reserve.
- The time lag before the impact of a monetary policy action is felt can vary significantly. Federal Reserve actions that change expectations can have an immediate effect, while those that must work through a multiplier process will take much longer to be fully felt.
- Technological changes in banking (like the introduction of the ATM and automatic overdraft protection for checking accounts) blur the distinction between M1 money and near-monies. This makes it difficult to know if monetary targets are actually being met.

Monetarists therefore argue that monetary policy should concentrate on meeting the long run goal of a steady rate of growth in the money supply. All sorts of potential problems in the macro economy can be avoided if the money supply grows at the same rate as real GDP over the long run. Short-run fluctuations (whether caused by changes in demand or changes in supply) are unimportant. They will balance out in the long run. Attempts by the Fed to react to these temporary changes are unlikely to be successful, and run the danger of damaging the credibility of the Fed's long term goal.

The chart below shows that this monetarist prescription for monetary policy has not been followed very closely. Over the past fifty years, the rate of growth in the money supply has been quite volatile—often increasing much faster than the rate of growth of real GDP, and several times actually declining.

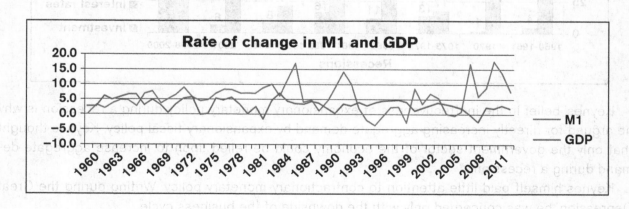

The average annual rate of growth in real GDP over this period was 3.1%. The average annual rate of growth in the M1 money supply over the same period was 5.7%

Monetarists argue that problems happen when the money supply does not grow at the same rate as real GDP.

When the money supply grows faster than real GDP, it creates inflation. The idea here is that when consumers have more money, they want to spend more. If there are more goods and services to buy, then prices don't have to change. But if the demand to buy (the money supply) increases faster than the supply of goods to buy (real GDP), then the excess demand will push up prices.

The chart below shows the relationship between growth in the money supply and inflation over the past fifty years. A direct relationship between the two is clearest in the 1960s and 1970s, when a rising rate of growth in the money supply was matched by a rising rate of inflation. Money growth became more volatile after 1980; though generally declining rates of growth in M1 money are matched by generally declining inflation.

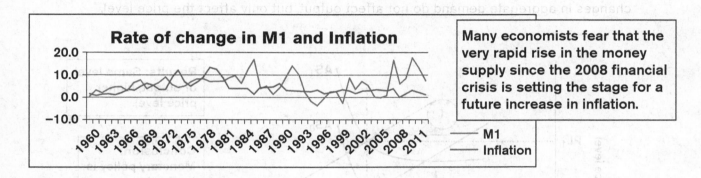

Many economists fear that the very rapid rise in the money supply since the 2008 financial crisis is setting the stage for a future increase in inflation.

On the other hand, when the money supply grows slower than real GDP, it causes a recession. The idea here is that too slow a rate of money growth results in a shortage of loanable funds for investors. This drives up interest rates, reduces planned investment, and sets off a downward multiplier process.

- Two dramatic examples of this are the early years of the Great Depression (when a lack of funds drove many otherwise sound banks into bankruptcy) and the financial panic of 2008 (when the supply of new bank loans dried up and threatened wholesale financial meltdown).

Is the Federal Reserve monetarist? There are some monetarist tendencies in the Fed. For example:
- The Fed does set targets for growth rates in the M1 and M2 measures of the money supply.
- Money supply statistics are closely watched by investors attempting to anticipate future monetary policy actions by the Fed.
- Economists from the monetarist school are employed by the Fed (most notably at the Kansas City Federal Reserve Bank).

However, the Fed's targets for the money supply are seldom met, the rate of growth in the money supply greatly exceeds the rate of growth in real GDP, and the Fed pays a great deal of attention to short- run fluctuations in the economy. None of these would be true if the Fed was truly monetarist.

5. CLASSICAL VIEW OF MONETARY POLICY

The Classical view of monetary policy is that it can't affect real values, but can only affect the price level. The classical quantity theory of money depends on the equation of exchange and the stability of the velocity of money.

The Classical view of monetary policy is that it can't affect real values, but can only affect the price level. Classical economists argued that real variables (output and employment) can only be affected by other real variables (changes in resources or technology). Because monetary policy acts on financial variables (money supply, interest rate), it can only affect other financial variables (price level).

- With the long-run aggregate supply curve being a vertical line at the level of potential GDP, changes in aggregate demand do not affect output, but only affect the price level.

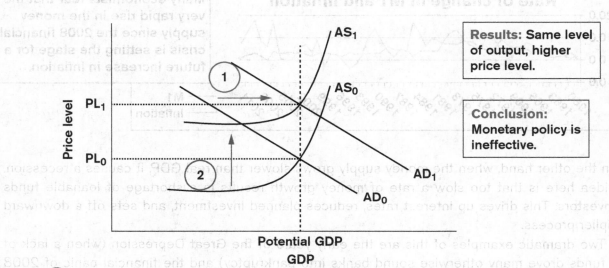

Results: Same level of output, higher price level.

Conclusion: Monetary policy is ineffective.

1 An expansionary monetary policy succeeds in increasing aggregate demand.

2 Resource prices rise, shifting the short-run aggregate supply curve upward.

Classical monetary theory is called the quantity theory of money. The heart of this theory is the equation of exchange:

Money Supply times Velocity of Money = Price Level times Real GDP

The predictions of the quantity theory of money depend upon the velocity of money being stable in the short run.

5.1. VELOCITY OF MONEY

The velocity of money is the average number of times a dollar is spent over the year: aggregate expenditures divided by the money supply. Classical theory views velocity as very stable, determined by institutional factors in the economy.

The velocity of money is the average number of times a dollar is spent over the course of a year. It is calculated as aggregate expenditures divided by the money supply.

> **Velocity of money for an individual**
>
> John normally keeps $300 on hand in currency, and keeps an average of $1200 in his checking account. His total expenditures are $60,000 per year.
> - John's velocity of money is 40.   60,000 / (300 + 1,200) = 40
>
> George normally keeps $1000 on hand in currency, and keeps an average of $5000 in his checking account. His total expenditures are also $60,000 per year.
> - George's velocity of money is 10.   60,000 / (1,000 + 5,000) = 10

> **Velocity of money for the United States as a whole**
>
> In March 2014, the M1 money supply was $2.744 trillion, and nominal GDP was $17,150 trillion.
> - The U.S. velocity of money is 6.25.   17,150/2.744 = 6.25

Classical monetary theory views the velocity of money as being very stable in the short run. They argue that the velocity of money is determined by institutional factors in the economy, and that these institutional factors change very slowly.

The most important institutional factors for influencing the velocity of money are the timing of payments to factors of production and the cost of converting near-monies to medium of exchange money.
- The timing of payments matters because it affects average money holdings. Assume a worker lives from paycheck to paycheck, budgeting expenses so that one paycheck is fully spent when the next paycheck is received. If workers get paid monthly, their average money on hand will be half of their monthly salary. But if they are paid weekly, their average money on hand will be much less (half of their weekly salary). The velocity of money will be higher when payments are more frequent.
- The cost of converting near-monies to medium of exchange money matters because this also affects average money holdings. The more expensive it is to convert near-monies to M1 type money, the less often people will do it, and the larger will be the amount of M1 money they typically keep on hand. As the cost of converting near-monies goes down, the velocity of money will increase.

5.2. EQUATION OF EXCHANGE

The equation of exchange is: MV = PQ. Money supply times velocity equals price level times real GDP. The equation of exchange is both an accounting identity and a powerful macro model.

The equation of exchange is: MV = PQ

>   M = Money Supply : This could be measured either as M1 (medium of exchange money) or as M2 (including near-monies).

>   V = Velocity of Money : Velocity can also be measured in terms of either M1 or M2.

>   P = Price Level : This is measured with a general price index; perhaps the Consumer Price Index or the GDP deflator. Note: to convert a price index to a price level, divide by 100.

>   Q = Real GDP : It doesn't matter what year's dollars real GDP is expressed in.

The equation of exchange is an accounting identity. The equation is true by definition.
- MV is the number of dollars multiplied by the average number of times each dollar is spent. This is aggregate expenditures. For example, if you have 100 dollars, and spend each dollar 5 times, you have spent $500.
- PQ (real GDP times the price level) is simply nominal GDP. It is the market value of all final goods and services produced in the country during the year. GDP = C + I + G + NE : this is also aggregate expenditures.

The two sides of the equation of exchange are simply two different ways to calculate the same thing.

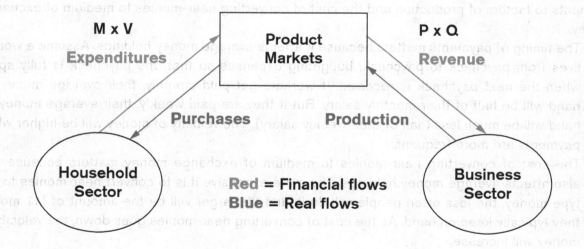

However, with a couple of reasonable-seeming assumptions, the equation of exchange becomes much more than an accounting identity: it becomes a powerful macroeconomic model.

Classical theorist assumed:

1. Real GDP is constant in the short run.
   - Real GDP is determined by the quantity and quality of resources available to the economy, and by the level of technology.
   - Real GDP can grow only if the real resources available to the economy grow. For example, if the labor force expands, if new factories and machinery are built, if additional natural resources are discovered, if there are new inventions or improvements to existing technology.
2. The velocity of money is constant in the short run.
   - Velocity is determined by institutional factors: payment methods and the cost of converting near-monies to M1 money.
   - These institutional factors change only slowly. It is disruptive and expensive for businesses to change how frequently they pay their workers, so they make such changes infrequently. The cost of converting near-monies is affected by government regulation of the financial sector and by technological change in the banking industry. Regulators and bankers are both stereotypically conservative and slow to change.

With these two assumptions, the equation of exchange now predicts a direct and proportional relationship between the money supply and the price level.

Assume that:
$M = 100; V = 10; P = 1; Q = 1000$
$$MV = PQ : (100)(10) = (1)(1000)$$
Now let the money supply double to 200
$$MV = PQ : (200)(10) > (1)(1000)$$
Something has to change to make the equation balance again. But velocity is constant, and real GDP is constant, so the only thing that can change is the price level.
$$MV = PQ : (200)(10) = (2)(1000)$$

Any change in the money supply causes a direct and proportional change in the price level. In this example the doubling of the money supply leads to a doubling of the price level.

So the equation of exchange provides additional justification for the Classical belief that financial variables cannot affect real variables.

5.3. HOW STABLE IS THE VELOCITY OF MONEY?

The equation of exchange is meaningful only if the velocity of money is stable. If velocity is variable, this breaks the link between money supply and price level. Historical data seem to say that velocity is not very stable.

The equation of exchange is meaningful as a macroeconomic model only if the velocity of money is stable. If the velocity of money is highly variable, this breaks the link between the money supply and the price level. A simple example shows why.

Assume that:

M = 100; V = 10; P = 1; Q = 1000

$$MV = PQ : (100)(10) = (1)(1000)$$

Now let the money supply double to 200. If velocity is constant, the price level must also double.

$$MV = PQ : (200)(10) = (2)(1000)$$

But if velocity can vary, then there is no way to predict what the price level will do.

$$MV = PQ : (200)(5) = (1)(1000)$$
$$Or : (200)(8) = (1.6)(1000)$$
$$Or : (200)(4) = (0.8)(1000)$$

If the velocity of money is not stable, then the equation of exchange is nothing more than an accounting identity.

Historical data seem to show that the velocity of money is not particularly stable. Over the past fifty-plus years, the velocity of money rose from a low of 3.73 in 1959 to a high of 10.53 in 2007, and then fell again to 6.36 in 2013.

- The velocity changed by an average of nearly five percent a year. There are three years when velocity changed by more than ten percent.

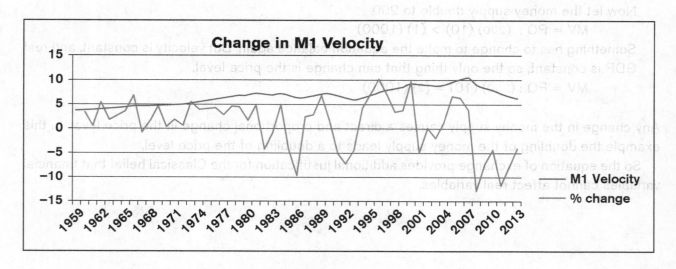

In the first half of the twentieth century, the velocity of M1 money was quite stable. So what has changed since then? The two factors identified by Classical theorists as determining the velocity of money are payment methods and the cost of converting near-monies to M1 money.

Payment methods have not changed greatly over the last 100 years. Early in the twentieth century most workers received paychecks on a weekly, bi-weekly, or on a monthly basis. The same is still true today. The major differences in payment methods today are:
- Automatic withholding for income taxes, health insurance, and employees' contributions to other types of benefits
- Income spreading for employees in seasonal occupations (like teachers)
- Direct deposit to a bank account (eliminating physical checks)

None of these changes have had a significant impact on the velocity of money.

On the other hand, the cost of converting near-monies to M1 money has changed greatly over time.
- The number of bank branches has grown, and the hours when banks are open have expanded. Seldom does anyone need to take time off from work to visit a bank anymore.
- Proliferation of ATMs reduces time and effort needed to withdraw cash from a savings account.
- Transfers between accounts can be done online or with a mobile device, eliminating the need for many bank visits.
- Many banks offer automatic transfers from a savings account to protect against overdrafts in a checking account.

All of this makes it quick, easy, and cheap to convert near-monies today. The effect of this can be seen in the chart of M1 velocity, which increased steadily between 1959 and 2007.

With the major institutional change being the dramatically lower cost of converting near-monies, velocity in terms of M2 should be more stable than velocity in terms of M1. This is in fact the case.

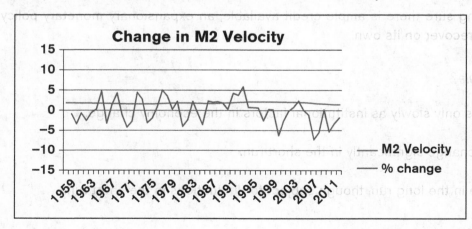

Even so, M2 velocity changes an average of almost 2.5% per year. There are 5 years when M2 velocity changed by more than 5%.

6. COMPARISON OF MONETARY SCHOOLS OF THOUGHT

The Classical school held that monetary policy can only affect the price level. Both Keynesians and Monetarists think that monetary policy can be used to affect real variables, but disagree as to whether it should be so used.

The Classical, Keynesian, and Monetarist schools of economic thought have very different opinions about both the role and the effectiveness of monetary policy.

Can monetary policy be used to affect real variables?

Classical: No; because monetary policy works on financial variables, it can only affect financial variables, not real variables.

Keynesian: Yes; monetary policy can affect the interest rate, and changes in the interest rate affect output and employment.

Monetarist: Yes; too slow a growth of the money supply will cause a shortage of loanable funds and restrain the growth of output.

Can an expansionary monetary policy help bring the economy out of a recession?

Classical: No; the economy will recover on its own; an expansionary monetary policy will only create inflation.

Keynesian: No; banks will not support new investment during a recession; they will absorb the new funds by increasing their excess reserves instead; investors will not respond to lower interest rates during a recession anyway.

Monetarist: Yes; by making sure there is ample credit available, an expansionary monetary policy helps the economy to recover on its own.

Is the velocity of money stable?

Classical: Yes; changes only slowly as institutional factors in the economy change.

Keynesian: No; it can change significantly in the short run.

Monetarist: Yes; stable in the long run, though subject to fluctuations in the short run.

Can a contractionary monetary policy help to slow down an overheated economy?

Classical: No; the economy will cool off on its own; a contractionary monetary policy will only create deflation.

Keynesian: Yes; raising the interest rate will restrain investment and lower output.

Monetarist: Yes; but there is a danger that the policy will go too far and put the economy into a recession.

What was the cause of the Great Depression?

Classical: The Great Depression was merely another example of the regular cycle of boom and bust that is the natural condition of the economy; during a recession the economy works out the excesses of the boom times.

Keynesian: The economy is inherently unstable; loss of investor confidence crashed the stock market and set off a downward multiplier process.

Monetarist: The Great Depression would have been a normal recession, but the Federal Reserve foolishly allowed the money supply to shrink, which led to many bank failures, and made the economy situation much worse.

What should be the main goal of monetary policy?

Classical: To maintain a stable price level. This is really all that monetary policy can do. Output in the long run will be at the level of potential GDP; the only question is what the price level will be.

Keynesian: To maintain full employment by helping to stabilize the macro economy in the short run. Monetary policy needs to recognize and respond to short-run deviations from potential GDP, since the economy will not automatically bring itself back to this point.

Monetarist: To maintain a steady rate of growth of the money supply; to encourage long run stability in the economy. Monetary policy tools are too crude to be reliable in the short run.

7. WHAT IS THE BEST MONETARY POLICY?

Monetary policy affects real variables only indirectly, and there are serious operational problems in implementing it. The historical record of the past 100 years of monetary policy results is not very good. A cautious approach to monetary policy is probably best.

The ultimate goal of monetary policy is to keep the economy running smoothly and growing steadily; to avoid the disruptive swings of the business cycle. The "best" monetary policy is the one that comes closest to meeting this goal. An effective monetary policy will acknowledge the limitations of the various monetary policy tools and will not overreach itself.

A real complication to monetary policy is that it affects real variables only indirectly. Monetary policy acts through financial variables (money supply, interest rate). The paths by which changes in these financial variables affect real variables like output and employment are many and varied, but generally weak, often convoluted, and not always well understood.

- The main path is from money supply to interest rate to investment. An expanding money supply leads to falling interest rates, which induces business firms to increase their investment.
- Falling interest rates can also affect household consumption—with a lower reward for saving, consumers may choose to spend more. On the other hand, consumers with a fixed savings goal might save more now to offset lower interest earnings on their savings.
- Lower interest rates reduce interest payments on the federal debt, which (all else being equal) reduces government expenditures.
- If growth in the money supply causes an increase in the rate of inflation, this will tend to reduce exports and increase imports, thereby reducing net exports.

There are serious operational problems in implementing monetary policy. Unlike fiscal policy (which can operate directly on the government expenditures component of GDP), the Federal Reserve must run its monetary policy through the banking, business, and household sectors of the economy.

- The money supply only grows if banks are willing to make new loans—The Federal Reserve can encourage this money creation, but it can't require it.
- Investment and consumption only grow if business firms are willing to invest more and households are willing to spend more in response to lower interest rates—the Fed can encourage this, but again it can't require it.

A particularly tricky problem for short-run monetary policy is that there are lags between the use of a monetary policy tool and the resulting impact on the economy. And the lags can be variable in length.

- It is hard to decide what policy might be appropriate for the next three months if actions taken today might impact financial markets for six months to come, but might just as well have no further impact after only one month.

The historical record of the first 100 years of monetary policy in the United States does not inspire a lot of confidence in the Federal Reserve's ability to stabilize the economy.

- At the start of the Great Depression in 1929 and 1930, the Federal Reserve allowed the money supply to shrink. In the face of mounting bank failures and runs on banks, the Fed did not offset the drains on bank reserves. The Fed chose to not practice expansionary monetary policy. These actions (and inactions) made the economic downturn much worse than it otherwise would have been.
- Inflation grew steadily from the late 1960s to the late 1970s. The Fed accommodated this steady increase in the price level, as they persisted with expansionary monetary policies and consistently exceeded their targets for growth in the money supply.
- The Federal Reserve did not foresee the house price bubble of 2007 and 2008. Nor did the Fed foresee the widespread financial panic that followed the bursting of the housing bubble.

Part of the difficulty facing the Federal Reserve is the large role that expectations play in financial markets.

- Stock prices depend on expectations of future dividend payments.
- Investment depends on expectations of future business conditions.
- Nominal interest rates depend on expectations of future inflation.

Participants in financial markets watch the Fed closely, and change their expectations (and their current behavior) based not only upon actions the Fed takes but also upon signals they think they see the Fed sending as clues to future Fed actions. This sensitivity of expectations to any Fed actions increases the volatility of financial markets.

There are some things the Federal Reserve does well.

- As the lender of last resort to the banking industry, the Fed can act to maintain liquidity during crises. The Fed's quick and strong action to provide funds to cash-strapped financial institutions in 2008 helped prevent that crisis from being even more damaging.
- The Fed can be a source of calm, helping to stop financial panics before they start. When banks are confident that the Fed will provide support, they are less likely to rush into rash action.
- Deposit insurance (the promise by the government to make good depositor losses from a bank failure) is a dramatic example of an institution that brings stability to financial markets. Runs on banks are a thing of the past, because depositors now are confident that their money is safe.

Bottom line: A cautious approach to monetary policy is probably best. The Federal Reserve should aim for stability and predictability in its policies, acting decisively only in extreme circumstances. As Keynes put it: "If economists could manage to get themselves thought of as humble, competent people on a level with dentists, that would be splendid."

SUMMARY OF CHAPTER 12

Monetary policy starts on the financial side of the economy, but then influences real variables. Monetary policy first impacts the money supply, which influences interest rates, which impacts investment and aggregate demand.

Modern monetary policy started with the formation of the Federal Reserve System in 1914. In early years monetary policy from the Fed was quite timid, but it has become much more aggressive over time.

Keynes thought that monetary policy would be ineffective in ending a recession. He argued that, during a recession, banks would be unlikely to make new loans, and that lower interest rates would not draw forth new business investment.

Monetarists view monetary policy as too crude a tool to be useful in the short run. They argue that the only safe monetary policy is for steady growth in the money supply over the long run.

Both Keynesians and Monetarists think that monetary policy can be used to affect real variables, but disagree as to whether it should be so used.

The Classical view of monetary policy is that it can't affect real variables, but can only affect the price level. The Classical quantity theory of money depends on the equation of exchange and the stability of the velocity of money.

The velocity of money is the average number of times a dollar is spent over the year: aggregate expenditures divided by the money supply.

The equation of exchange is: M V = P Q. Money supply times velocity equals price level times real GDP. The equation of exchange is both an accounting identity and a powerful macro model.

The equation of exchange is meaningful only if the velocity of money is stable. If velocity is variable, this breaks the link between money supply and price level.

Monetary policy affects real variables only indirectly, and there are serious operational problems in implementing it. The historical record of the past 100 years of monetary policy results is not very good.

CH

THIRTEEN

SUPPLY-SIDE POLICIES

Both Classical and Keynesian economists tended to ignore the aggregate supply curve; Keynesians because of their emphasis on aggregate demand, and Classicists because of their belief that the long-run aggregate supply curve was vertical at the level of potential GDP.

The behavior of suppliers in resource markets is influenced by net benefits (that is, after taxes). Tax policy can cause shifts in the aggregate supply curve.

There is considerable controversy over the size of supply-side effects. It seems likely that supply-side effects are relatively small in the short run, but could be quite large in the long run.

1. DOES THE AGGREGATE SUPPLY CURVE MATTER?

Both Classical and Keynesian economists tended to ignore the aggregate supply curve, though for different reasons. More recent economic thinking has been paying more attention to aggregate supply.

Both Classical and Keynesian economists tended to ignore the aggregate supply curve, though for different reasons.

Classical economists tended to ignore the aggregate supply curve because they viewed it as being constant in the long run and quickly self-adjusting in the short run.

- In the long run, the aggregate supply curve is a vertical line at the level of potential GDP. Aggregate supply is determined by real factors—quantity and quality of available resources—and will change only as those real factors change.
- In the short run the aggregate supply curve does slope upward, but the only point along the short run AS curve that matters is at the level of potential GDP. If aggregate demand intersects aggregate supply at any point other than at potential GDP, the short-run AS curve shifts up or down until the intersection is at potential GDP again.

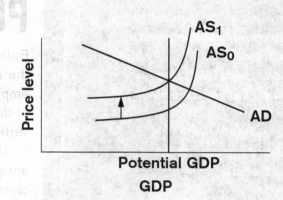

Keynesian economists tended to ignore the aggregate supply curve because Keynes himself ignored it. Keynes recognized that wages are sticky downward, so that during a recession the short-run aggregate supply curve would not shift downward enough to restore equilibrium at potential GDP. The remedy for a recession lies in the aggregate demand curve, not the aggregate supply curve.

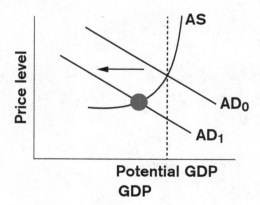

> The intersection of AD_1 and the stable AS curve is a recessionary equilibrium.

The shape of the long-run AS curve did not concern Keynes, because he thought that the short run was the relevant time period. After all; "In the long run we are all dead."

More recent economic thinking has been paying more attention to aggregate supply. Rather than simply taking aggregate supply as fixed, policy makers have been looking for ways in which the AS curve can be shifted.

The attraction of such supply-side policies is that they can foster economic growth and reduce inflation at the same time.

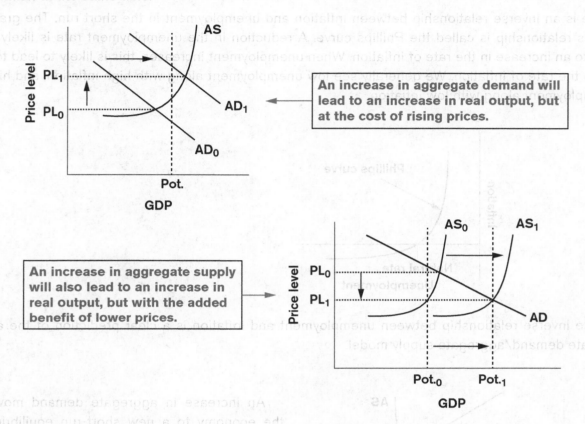

An increase in aggregate demand will lead to an increase in real output, but at the cost of rising prices.

An increase in aggregate supply will also lead to an increase in real output, but with the added benefit of lower prices.

The main impetus for the new attention being given to aggregate supply is a growing awareness of the limitations to policy actions directed at aggregate demand. Considerations which limit the effectiveness of fiscal policy include:

- The significant lags inherent to discretionary fiscal policy often results in fiscal policy actions which are badly timed.
- Government spending and tax programs generally are enacted only if they are thought to have value in themselves; that is, macroeconomic stabilization typically is a secondary goal at best.
- Increases in government spending are likely to be offset by decreases in business investment, as investors get "crowded out" of credit markets by new government borrowing that soaks up the available loanable funds.
- Reliance on fiscal policy tends to increase the relative size of the government sector over time.

If fiscal policy is insufficient to counteract the business cycle, it makes sense to see if supply-side policies can help.

2. RELATIONSHIP BETWEEN INFLATION AND UNEMPLOYMENT

There is an inverse relationship between inflation and unemployment in the short run. The AD/AS model predicts this clearly. It is also a clear consequence of the business cycle.

There is an inverse relationship between inflation and unemployment in the short run. The graph of this relationship is called the Phillips curve. A reduction in the unemployment rate is likely to lead to an increase in the rate of inflation. When unemployment increases, this is likely to lead to a fall in the rate of inflation. We generally see low unemployment along with high inflation, and high unemployment along with low inflation.

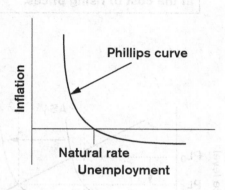

The inverse relationship between unemployment and inflation is a clear prediction of the aggregate demand/aggregate supply model.

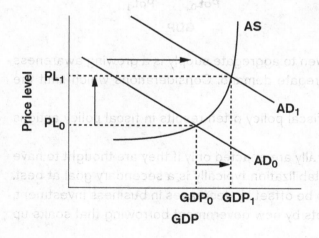

An increase in aggregate demand moves the economy to a new short-run equilibrium position. Output expands from GDP_0 to GDP_1. In order to produce the additional output, businesses must hire more workers. This reduces the unemployment rate.

At the same time, the price level rises from PL_0 to PL_1. Lower unemployment, but higher inflation.

Business cycle theory also predicts the same inverse relationship.

- During a contraction, output falls and workers get laid off, so unemployment rises. Aggregate demand falls, putting downward pressure on the prices of goods and services. High unemployment and low inflation.
- During an expansion, output increases and new workers get hired, so unemployment falls. Aggregate demand increases, putting upward pressure on the prices of goods and services. Low unemployment and high inflation.

During Expansions:	Inflation Rises	Unemployment falls
1999-2000 2004-2005	From 1.6% to 3.4% From 1.9% to 4.0%	From 4.4% to 3.9% From 5.7% to 4.7%
During Recessions:	Inflation Falls	Unemployment rises
3 '01 - 11 '01 6 '07 - 10 '09	From 2.9% to 1.9% From 2.7% to -0.2%	From 4.3% to 5.5% From 4.6% to 10.0%

This short-run inverse relationship between inflation and unemployment does not hold in the long run. The long-run aggregate supply curve is a vertical line at the level of potential GDP. In the long run, unemployment will return to the natural rate no matter what the rate of inflation might be.

So which is the more appropriate view for policy makers, the short run or the long run? The answer depends upon the situation the policy makers are facing. Crises tend to happen in the short run, and they need to be dealt with NOW! Knowing that a good harvest will eventually come is little comfort to someone who is starving today. This is why Keynes, writing in the depths of the Great Depression, said: "In the long run, we are all dead." The point was to get the economy moving right then, because further delay would only extend people's current suffering. On the other hand, if you eat your seed grain today, the good harvest will never come. Policies that look good in the short run can have seriously negative long-term consequences.

> It is hard to remember that your goal is to drain the swamp, when you are surrounded by hungry alligators!

A real consideration for the macro economy is whether the long run ever really arrives. In theory there is both a short-run and a long-run reaction to an external shock to the economy—both an immediate reaction to the newly changed conditions, and a more widespread impact after all markets have had time to adjust to new equilibrium positions. But in the real world, perhaps what actually occurs is a series of short-run reactions to one external shock after another, with the economy never getting the time to reach the long run.

3. THE PHILLIPS CURVE

The original Phillips curve shows the relationship between wage inflation and unemployment in individual labor markets. Excess supply or excess demand for labor causes changes in the wage rate. The greater the excess, the faster the change.

The Phillips curve did not start out in its current form. The original Phillips curve shows the relationship between wage inflation and unemployment in individual labor markets.

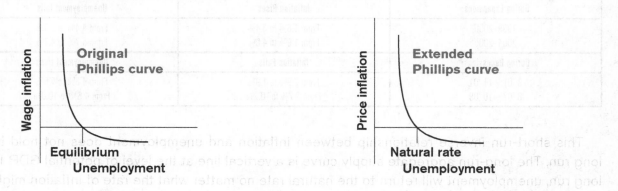

When a labor market is in equilibrium, the wage rate does not change. To the left of that equilibrium there is excess demand for labor, so the wage rate gets bid up. To the right of that equilibrium there is an excess supply of labor, and the wage rate falls.

- Note: The flatter slope of the curve to the right of equilibrium is the idea of wage rates being sticky downward again.

A.W. Phillips (1914—1975) was a New Zealand economist who spent most of his academic career at the London School of Economics. Phillips led a varied and active life, including time spent as a youth as a crocodile hunter.

Phillips, with his MONIAC computer.

Phillips' war-time experiences includes escape from the Japanese invasion of China, crossing Asia on the Trans-Siberian Railway, joining the British Royal Air Force, being present for the fall of Singapore and the fall of Java, and three-and-a-half years in a Japanese prisoner-of-war camp. He learned Chinese from other prisoners, repaired and miniaturized a secret radio, and fashioned a secret water boiler for tea. In 1946, he was made a Member of the Order of the British Empire for his war service.

Phillips studied at the London School of Economics, and was offered a position there after impressing the faculty with his creation of an analogue computer which used hydraulics to model the workings of the British macro economy. Had he lived longer, he probably would have been awarded a Nobel Prize in economics.

Here is Phillips' model for wage inflation:

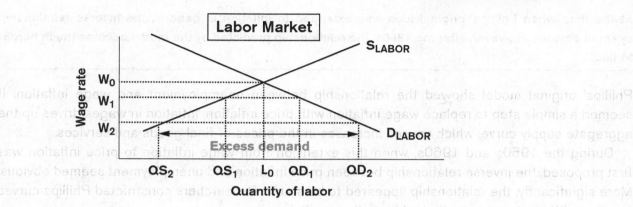

When the wage rate is lower than W_0, there is excess demand for labor. For example, at W_2, the quantity of labor demanded is QD_2 and the quantity of labor supplied is QS_2, with $QD_2 > QS_2$. Employers want to hire more workers at a wage of W_2 than there are workers willing to take a job at a wage of W_2.

The excess demand for labor puts upward pressure on the wage rate. The excess demand for labor is not eliminated until the wage rises to W_0. How much and how quickly will the wage rise? That is directly related to the size of the excess demand for labor. The greater is the excess demand for labor, the stronger is the force pushing the wage rate up, and the larger will be the rate of wage inflation.

- For example, excess demand is higher at W_2 than at W_1, so the wage rate will be rising faster at W_2 than at W_1.

It is not difficult to extend Phillips' model from a single labor market to all labor markets. We can estimate excess demand for labor with the unemployment rate. The lower the unemployment rate, the greater the excess demand for labor. Excess demand will be zero at the natural rate of unemployment.

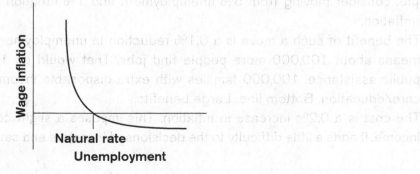

4. HISTORICAL DATA ON THE PHILLIPS CURVE

At the time when Phillips' original idea was extended to inflation in general, the inverse relationship seemed obvious. However, after the 1960s, the relationship predicted by the model became much harder to find.

Phillips' original model showed the relationship between unemployment and wage inflation. It seemed a simple step to replace wage inflation with price inflation. Inflation in wages drives up the aggregate supply curve, which causes increases in the prices of final goods and services.

During the 1950s and 1960s, when this extension from wage inflation to price inflation was first proposed, the inverse relationship between price inflation and unemployment seemed obvious. More significantly, the relationship appeared to be stable. Researchers constructed Phillips curves for many different nations, with highly similar results.

Here are ordered pairs for inflation and unemployment in the United States in the 1960s.

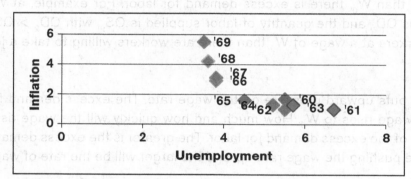

> The general downward sloping shape of the Phillips curve is clear.

Government macroeconomic policy makers looked at the Phillips curve and saw a menu of policy options. They could choose, for example, 5% unemployment and 1% inflation (as in 1962) or 4% unemployment and 3% inflation (as in 1966). The problem for policy makers was how to determine the "best" combination of unemployment and inflation to choose from the Phillips curve menu of options.

It turns out that it is relatively easy to choose between any two options. One must only estimate the likely marginal benefits and marginal costs of choosing one combination over another. For example: consider moving from 5% unemployment and 1% inflation to 4.9% unemployment and 1.2% inflation.

- The benefit of such a move is a 0.1% reduction in unemployment. For the U.S. in 1960, this means about 100,000 more people find jobs. That would be 100,000 less people getting public assistance, 100,000 families with extra disposable income for better housing/health care/education. Bottom line: Large benefits.
- The cost is a 0.2% increase in inflation. This imposes a slight cost on people living on fixed income. It adds a little difficulty to the decisions of investors and savers. Bottom line: Small costs.

It is an easy choice for policy makers; the benefits of a little lower unemployment is always greater than the cost of a little more inflation. That choice was repeatedly made in the 1960s. The chart above shows a steady move to lower unemployment and higher inflation over the decade.

After the decade of the 1960s, the relationship predicted by the Phillips curve model becomes much harder to find.

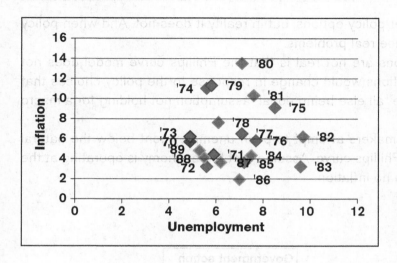

The Phillips curve appears to shift outward in the late 1970s and early 1980s.

It then appears to shift back inward in the late 1980s.

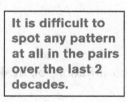

It is difficult to spot any pattern at all in the pairs over the last 2 decades.

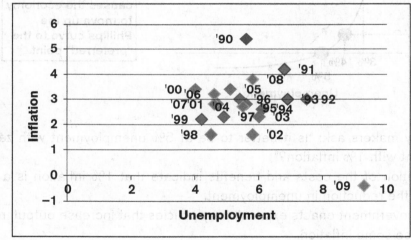

It appears that the Phillips curve for the U.S. became unstable after the 1960s. This presented government policy makers with a much less desirable menu of policy options.

▪ Given the outward shift in the Phillips curve, the economy now endures a higher rate of inflation to enjoy the same low level of unemployment that previously could be achieved with less inflation.

However, the cost/benefit analysis gives the same result as before: the benefits of lower unemployment still are greater than the costs of higher inflation.

5. PROBLEMS WITH THE PHILLIPS CURVE MODEL

The basic problem with the Phillips curve model is that it did not take into account how people's expectations would change. As people experience a changing price level, their expectations about the price level in the future change accordingly, and this affects the position of the Phillips curve.

The Phillips curve model appears to offer policy options, but in reality it does not. And when policy makers act on this appearance, they cause real problems.

The reason the apparent policy options are not real is that the Phillips curve model does not take into account how people's expectations would change in response to the policy choices that are made. This is another example of the "all else being equal" assumption not holding for a macro model.

Consider what happens when policy makers attempt to push unemployment below the natural rate. Here is the original position of the Phillips curve. Assume that the economy is operating at the natural rate of unemployment (5%), with no inflation.

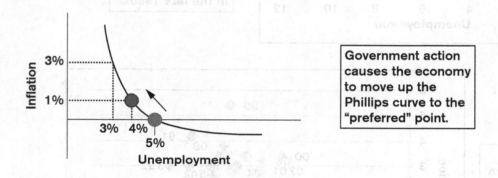

> **Government action causes the economy to move up the Phillips curve to the "preferred" point.**

Now policy makers ask: "Is it better to be at 5% unemployment with zero inflation, or at 4% unemployment with 1% inflation?"

- Examination of the costs and benefits indicate that 1% inflation is a small price to pay to achieve the reduction in unemployment.
- So the government enacts expansionary policies that increase output, reduce unemployment, and cause some inflation.

Prior to this action, people were experiencing a stable price level. This experience leads them to expect that prices will continue to stay level in the future. Expecting no loss in the real purchasing power of their paychecks, workers do not push hard for increases in their nominal wage rate. The prices of inputs stay the same; the aggregate supply curve does not shift.

However, because of the choice by policy makers to move up the Phillips curve, people now begin to experience inflation. This leads them to expect further inflation in the future. Workers, expecting that the real purchasing power of their paychecks will be smaller in the future, push hard for increases in their nominal wage rate. The prices of inputs rise; the aggregate supply curve shifts upward.

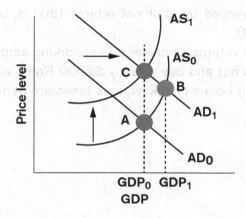

The policy choice is to move from point A to point B (lower unemployment, higher inflation).

Expectations of future inflation shift the aggregate supply curve upward, and the economy moves from point B to point C. The economy has returned to the original level of unemployment, but now at a higher rate of inflation. It looks to policy makers as though the Phillips curve has shifted outward.

Government policy makers were trying to pick options from the short-run Phillips curve. But their options were not sustainable in the long run.

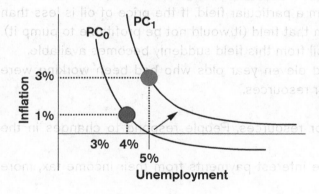

The policy options on the Phillips curve menu are now not as attractive. And if they keep trying to trade less unemployment for more inflation, the options will continue to get worse.

- And because expectations can change very quickly, the long run in this case does not have to be very far into the future.

The long-run Phillips curve is a vertical line at the level of the natural rate of unemployment. The actual trade-off is not between inflation and unemployment, but between different rates of inflation at the natural rate of unemployment.

6. MARGINAL TAX RATES

The behavior of suppliers in resource markets is influenced by net benefits (that is, after taxes). This means that tax policy can cause shifts in the aggregate supply curve. People respond to changes in the marginal tax rates they face.

The behavior of suppliers in resource markets is influenced by their net returns (that is, by the increase in their income after taxes have been removed).

To see the difference between gross returns and net returns, consider a hardworking employee who receives a $2000 bonus. Can this person now go out and buy a fancy $2000 Rolex watch? They had better not. Before the employee receives their bonus check, various taxes are deducted from it.

- Federal income tax : at 33% = $666
- State income tax : at 5% = $100
- Social Security tax : at 8% = $160
- Medicaid tax : at 1.5% = $30

Total deductions = $956. Gross bonus = $2000. Net bonus check the employee receives = $1,044.

Because behavior is influenced by after-tax returns, changes in tax policy can cause shifts in the aggregate supply curve. The level of aggregate supply is determined by the quality and quantity of the resources available to the economy. But "available" means, provided at the going price. The amount and type of resources available will vary as their prices change. For example:

- Assume it costs $60/barrel to pump oil from a particular field. If the price of oil is less than $60/barrel, then no oil will be available from that field (it would not be profitable to pump it). But if the price of oil rises to $100/barrel, oil from this field suddenly becomes available.
- When child labor was made illegal, ten and eleven year olds who had been working were suddenly no longer available to provide labor resources.

Changes in tax policy affect the net price for resources. People respond to changes in the marginal tax rates they face.

- Because homeowners can deduct mortgage interest payments from their income tax, more people buy homes than otherwise would.
- Raising the tax rate on capital gains will lead to fewer investments that might earn capital gains.
- Raising the excise tax on cigarettes causes some people to stop smoking.

The average tax rate is total tax paid divided by gross income. People's behavior, however, is affected by the marginal tax rate, which is the percentage of any additional income earned which is paid in taxes.

Comparison of average and marginal tax rates:

Income	Tax paid	Average tax rate	Marginal tax rate
10,000	0	0%	-
20,000	1,000	5%	10%
30,000	3,000	10%	20%
40,000	6,000	15%	30%
50,000	10,000	20%	40%

> For example, when income rises from $20K to $30K, taxes rise from $1K to $3K. $2K in taxes out of an additional $10K in income is a marginal tax rate of 20%.

In a progressive income tax system, marginal tax rates always are higher than average tax rates. Higher marginal tax rates discourage people from working, because they reduce the net return from working.

- For example, assume someone is willing to work if they can earn $10/hour. They are offered a job where the gross pay is $12/hour. If their marginal tax rate is 10%, they will take the job ($12 minus 10% for taxes = $10.80). But if their marginal tax rate is 20%, they won't take the job ($12 minus 20% for taxes = $9.60).

> Federal tax brackets in U.S.: Income up to $9K = 10%
>
> $9–$36K = 15%
> $36–$88K = 25%
> $88–$183K = 28%
> $183–$400K = 33%
> Above $400 K = 39.6%

The work disincentive effect of higher marginal tax rates can have a strange effect on tax revenue. It is possible that, by lowering marginal tax rates, the government might actually collect more total tax revenue. The lower marginal tax rate might encourage so much additional work effort that a lower percentage of a higher tax base could actually yield higher tax revenue. The relationship between marginal tax rate and total tax receipts is called the Laffer curve.

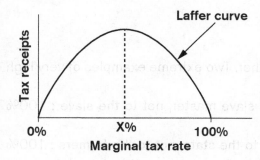

> There is some marginal tax rate (X% in the graph) above which raising the tax rate results in less tax revenue rather than more.

At a zero marginal tax rate, tax receipts are zero (zero percent of anything is zero).

At a 100% marginal tax rate, tax receipts are also zero. No one will voluntarily work if they get to keep nothing of what they earn (one-hundred percent of zero is still zero).

7. WORK DISINCENTIVES

Labor supply curves slope upward. This means that higher marginal tax rates will lead to less labor being supplied. Very high marginal tax rates can discourage work altogether. This is the unfortunate effect of means-tested welfare programs.

Labor supply curves slope upward. This means that higher marginal tax rates will lead to less labor being supplied. Workers are not so much interested in the size of their paycheck, but rather in how much of that paycheck they get to keep. The marginal tax that a worker pays reduces the amount of their paycheck that they get to keep. The graph below shows how this affects the labor supply curve.

- At a gross wage rate of 20 and a marginal tax rate of 0%, the net wage is also 20, and the quantity of labor supplied is 100.
- At the same gross wage rate of 20, but with a 25% marginal tax rate, the net wage rate is 15, and the quantity of labor supplied is 80.
- At the same gross wage rate of 20, but with a 50% marginal tax rate, the net wage rate is 10, and the quantity of labor supplied is 60.

Raising the marginal tax rate is equivalent to an inward shift of the labor supply curve.

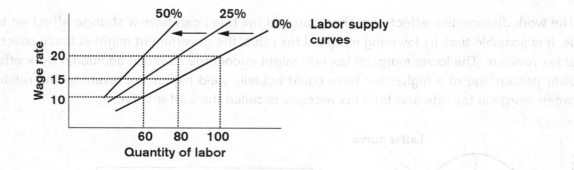

Very high marginal tax rates can discourage work altogether. Two extreme examples of very high marginal tax rates are slavery and Soviet collective farms.

- Under slavery, the output of the slave belongs to the slave master, not to the slave : 100% marginal tax rate
- With a collective farm, the output of the farm belongs to the state, not to the farmers : 100% marginal tax rate

Neither the slave nor the worker in the collective farm gets to keep any of their output; hard work brings no reward. Work effort is not given voluntarily; it must be forced. Forced labor is always much less productive than voluntary labor.

> It is estimated that collective farm earnings were only one fourth of the cash income from private plots on Soviet collective farms.

Although we no longer have slave labor, modern means-tested welfare programs come with confiscatory high effective marginal tax rates. The unintended effect of this is to discourage people who are getting government assistance from finding jobs.

Means-tested welfare programs have two general features:
1. They provide some base level of support. When the person has no income, they receive the base level of support.
2. There is a phase-out rate for support. As the person's income rises, the amount of support they receive diminishes. When their income exceeds the means-test, they are no longer eligible for support.

The problem with this approach is:
- If the phase-out rate is set low, then support payments will go to persons who don't need them: the cost of financing the welfare program will be high.
- If the phase-out rate is set high, it imposes a very high marginal tax rate: work disincentive effects are severe.

The following example is hypothetical, but illustrates the problem.

Support Program	Base level of support	Phase-out rate	Means-test upper limit
Food stamps	5,000	25%	20,000
Child care	4,000	20%	20,000
Housing subsidy	10,000	50%	20,000

Assume a marginal tax rate of fifteen percent on income above 10,000.

Earned income	Food stamps	Child care	Housing subsidy	Income plus support	Income tax	Disposable income	Effective marginal tax rate
0	5,000	4,000	10,000	19,000	0	19,000	
5,000	3,750	3,000	7,500	19,250	0	19,250	95%
10,000	2,500	2,000	5,000	19,500	0	19,500	95%
15,000	1,250	1,000	2,500	19,750	750	19,000	110%
20,000	0	0	0	20,000	1,500	18,500	110%
25,000	0	0	0	25,000	2,250	22,750	15%

In this example, persons with no earned income do not make themselves better off by getting low-paying jobs—most of what they earn is offset by decreased support payments. Once they begin to earn enough to pay income tax, working harder actually makes them worse off. Why should such persons try hard to find jobs? Means-tested welfare programs impose high marginal tax rates, and have strong work disincentives.

How can this problem be fixed? It can't be—it is inherent to how such programs work.

8. SIGNIFICANCE OF SUPPLY-SIDE EFFECTS

There is considerable controversy over the size of supply-side effects. It seems likely that supply-side effects are relatively small in the short run, but could be quite large in the long run.

There is considerable controversy over the size of supply-side effects. If marginal tax rates are cut, will economic activity increase by a little or by a lot?

Advocates of supply-side policies say things like:

- Arthur Laffer: "Government spending is taxation. When you look at this, I've never heard of a poor person spending himself into prosperity; let alone I've never heard of a poor person taxing himself into prosperity."
- Ronald Reagan: "Government's view of the economy could be summed up in a few short phrases: If it moves, tax it. If it keeps moving, regulate it. And if it stops moving, subsidize it."

Opponents of supply-side policies say things like:

- Geraldine Ferraro: "I'd call it a new version of voodoo economics, but I'm afraid that would give witch doctors a bad name."
- Frances O'Grady: "The difficulty for the Government is there's this ideological straitjacket of the market will provide, let the market rip and everything will work out... It's back to trickle-down economics, which, it's plain to see, have not delivered."

Supply-side effects are probably relatively small in the short run. There are several reasons to think this:

- It takes time for both workers and employers to modify their behavior in response to changes in marginal tax rates. Workers can't instantly switch from part-time to full-time jobs. Employers can't instantly hire new workers, or instantly change procedures for overtime. New entrants to the labor market can't ignore non-market responsibilities, and won't instantly find jobs.
- Institutional arrangements may make marginal adjustments difficult. Employers seldom make changes to their companies' standard workweek. For some occupations minimum/maximum hours of work are set by law or contract.
- Workers may be reluctant to adjust their behavior until confident that the change in marginal tax rates is permanent.

Supply-side effects could be quite large in the long run. There are several reasons to think this.

- Given enough time, people do respond to changed incentives.
- The longer people have to enjoy the benefits of a lower marginal tax rate, the greater the total benefits become.
- There is considerable unused capacity for any resource. For example, the labor force participation rate in the U.S. is well below seventy percent—about 1/3 of the potential labor force chooses not to participate. Policies that increase the benefits of work have a large pool of potential workers to attract.

The best historical example of supply-side policies is the Reagan supply-side tax cuts in 1981 and 1982.

The decade of the 1970s was a period of rising inflation and sluggish growth for the United States. Expansionary fiscal and monetary policies designed to increase aggregate demand had contributed to rising inflation without greatly stimulating the economy. President Reagan's policies attempted to shift the aggregate supply curve instead.

The heart of the supply-side policy was significant cuts in marginal tax rates on income and capital gains. The top marginal tax rates for federal income tax fell from 70% to 28%. The marginal tax rate on capital gains fell from 28% to 20%. Income ranges for the various marginal tax rates were indexed to inflation to prevent future "bracket creep." The intent of these changes was to encourage additional economic activity and growth.

There is considerable controversy over the success of these supply-side policies. There is no doubt that, following the end of the 1981–82 recession, economic growth was strong for the rest of the decade. There is also no doubt that both inflation and unemployment fell sharply over this period. Supply-side proponents claim that these happy results were due to the cuts in marginal tax rates. Critics point out that federal tax receipts initially fell after the 1981 tax cuts, and argue that inflation was controlled by the Fed's contractionary money policy and that growth after the end of the recession would have occurred anyway.

President Reagan explaining his supply-side policies.

Recent supply-side changes in tax policy include:
- Presidents George H. Bush, Bill Clinton, and George W. Bush all enacted cuts to marginal tax rates for businesses and investors.
- President Obama cut marginal payroll tax rates.

Supply-side policies can work through channels other than marginal tax rates. For example:
- Investment on job retraining, education, and other forms of human capital.
- Reform of means-tested welfare programs to set time limits on eligibility to receive support.
- Investment in physical infrastructure.
- Reducing regulations which increase the cost of labor.

That last approach has proven to be especially difficult to implement. There are many government regulations which increase the cost of labor. For example: minimum wage laws, requirements for maternity leave, occupational safety and health regulations. These laws and regulations are often very popular with voters, and so are unlikely to be repealed, regardless of their effect on aggregate supply.

SUMMARY OF CHAPTER 13

Both Classical and Keynesian economists tended to ignore the aggregate supply curve: Keynesians because of their emphasis on aggregate demand, and Classicists because of their belief that the long run aggregate supply curve was vertical at the level of potential GDP.

There is an inverse relationship between inflation and unemployment in the short run. Both the aggregate demand/aggregate supply model and business cycle theory predict this. The Phillips curve models this relationship.

The original Phillips curve shows the relationship between wage inflation and unemployment in individual labor markets. Excess supply or excess demand for labor causes changes in the wage rate. The greater the excess, the faster the change.

At the time when Phillips' original idea was extended to inflation in general, the inverse relationship seemed obvious. However, after the 1960s, the relationship predicted by the model became much harder to observe.

The basic problem with the Phillips curve model is that it does not take into account how people's expectations will change in response to the policy choices of government decision makers. As people experience a changing price level, their expectations about the price level in the future change accordingly, and this affects the position of the Phillips curve. The long-run Phillips curve is a vertical line at the natural rate of unemployment.

The behavior of suppliers in resource markets is influenced by net benefits (that is, after taxes). This means that tax policy can change people's behavior and cause shifts in the aggregate supply curve.

People respond to changes in the marginal tax rates they face. Higher marginal tax rates will lead to less labor being supplied. Very high marginal tax rates can discourage work altogether. This is the unfortunate effect of means-tested welfare programs.

There is considerable controversy over the size of supply-side effects. It seems likely that supply-side effects are relatively small in the short run, but could be quite large in the long run.

Credits

Fig 13.9: "MONIAC computer," https://commons.wikimedia.org/wiki/File:Phillips_and_MONIAC_LSE.jpg. Copyright in the Public Domain.
Fig 13.21: "President Reagan," http://www.reaganlibrary.gov/images/Major_Speeches/c3241-20.jpg. Copyright in the Public Domain.

CH
FOURTEEN
ECONOMIC GROWTH

Economic growth is measured in terms of the rate of change in real GDP. Over the past 100 years, the U.S. economy has grown at an average rate of about three percent per year.

Economic growth is driven by increases in the quantity of resources available to the society, improvements in the quality of resources available, and advancements in technology.

The best prediction for the near future is that it will be like the present. The best prediction for the far future is that it will be different from the present, in unexpected ways. Any prediction is flawed if it ignores market reactions to changing incentives.

1. GROWTH OF THE U.S. ECONOMY

Economic growth is measured in terms of the rate of change in real GDP. Over the last 100 years, the U.S. economy has grown at an average rate of about three percent per year.

Economic growth is measured in terms of the rate of change in real GDP.
- Rate of growth = Real GDP in year 2/Real GDP in year 1 − 1

> Real U.S. GDP was 15,470.7 in 2012, and 15,761.3 in 2013, so the U.S. economy grew by 1.9% in 2013.
>
> **(15,761.3/15,470.7) − 1 = 0.01878, or 1.9% growth**

Per capita GDP is real GDP divided by the population. It is the average share of total output going to each individual. The rate of growth in per capita GDP is generally considered a measure of the improvement in the average person's standard of living. When the population is growing, per capita GDP grows at a slower rate than does the economy as a whole.

The size of the labor force is an approximation for the total resources available to the economy. Labor is not the only resource, but it is the most important one. Adam Smith, the founder of modern economics, said in 1776 that the source of the wealth of nations is the quality of its labor force. Labor productivity is output per worker: real GDP divided by the number of persons in the labor force. It is possible to calculate the productivity of capital, of land, and of any other resource. However, labor productivity is the most important for measuring growth.

Year	Real GDP (A)	Population (B)	Labor force (C)	GDP per capita (A/B)	Labor productivity (A/C)
2012	15,470.7	316.4	143.2	48,896	108,136
2013	15,761.3	317.8	144.6	49,595	108,999

Growth rate of: Real GDP = 1.9%   Population = 0.4%   Per capita GDP = 1.4%
- Growth rate of per capita GDP = Growth rate of real GDP − Growth rate of population

Growth rate of: Labor force = 1.0%   Labor productivity = 0.8%
- Growth rate of labor force + Growth rate of labor productivity = Growth rate of real GDP

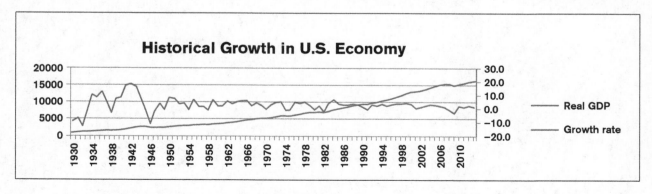

Growth can be visually depicted by macroeconomic models.

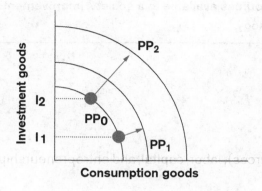

The production possibilities curve shows the possible combinations of 2 goods that a society could produce.

When the two goods in a production possibilities curve are defined as consumption goods and investment goods, the curve becomes a model of economic growth. Investment goods increase the resources available to the society, and so increase the future production possibilities for the society.

- If the society chooses to produce relatively few investment goods (I_1 in the graph above), then future production possibilities will shift out only a little; economic growth is slow.
- If the society chooses to produce a larger quantity of investment goods (I_2 in the graph above), then future production possibilities will shift out more; economic growth is faster.

In the aggregate demand/aggregate supply macroeconomic model, growth is shown by an outward shift in potential GDP.

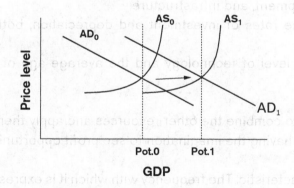

The larger the outward shift in potential GDP, the faster the rate of economic growth.

Both of these models are visual depictions of economic growth. Neither is a deterministic model. That is, they merely show that a growing economy gains more resources; they do not describe the policy actions that might lead to this result.

2. FACTORS THAT AFFECT GROWTH

Economic growth is driven by increases in the quantity of resources available to a society, improvements in the quality of resources available, and advances in technology.

Economic growth is driven by three factors:
- Increases in the quantity of resources
- Improvements in the quality of resources
- Advances in technology

The four basic types of resources are land (natural resources), labor, capital, and entrepreneurship.

Natural resources are useful things provided by nature itself—unlike the other types of resources, natural resources exist independent of human activity.
- The quantity and quality of natural resources are largely inherent to the environment. A nation either has mineral deposits, or it doesn't; a nation either gets abundant rainfall, or it doesn't.
- Human activity can improve the productivity of natural resources. The quantity of arable land is increased when a swamp is drained; the productivity of farmland is increased by irrigation.

Labor resources are the physical and mental abilities of a nation's work force.
- The quantity of labor is determined by the size of the population, the age distribution of the population, and the labor force participation rate.
- The quality of labor is determined by the level of investment in human capital: education and training.

Capital resources are man-made structures, equipment, and infrastructure.
- The quantity of capital is determined by the rates of investment and depreciation, both at present and in the past.
- The quality of capital is determined by the level of technology and the average age of the existing capital stock.

Entrepreneurship is the special human ability to combine the other resources and apply them to productive economic activity. Entrepreneurship is having the imagination to see profit opportunities and the gumption to take on the risk they entail.
- Entrepreneurship is an inherent human characteristic. The frequency with which it is expressed is determined by the extent to which a society rewards innovative risk-taking behavior.

Various economic growth models treat the four types of resources differently.

The production possibilities model of growth holds labor resources and natural resources constant, and then varies the rate of growth of capital resources.

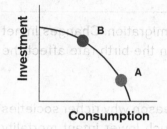

The rate of growth of capital is shown by the position along the curve. Combinations closer to the consumption axis (point A) have slower growth of capital. Combinations closer to the investment axis (point B) have faster growth of capital.

In a normal production possibilities curve (showing the various combinations of two different goods that could be produced), an increase in any resource is shown by an outward shift in the curve. Unlike the growth model, the outward shift is the same regardless of where the society chooses to operate along the curve.

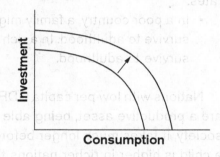

The aggregate demand/aggregate supply graph below shows an equal increase in both aggregate demand and aggregate supply, so that the economy is enjoying growth with stable prices.

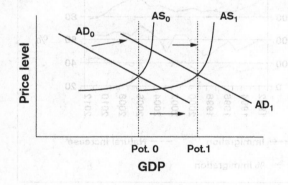

This type of change might be caused by population growth.

- Aggregate demand increases because the number of consumers has grown.
- Aggregate supply increases because the quantity of labor resources has grown.

3. GROWING QUANTITY OF RESOURCES

Population growth increases labor resources. Investments build up the stock of capital. The quantity of natural resources available varies with advances in technology and changes in the price of the resource.

Growth in the quantity of labor is affected by the birth rate and by net immigration. Changes in net immigration affect the size of the labor force in the short run. Changes in the birth rate affect the size of the labor force in the long run.

Birth rates tend to decline with growth in per capital GDP. Part of the reason why richer societies have lower birth rates is because of better medical care, resulting in much lower infant mortality rates.

- In a poor country, a family might need to have six children in order to be confident that two will survive to adulthood. In a rich society, a family with two children can be confident that both will survive to adulthood.

Nations with low per capita GDP tend to be heavily agricultural. For an agricultural family, children are a productive asset, being able to perform useful farm duties from an early age. In an industrial society, it takes much longer before a child is a productive asset to the family. Since the net cost of a child is higher in richer nations than in poorer ones, families in richer nations tend to have fewer children.

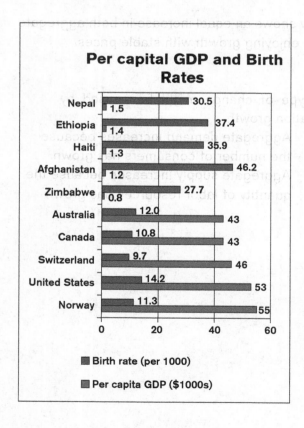

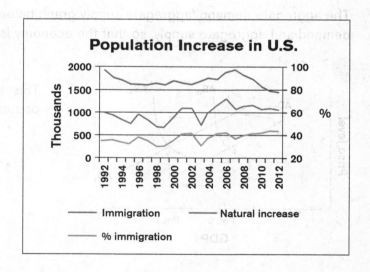

Net immigration to a country (both legal and illegal) is largely a matter of government policy. U.S. policy has generally encouraged immigration, though there have been exceptions.

Growth in the quantity of physical capital is driven by business investment and by public investment in infrastructure. Business investment is largely driven by expectations of future business conditions. Thus the level of business investment tends to fluctuate with the business cycle, rising during boom times and falling during recessions.

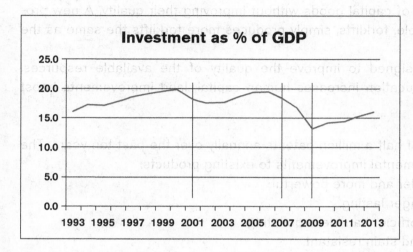

Investment as % of GDP

Note the drop in investment during the recessions of 2001 and 2007–2009.

The quantity of natural resources available is assumed to be fixed, given the existing level of technology and the existing prices for resources. Over time the quantity of a natural resource can shrink (by depletion of existing supplies of the resource) or grow (by discovery of new deposits of the resource).

Much more significant for future quantities of a natural resource are advances in technology and changes in the price of the resource. New technology can increase the available quantity of a natural resource.

- A recent example of this is the development of hydraulic fracturing for oil and natural gas production. A liquid mixture is injected at high pressure into a wellbore, creating small fractures in deep rock formations. Oil and gas seep through the cracks into the well. This process allows the extraction of immense quantities of previously inaccessible hydrocarbons.

Changes in the price of a natural resource can also affect the quantity available. A rising price for a natural resource encourages exploration and discovery of new sources for the natural resource. A rising price also makes it economically attractive to extract the resource from more costly sources and by more costly methods.

- A recent example of this is the dozens of old gold mines that reopened in California in response to rising prices for gold.

4. GROWING QUALITY OF RESOURCES

Much investment is designed to improve the quality of the available resources. Inefficient machinery is replaced, education increases human capital, land improvements boost productivity.

Investment can increase the quantity of capital goods without improving their quality. A new production line manufacturing, for example, forklifts, simply produces more forklifts the same as the existing forklifts.

However, much investment is designed to improve the quality of the available resources. Inefficient machinery is replaced, education increases human capital, land improvements boost productivity.

Americans have filed an average of half a million patents annually over the past ten years. The great majority of these were for incremental improvements to existing products.

- Electronic devices become smaller and more powerful.
- Batteries become lighter and longer lasting.
- Car engines become more fuel efficient and less polluting.
- Fabrics become more durable and stain resistant.
- Sutures absorb into the body rather than having to be removed.
- Motion pictures talk, then are in color, then are in 3D.
- Frozen foods last longer and taste better.

Two dramatic recent examples of improving quality are personal computers and digital cameras.

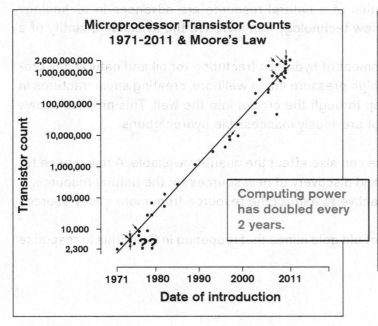

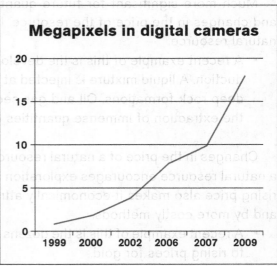

Americans invest billions of hours in formal education every year. On top of that are the millions of workers who receive on-the-job training, remedial education, or retraining for new careers. Such investment in human capital improves the quality of the labor force and increases worker productivity.

Persons with more years of schooling have higher average earnings and lower average unemployment rates.

Years of schooling	Unemployment rate	Median weekly earnings
< high school	11.4%	$480
High school	7.2%	$660
Some college	6.0%	$756
College graduate	3.6%	$1,199

On-the-job training is an important source of human capital. Even a minimum wage job develops skills that increase a worker's value.

- Getting to work on time
- Dressing appropriately
- Following instructions
- Presenting a good attitude

Even land (the ultimate fixed resource) can be improved by human efforts. Swamps can be drained, mountainsides can be terraced, arid lands can be irrigated. As an example, the chart below shows that arable land in Brazil has nearly doubled over the past fifty years.

Arable land in Brazil

Increases in agricultural productivity mean that the U.S. food supply is produced by an ever smaller proportion of the total labor force: 150 years ago, 70-80% of the U.S. population was engaged in agriculture. Today that number is less than 1%.

Sources of agricultural productivity include:
- Crop rotation
- Contour plowing
- Mechanized farm equipment
- Fertilizers
- Irrigation
- High yield seeds

5. GROWING TECHNOLOGY

Applied research and development seeks incremental improvements to existing processes. Basic research generally has more long-term payoffs, often in unexpected areas.

Technological change is notoriously hard to predict. The list of long-anticipated but not yet achieved technological advances includes:

- Flying cars
- A cure for the common cold
- Fusion reactors
- Travel to other planets

On the other hand, no one anticipated until it was developed things like:

- DNA manipulation
- Plastics
- The internet
- Lasers

Most research and development investment is applied R&D. Applied R&D activity seeks incremental improvements to existing processes. For example:

- Modifications to the shape of airplane wings and propellers to make them more aerodynamic
- Improvements to internal combustion engines to provide more horsepower

"Incremental" changes do not have to have small impacts.

- Henry Ford's adaptation of assembly line techniques to auto manufacturing lowered the cost of a car to the point where the average worker could afford to buy one.
- Replacing iron with steel in plow blades opened up the American Great Plains to agriculture.

Applied research works toward a definite known goal. For example:

- A pharmaceutical company researching for a vaccine against a particular disease
- World War I aircraft engineers figuring out how to make a machine gun shoot through a spinning propeller
- Thomas Edison trying thousands of different materials before he found a working filament for his incandescent light bulb

Accidental discoveries do happen in applied research. For example:

- Corn flakes were invented when Will Kellogg accidentally left boiled wheat sitting out for several hours.
- The idea for the microwave oven came when its inventor stood next to a magnetron, and a candy bar in his pocket melted.
- Wilson Greatbatch invented the pacemaker when he accidentally installed the wrong transistor in a heart monitor.

Basic research and development generally has more long-term payoffs. The profit motive still operates, but direct commercial applications are generally not known in advance. The payoffs from basic research often come in unexpected areas.

Lasers are an excellent example of how payoff from basic research can come in unexpected areas. No one set out to invent a laser; in fact, no one even thought it was possible until a few years before the first one was built. The discoveries that led to the invention of lasers were the result of basic research into the nature and behavior of light. The knowledge gained through that basic research into light led to totally unexpected practical applications in communications, manufacturing, medical care, and entertainment.

Research and development is performed by government agencies, by business firms, and by academic institutions. In the United States, government provides most R&D funds. Academic institutions are more likely to engage in basic research, while both government and business are more likely to pursue applied research.

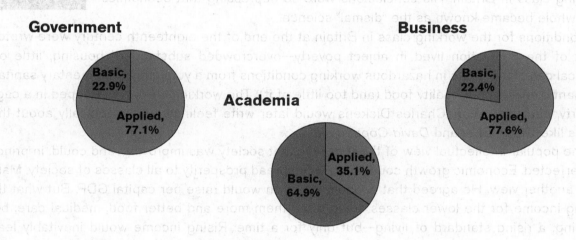

The distinction between applied and basic research is sometimes blurred. Consider the Manhattan Project—probably the largest R&D project in world history. This was the World War II effort to create an atomic bomb. The Manhattan Project had a definite known end—development of a bomb of unprecedented destructive power. However, the project pioneered totally new processes rather than making improvements to existing processes. Although the desired end was achieved (the atomic bombs that brought the war to an end), the knowledge of nuclear fission gained by the research found uses in unexpected areas (nuclear medicine, nuclear power plants, high-energy physics basic research).

6. CASE STUDY IN GROWTH - MALTHUS

Thomas Malthus studied the growth of population and food production, and reached rather dire conclusions. As a result of his theory, economics became known as the "dismal" science.

Thomas Malthus studied the growth of population and food production, and reached rather dire conclusions.

Malthus (1766–1834) was an English cleric and scholar. An early macroeconomist, he argued that the long-run stability of the economy was more important than short-run expediency. He is best known for "An essay on the Principle of Population"—of which there were six editions between 1798 and 1826.

Malthus studied the impact of economic growth on the well-being of the working class in Britain. His conclusions were so depressing that economics as a whole became known as the "dismal" science.

Conditions for the working class in Britain at the end of the eighteenth century were wretched. Most of the population lived in abject poverty—overcrowded substandard housing, little or no medical care, long hours in hazardous working conditions from a young age, rudimentary sanitation, rampant disease, poor quality food (and too little of it). The working class was trapped in a cage of poverty, near starvation. Charles Dickens would later write feelingly and graphically about this in works like *Oliver Twist* and *David Copperfield*.

The popular intellectual view of the time was that society was improving, and could, in principle, be perfected. Economic growth could bring widespread prosperity to all classes of society. Malthus took another view. He agreed that economic growth would raise per capital GDP. But what then? Rising income for the lower classes could bring them more and better food, medical care, better housing, a rising standard of living—but only for a time. Rising income would inevitably lead to rising population (fewer children would die as babies). Rising population would again drive down per capita GDP. All the gains of the working class would be lost, and they would once again live in poverty, near starvation.

As Malthus put it:

"That the increase of population is necessarily limited by the means of subsistence, that population does invariably increase when the means of subsistence increase, and that the superior power of population is repressed, and the actual population kept equal to the means of subsistence, by misery and vice."

Malthus argued that there is a basic imbalance between growth in population and growth in food production.

- Population grows geometrically; with a constant birth rate, more women of child bearing age necessarily means more children will be born.
- Food production grows arithmetically; the limiting factor is the fixed amount of land.

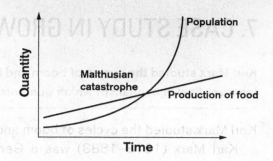

Mathus' prediction:

Since continual population growth is not sustainable (the growth in food production can't forever keep up with it), the population will be held within its resource limits by positive checks that increase the death rate; hunger, disease, and war.

- Societal miseries will continue unchecked, and economic growth cannot solve this.

Malthus, fortunately, was wrong. His model is logically consistent, within its assumptions. The error is Malthus' assumption that rising per capita GDP causes rising rates of population growth. What he did not foresee was that rising living standards also lead to lower birth rates.

- Rate of population growth = Birth rate - Death rate
- If the birth rate remains the same when death rates fall (due to higher per capita GDP), then the rate of population growth will indeed rise.
- But if the birth rate also falls when per capita GDP rises, then the rate of population growth could stay the same, or even fall.

The reason that birth rates fall when there is economic growth is that rising living standards change the incentives for bearing and rearing children—and people's behaviors change in response to changing incentives.

Malthus recognized that preventive checks to population growth (abortion, birth control, prostitution, postponement of marriage, celibacy) could allow a higher standard of living for all. He simply didn't believe that enough of the working classes would use such preventive checks to make any real difference.

Malthus scientifically "proved" that nothing could be done to permanently alleviate the suffering, misery, and moral degradation of the working classes. No wonder economics became known as the dismal science!

7. CASE STUDY IN GROWTH - MARX

Karl Marx studied the cycles of boom and bust in capitalist economies. He thought he had discovered an inherent flaw in capitalism which guaranteed its eventual destruction.

Karl Marx studied the cycles of boom and bust in capitalist economies.

Karl Marx

Karl Marx (1818–1883) was a German philosopher, economist, and revolutionary socialist. Marx argued that human societies progress through class struggle: a conflict between an ownership class that controls production, and a dispossessed working class that provides the labor for production. His most famous work is *Das Kapital* (1867).

Marx thought that he had discovered an inherent flaw in the capitalist system which guaranteed its eventual destruction. He modeled capitalism as a series of booms and busts (the business cycle). This economic instability is a product of relentless competition among capitalists to always increase productivity and reduce costs.

- Marx was strongly influenced by his observation of the panic of 1857, an international economic crisis that started in the United States and spread to European nations.

Each boom period is fueled by innovation and investment in new technologies and capital equipment. Each bust period sees weaker firms swallowed up by stronger ones. Thus each cycle will lead to an ever-increasing concentration of industry; the means of production gathered into ever-fewer hands. And an ever-increasing impoverishment of the working class, as the successful capitalists squeeze ever more profit from labor. The cycle of growth, collapse, then more growth will become ever more severe. It will stop only when the oppressed workers rise in revolution and overthrow the entire system.

The internal inconsistency in capitalism is that it draws its profit from the labor of workers, but is also driven to abuse and exploit those workers. This process of exploitation is not sustainable in the long run—but it is inherent to the capitalist system. No single capitalist firm can buck the process and act humanely toward their workers, because to do so would raise their costs and lower their profits. Cut-throat competition from more exploitative firms would drive the humanely acting firm out of business.

> For example, consider a textile manufacturer who believes that children belong in school rather than in factories, and who acts on those beliefs by employing only adults in his factory. There are tasks in textile manufacturing where the small fingers of a child work better than the large fingers of an adult. Adults can do these tasks, but more slowly and less accurately than children. Per-unit costs are higher among the adults-only workforce; his competitors (who still employ children) undercut his costs, lure away his customers, and drive him out of business.

Marx was not shy in his call for revolution:

> Workers of the world unite; you have nothing to lose but your chains.

> Capital is reckless of the health or length of life of the laborer, unless under compulsion from society.

> Capital is dead labor, which, vampire-like, lives only by sucking living labor, and lives the more, the more labor it sucks.

> The rich will do anything for the poor but get off their backs.

> The more the division of labor and the application of machinery extend, the more does competition extend among the workers, the more do their wages shrink together.

Marx was compelling in his rhetoric, and his economic model is elegant and internally consistent. However, his predictions of growing concentration of economic power and worsening conditions for workers were wrong. His error was two-fold.

First, Marx implicitly assumed that economies of scale have no end—that larger firms will always have lower average costs of production. He did not recognize that diseconomies of scale would put a check on the growth of firms. The most important diseconomy of scale is the growing difficulty of managing a firm as it becomes larger. If sheer size guaranteed success, the world would still be ruled by dinosaurs.

Second, Marx did not foresee that problems could be remedied within the system by collective action. Marx viewed government as a tool of the ruling class, but in fact government has played a critical role in improving conditions for the working class. Marx was correct that any capitalist, acting alone, was powerless to improve general working conditions. That kind of change required collective action, with government acting to enforce the collective decisions.

Collectively agreed changes to nineteenth century working conditions include:
- Elimination of child labor
- Elimination of slave labor
- Reduction in hours of work (from a standard 14-hour work day, to 12, to 10, to 8-hour)
- Workplace safety regulations
- Anti-discrimination rules
- Paid vacation time; paid sick leave
- Right to collectively bargain (to form a union)
- Compensation for workplace injury
- Unemployment insurance

8. CASE STUDY IN GROWTH – EHRLICH

Paul Ehrlich argued that unchecked human population growth would inevitably lead to worldwide disaster. Many other environmental factors will also lead to disaster, if current trends continue.

Paul Ehrlich argued in his 1968 book *The Population Bomb* that unchecked human population growth would inevitably lead to worldwide disaster. Here is how his book begins:

Paul Ehrlich

> *"The battle to feed all of humanity is over. In the 1970s hundreds of millions of people will starve to death in spite of any crash programs embarked upon now. At this late date nothing can prevent a substantial increase in the world death rate..."*

Ehrlich's argument is quite simple and intuitively compelling:

1. The rate of growth in the world's population has been increasing.
   - World population reached 1 billion in 1804. It took 123 years to double to 2 billion in 1927, but only 47 years to double again to 4 billion in 1974, and currently has nearly doubled again to over 7 billion.

2. The world's resources to support this population are limited.
   - There is only so much arable land, only so much fresh water, only so much petroleum, and so on.

3. Unchecked population growth will overwhelm the world's resources, and lead to disaster on an unprecedented scale.

This is Malthus all over again. Ehrlich has done two things differently.

- Where Malthus explained the sources of population growth, Ehrlich merely documents the observed rate of population growth, and projects that rate into the future.
- Where Malthus concentrated on food production as the check on human population, Ehrlich expands beyond food production to argue that the environment as a whole puts a check on human population.

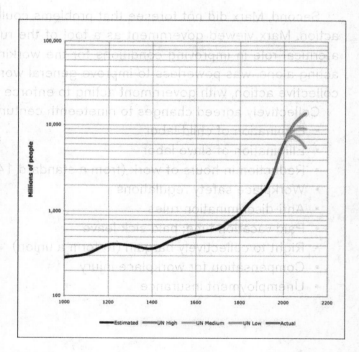

Ehrlich focuses on population growth, but many other environmental factors will also lead to disaster, if current trends continue. For example:

- If air pollution continues to worsen, eventually we will choke to death on the toxic fumes.
- If cutting of rain forests continues at the current pace, eventually the rain forests will all be gone.
- If whaling continues at its current rate, eventually all whales will be extinct.
- If global warming continues, eventually the ice caps will melt and all coastal cities will drown.
- If traffic congestion continues to worsen, eventually we will spend our lives crawling to and from work.
- If disposable diapers continue to be dumped in landfills at the current rate, eventually the whole country will be thirty feet deep in baby poo.

One can take any existing trend and project it forward, and eventually it will cause the system to crash and burn.

Ehrlich (and all other environmental disaster predictors) are wrong on two counts.

First, they assume that technology will remain constant. A problem that appears insurmountable with existing technology, may turn out to be trivial with improved technology.

- For example, the world currently depends upon fossil fuels (oil and coal) for most energy. Think how dramatically that would change if someone invented an efficient means to gather solar energy.

Secondly, and more importantly, Ehrlich ignores market adjustments. With well-functioning markets, it is impossible to completely use up a natural resource.

- As the quantity of the resource available declines, the price of the resource rises. The higher price both reduces the quantity of the resource demanded and increases the quantity of the resource supplied. A rising market price causes people to change their behavior: producers have an incentive to increase exploration to discover new sources of supply, and consumers have an incentive to conserve and use the current supply more efficiently.

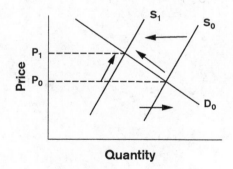

Supply falls from S_0 to S_1. The market price rises from P_0 to P_1. Both suppliers and consumers change their behavior in response to the higher price.

9. PREDICTING THE FUTURE

The best prediction of the near future is that it will be like the present. The best prediction for the far future is that it will be different from the present, in unexpected ways. Any prediction is flawed if it ignores market reactions to changing incentives.

Predicting the future is a losing proposition. The future is inherently unknowable in advance, so that predictions of future events or conditions (whether developed from rigorous economic models, intuition, or casting of bones) are never any more than educated guesses. Economists make such educated guesses about the future all the time, but without notable success.

The following statements may be funny, but they are also true:
- An economist is an expert who will know tomorrow why the things he predicted yesterday didn't happen today.
- An economist is a trained professional paid to guess wrong about the economy.
- Economists have forecasted nine out of the last five recessions.

There is real value in knowing in advance the future values of economic variables.

For example:
- Knowing what the inflation rate will be in the future would allow investors to identify the real value of the interest rate they are earning, would allow union negotiators to identify what nominal wage rate in a new contract would preserve the real purchasing power of their members' wage, would allow savers to estimate how much they need to put aside today to meet their desired goals in the future.
- Knowing the future level of demand for a product would let producers identify if they need to modify their production capacity.
- Knowing how input prices will change in the future (for example, if crude oil prices will rise or fall over the next year) would let manufacturers estimate their future costs, design their future pricing strategies, and decide whether or not to change production processes.

Because knowledge of future economic conditions and variables would be so valuable, people invest significant time and effort on prediction.

The best prediction of the near future is that it will be like the present. Most change is incremental and takes place at the margin, so major dramatic events are rare in the short run. Dramatic change can occur suddenly and unexpectedly (most volcanoes do not erupt very often, but when they do it is a big deal!), but it usually doesn't.

Because the near future is usually a lot like the present, small changes in economic variables take on a larger importance.

- If the current unemployment rate is 6.5%, then the prediction that next month it will be 6.4% is very different from the prediction that it will be 6.6%. The first prediction says that the employment situation will improve, while the second says that it will get worse.

- If the current price of gold is $1500/ounce, then the prediction that next month it will be $1450/ounce is very different from the prediction that it will be $1550/ounce. The first prediction says that now is a good time to sell your gold, while the second says that it is a good time to buy more.

Of course, the more detailed the prediction, the more likely it is to be wrong. For example, assume the current value of the CPI is 220.156. If you predict that next month the CPI will have a value:

- Between 218 and 225 : you will probably be correct
- Between 221 and 222 : you might be correct
- 221.983 : you will almost certainly be wrong

The best prediction of the far future is that it will be different from the present, and in unexpected ways.

- Around 1750, it was "proven" that the maximum size of a city was 1 million inhabitants. The controlling factor for population in the analysis was horse manure—literally. At the time, horses were the main means of transporting people and goods. The researchers calculated that, at a population over 1 million, the number of horses necessary to transport the goods to sustain the population daily would produce more manure than could be removed in a day! The then unforeseen invention of the internal combustion engine changed the situation completely; today cities routinely have more than 1 million inhabitants, without drowning in horse manure.

Predictions of the far future are fun, but they are not a good guide for decision making.

Any prediction is fatally flawed if it ignores market reactions to changing incentives.

- In 1980, the economist Julian Simon entered into a wager with Paul Ehrlich concerning resource scarcity. Ehrlich picked five commodity metals, and (since he believed that overpopulation was depleting natural resources) bet that their prices would rise over the next ten years. Simon, believing that new discoveries and advances in extraction technology would increase supply, bet that their prices would fall. By 1990, prices for all five commodities had fallen. Ehrlich paid up, and declined to enter into a new wager with Simon.

SUMMARY OF CHAPTER 14

Economic growth is measured in terms of the rate of change in real GDP. Over the past 100 years, the U.S. Economy has grown at an average rate of about three percent per year.

Economic growth is driven by increases in the quantity of resources available to a society, improvements in the quality of resources available, and advances in technology.

Population growth increases labor resources. Investments build up the stock of capital. The quantity of natural resources available varies with advances in technology and changes in the price of the resource.

Much investment is designed to improve the quality of the available resources. Inefficient machinery is replaced, education increases human capital, land improvements boost productivity.

Applied research and development seeks incremental improvements to existing processes. Basic research generally has more long-term payoffs, often in unexpected areas.

Thomas Malthus studied the growth of population and food production, and reached rather dire conclusions. As a result of his theory, economics became known as the "dismal" science. Malthus failed to foresee that rising living standards lead to lower birth rates.

Karl Marx studied the cycles of boom and bust in capitalist economics. He thought he had discovered an inherent flaw in capitalism which guaranteed its eventual destruction. Marx did not foresee that problems could be remedied within the system by collective action.

Paul Ehrlich argued that unchecked human population growth would inevitably lead to worldwide disaster. Many other environmental factors will also lead to disaster, if current trends continue. All such predictions ignore market adjustments to changing prices.

The best prediction of the near future is that it will be like the present. The best prediction for the far future is that it will be different from the present, in unexpected ways.

Any prediction is fatally flawed if it ignores market reactions to changing incentives.

Credits